# BLACK MEN

## AND *Intimacy*

## VOICES FROM ACROSS THE DIASPORA

## THEREZ FLEETWOOD

Published by Luxury Romance Concierge™
Atlanta, GA
Copyright © 2020 by Therese Fleetwood

ISBN: 978-0-9968325-3-3 (Softcover)
ISBN: 978-0-9968325-4-0 (ebook)

Ordering Information: Quantity sales. Special discounts are available on
quantity orders by corporations and associations. For details, contact the
publisher at info@luxuryromanceconcierge.com

Luxury Romance Concierge, LLC
Visit our website at www.luxuryromanceconcierge.com

This book is dedicated to all the
BEAUTIFUL BLACK MEN
who have opened up their hearts and minds and entrusted me to
share their voices with women, giving them a closer look at how
men think and what they really want in a relationship.

# TABLE OF CONTENTS

# INTRODUCTION

There are countless clinical and therapeutic books regarding men and relationships that analyze and interpret their feelings about intimacy. However, there are few books that just focus on Black men's points of view. *Black Men and Intimacy - Voices From Across the Diaspora* is a raw, impactful and inspiring exploration about the complexities of relationships through the minds of men who give real, unequivocal answers to the questions all women want to know but are often too afraid to ask.

My first book was published on men and relationships in 2016 because of my own personal journey seeking to develop more intimacy in my life. I wanted more meaningful connections with the men that I dated. I wanted to go below the surface of my emotions and connect in more intimate ways, mentally, physically, and spiritually. Writing *Men and Intimacy - Real Talk, Real Answers* was both eye-opening and cathartic. It helped me understand that men are also seeking intimacy and real authentic connections with their partners. And, it helped me debunk the enigma that men, Black men, are difficult to understand. Black men are not raised to show or express their emotions and because of this, they are not always communicative. However, given the right platform, without judgment or interruption, they have a lot to say.

Over the past few years, I've met other women who've also wanted more intimacy in their lives. They felt disconnected from their partners and desired to create a deeper bond. These women love their men, but they don't always understand them. They spend countless hours asking other women for advice on their relationships when they should be going directly to the source. Even when talking to their men, there were still unanswered questions that women could never truly get their partners to open up and talk about. *Black Men and Intimacy - Voices From Across the Diaspora* was written to focus primarily on our Black men, our brothers, our fathers, our friends, our kings. This book is a tool that can be could be used as a catalyst for conversation. All the interviews were transcribed so that they personify each man's voice. Whether he is complex or simple in the way he shares his thoughts, it is his experiences that ring true as he navigates life.

Black men have been characterized by society's interpretation of who they are. I wanted to debunk the stereotypes of Black men and show their intimate side which is seldom, if ever, shown in the media or to their loved ones. This book provides a portal for men to express themselves freely, discussing issues that are real and prevalent in their lives. Only a man can truly tell us who he is and how he feels and each of these men share their own unique stories. They openly share that which they've often kept hidden when it comes to issues that may challenge their self-esteem and self-worth.

*Black Men and Intimacy - Voices From Across the Diaspora* helps to demystify the communication differences between men and women and gives a very real and transparent look "behind the curtain" of the male mind. It gives you insight into the Language of Men, how they think, and how they express themselves. It sheds light on the thought processes to help women understand why a man does what he does. These men offer several different opinions and experiences that are unique to each of them while providing valuable information that women need to know. This book is a must-read for anyone really seeking to intimately understand the thinking of a Black man when it comes to love, life, dating, communication, sex, intimacy, marriage, relationships, fears, mental health, and childhood traumas.

I interviewed fifty men. Most of the men were born in the United States, while others were immigrants from Africa and the Caribbean. They range in age from 25 to 66 and are of various socioeconomic classes. Sixteen of the men were married. Fourteen men were divorced. Three were engaged. Seven were in a relationship and ten of the men were single and either dating, choosing to be celibate or focusing on things other than a relationship. All the men were interviewed under the guise of anonymity. In order for these men to speak freely, many of them stressed the importance that they remain anonymous.

Their professions included: Actor, Bartender, Behavior Therapist, Body Builder, Business Owner, Chef, College Professor, Consultant, Creative Director, Dentist, Radio Personality, Entrepreneur, Exotic Dancer, Film Producer, Fitness Coach, Flight Attendant, IT Manager, Life Coach, Maintenance Technician,

Marketing Consultant, Medical Sales professional, Musician, Music Producer, NFL Player, Photographer, Pilot, Robotics Technician, Maintenance Engineer, Sales and Interior Design Consultant, Sound Engineer, Sous Chef, Stage Manager, Student, Stylist, Talent Manager, Television Developer, Television Editor, Truck Driver, Welder, and Writer.

Some men struggled with answering the questions while others were extremely self-expressed. They relished the opportunity to speak and have their voices heard. Some of them welcomed sharing their opinions and getting stuff off their chest. They shared that there are not many platforms in which Black men can truly be self-expressed when it comes to talking about intimacy as reflected in their lives. They shared that it was cathartic for them to speak their minds freely without judgment, hesitation, or disapproval. As Isaiah, age 35, stated, "One of the toughest things about being a Black male is that it's rare to find people who understand us". - ISAIAH, 35

*Black Men and Intimacy - Voices From Across the Diaspora* was written for Black women who truly desire to understand Black men better; Black men who are looking to find their voice of self-expression; parents raising Black boys; moderators discussing Black men; ministers, marriage counselors, therapists and people in other areas of social service that counsel Black men; book clubs who want to discuss Black men and relationships; couples wanting to enhance the intimacy in their relationships; and any woman married to or dating a Black man.

Black men have seldom been taught how to deal with their emotions. It has never been "cool" for them to share intimacy and their vulnerabilities in this way. Being cool, saving face, appearing to be in control no matter the circumstances, is a persona they gravitate to almost instinctively. *Black Men and Intimacy - Voices From Across the Diaspora* provides clarity to common misconceptions, and answers to questions about how Black men think and express themselves.

This book is not a theoretical analysis of Black men overall, nor is it written to stereotype or categorize Black men. This book is a compilation of personal one-on-one interviews with men sharing their opinions based on their own life experiences. Only Black men can tell their stories and this sentiment is perfectly stated by Malik, age 38, "Everybody automatically thinks that all us Black men are the same when it comes to everything, and we're not. I'm a different human being from the next guy".

My hopes with *Black Men and Intimacy - Voices From Across the Diaspora* is that it initiates a change in the way we view each other intimately. I hope that people use this book as a guide to understand and discover or re-discover each other. I hope that they are able to share their own unique experiences together and that they support each other through the process. I hope that Black women and men will come together and have important conversations about relationships.

With Love,

Therez Fleetwood

# Chapter 1

# WHAT IS INTIMACY TO MEN?

Intimacy is having the experience of mental, physical and spiritual closeness. It occurs when two people are able to share their 'inner worlds' with one another and reveal their true feelings, fears, and desires without shame or judgment. Intimacy also means deeply knowing another person and feeling deeply known. This level of understanding takes time, patience, and the willingness to be awkward and compassionate with one another. Both people have to agree to build and nurture the relationship for everlasting intimacy.

There are great benefits to fostering an intimate relationship. Intimacy allows both people to not only learn and understand their partner on a deeper level, but it also provides insight into one's own individual psyche. There is an emotional connection that happens when one feels safe enough to be vulnerable. When you expose your core beliefs and values, you are able to support each other's weaknesses and celebrate each other's strengths and this is when true intimacy occurs. Real intimacy makes us feel alive and free because we have allowed someone to peer into the depths of our soul and see us for who we really are.

Intimacy to me is being able to lay in the bed with my significant other; talk, express our feelings, laugh and joke, it's kissing (not necessarily to lead to intercourse) and making each other feel wanted. I can count on one hand how many women I've actually been intimate with in this way, on a non-sexual level and I do find passion in it. However, I do find it challenging to find women who are able to engage in intellectual conversations. This is what I find most stimulating because I'm an intellectual guy. But because I am an exotic dancer, women tend to care more about my penis size and if my stage performance can be done in the bedroom. If I meet a woman that I like, I want to talk and get to know her on an intellectual level. - **JOSHUA, 25**

Intimacy is a level of closeness that one individual could have towards another. It's not necessarily a physical connection, essentially. I believe that there could be intimacy of the mind, as well as intimacy with God. I have had various levels of intimacy with women as well as emotional in the space of really understanding one another. Intimacy is something that I definitely desire and hope to build in a relationship, but what I have found is this level of closeness comes along in time from experience and experiences. People say that to be intimate you must be vulnerable, however, if I'm being intimate with the right person then it doesn't feel like I'm being vulnerable. It's nice being able to be free to express what's on my mind without worrying about what the other person is thinking. - **SHAUN, 25**

Intimacy to me is a mental and physical connection between two people. It's when two people can bond mentally and have a good understanding of one another. Our mindsets and goals are in sync with what we want to create for our future together. It is also when two people are genuinely happy to see each other. We look forward to seeing each other and creating this type of happiness together. If this is the type of connection we are both looking for then we can build from that and feel positive about each other. - **LAWRENCE, 26**

I think of three things when I hear the word intimacy. First, I think its how two people communicate. The only way to build intimacy is by communicating. Having conversations, sharing ourselves, learning about each other. Secondly, I think it's creating a cozy, romantic setting. My lady likes when I light some candles and burn some aromatherapy oils. I know this might sound crazy but I dig this shit too! Man, it just totally relaxes a brother, LOL! And lastly, I think it's also about sex. But, if I have sex without an intimate connection, it can still be good but in the long run it's unfulfilling. - **DONNIE, 27**

Intimacy is two people that love each other without having sex. It's not really intimate unless there is love. Intimacy is another way of saying "love". It's being with another person showing loyalty, having a good chemistry, really knowing each other and knowing about each other. Not just sexually, but in all aspects. It's loving a woman in a way where you see the good in her. It's being open to the point where you put everything on the table and accepting each other for who we are. - **LOGAN, 28**

I would describe intimacy as an emotional connection between two parties that satisfies a subjective need. These subjective needs can vary because in my experience I know that people appreciate intimacy in different ways. I know that some people appreciate physical touch, some people appreciate quality time, some people appreciate different things like receiving gifts, so it's kind of skewed for me based on my own experiences in relationships. I found that different women need different types of intimacy, it varies from person to person. - **DAMIAN, 30**

Intimacy is me giving all of myself to my partner and vice versa. We are giving in all aspects - mentally, emotionally, spiritually, physically - giving everything. This opens a realm of trust by being open and honest with who we are in all aspects, it also opens up another dimension of romance. This goes beyond the physical aspects of romance that includes touching, feeling, and kissing. It is more about being comfortable and safe with her. When I give her a simple gift of a flower or a card, how will she receive it? Will she just look at it and throw it away or will she actually accept my "gift" and know that I'm thinking about her throughout my day. - **GIANNI, 31**

Intimacy to me is sharing and letting someone into me and trusting them enough to let them become close to me. It's opening myself up to be vulnerable. I've been open and vulnerable in the past and those relationships didn't work out for me, my trust was betrayed. I didn't want to take this kind of hurt into other relationships, and I'm not necessarily talking about romantic relationships, but any kind of relationship. It's like putting myself out there, jumping off a ledge, and putting my faith in God that I will not get hurt or taken advantage of. I don't think intimacy necessarily has to be between a man and a woman in a sexual way. Intimacy can be between any two people. It's opening ourselves up and getting to know each other, as well as me getting to know myself. - **JAMAR, 32**

Intimacy to me is when I can really be honest and open with my significant other. I can be honest and share my thoughts and feelings without her judging me or thinking that I am weak. As a man, at this point in my life if I'm with a woman and she doesn't know how to communicate with me and share her feelings then we will never work together in a relationship. It's a shame to see couples out to dinner and rather than talking to each other they are on their phones completely ignoring each other. Why bother to be together if you don't have anything to say. For the first time in my life, I'm in a relationship where she is interested in getting to know the man that I am and she's not with me just for my wallet. I think men do want emotional intimacy, we just don't talk about it. And the reason we don't talk about it is because we don't want to appear to be weak. I don't want to tell a woman too much because she may hold what I said against me. This happened to me before and I still have not gotten over it. I think it left me feeling like I can't trust another woman. There's just a little bit of trepidation there for me to really open up. - **HUGH, 32**

Intimacy can mean a lot of things. This is a complex question. Over the course of the past 3 years, I analyzed this from an unpopular perspective. I think that intimacy now-a-days is misrepresented on television, so this causes a lot of confusion. Intimacy to me is anything that obviously evolves emotion but it doesn't specifically relate to sex or money, first and foremost. It involves spending more focused, quality time with my significant other and opening myself up to a more in-depth version of an individual, and vice versa. Intimacy from the societal perspective seems to primarily deal with sex and with money. Some people feel that in order for something to be intimate they need to have certain things around them in that moment.

Intimacy is two people being naked (figuratively) and transparent with each other. I have this type of intimacy with the woman I'm engaged to now, and with one other woman in my past. When I opened myself up in the past with women, trying to cultivate intimacy, it wasn't well received. Unfortunately we have these biases that have been created based off of mis-representation. As a black man I am not expected to be so in touch with my feelings. Intimacy takes time to develop with some people and with other people it's just natural. - **ANDRE, 33**

I guess I would say it is more like a verb. I would randomly come up behind my wife and give her a hug and a kiss on the forehead, or randomly slow dance with her in the living room. Just spending quality time together. Watching TV shows together, doing things we like to do, doing things for her. To me, intimacy is doing simple things like this. When my wife and I are vibing and connecting intimately, there is a rush of love and emotions that comes through me. When this happens, I just want to connect and share with her and share my feelings towards her. This is why I do the random things that I do so she knows I love her. Being honest is being intimate because it helps build trust in relationships. It's being open enough to tell my wife something and knowing that we'll be fine. Being honest builds the intimacy, the trust and the comfort between us, and this allows us to open up to each other even more. - **ALONZO, 34**

Intimacy to me is a connection shared between two people sexually and how you maintain that connection throughout the relationship that you have together. We maintain this intimate connection with flowers, dim lights, candles, little "thank you's", kisses, a lot of affection and confirmation. Confirmation means reassuring words like, "I love you', "I'm always here for you", "I want to please you", and "I want to spend the rest of my life with you". To me intimacy requires a certain amount of vulnerability which is something I just don't feel comfortable with giving to everybody. - **KING, 34**

Intimacy to me is multiple things. It's about the connection between two people. It's not only how we feel about each other on a sexual level but also how we respond to each other's body and how we intertwine. To me it's more about the physical than almost anything else. It's the way it feels when the hair stands up on my neck. It's like hanging out at Piedmont Park with a woman and we're really into each other; talking, smiling and really enjoying each other's energy. It's like two people having a visceral response to each other's interactions, words, touch, and body language. It's love. And then that love can connect to the sex. - **ISAIAH, 35**

Intimacy to me is having the ability to be vulnerable and feel protected within. It's being in a space with someone where I can share things that I don't share with everyone. I can share some of my deepest fears or things that I may have anxiety about at the current moment or things that I may have been harboring from previous relationships, or my family, and even things from my childhood. Things that I haven't expressed to anyone else because I just don't feel comfortable. Or feel as though I wouldn't get an empathetic response. An empathetic response where a woman will seek to understand where I'm coming from and she chooses to work together, whether for guidance or just having that shoulder to lean on. Intimacy is being in that space with someone where I can relax and let my guard down and I can just be my authentic self without judgment. It's having moments where I can sit here and talk about something that I'm deficient in and feel comfortable, and not feel like I'm being judged. The issue is being comfortable with our layers. When we get to the point of calling it intimacy is difficult because how often do we take a step out of our own world in order to see each other, to feel each other, and to understand each other and all that we go through. - **BRYCE, 35**

Intimacy to me is not just physical, it's the intellectual conversation that we have with each other on our own time. It's learning from each other, getting to know each other's turn-ons and turn-offs, and things of that nature. In some cases there is vulnerability with sharing intimacy, but there is also a risk. For instance, if I don't talk to that woman anymore, she could use what I've told her against me and I'm like "damn I told her all my stuff!" I've dealt with this before, so sometimes there is a little hesitation with really opening up and sharing myself with women. If I'm asked certain questions, I'll tell her that I'll share that with her later as we get to know each other better. A lot of times women take this as if I'm being secretive, and it's not that, I just don't put all my eggs in one basket at first. - **RL, 36**

I know a lot of people say intimacy is touching, feeling, kissing and whatever. Because of my job, I'm not around my wife a lot of the time. I'm gone for six weeks at a time and when I come back I'm only home for two weeks. So intimacy for me is the closeness that we have when we're not together as well as when we're together. When we're apart, intimacy is the little stuff that she does for me, like sending me a sweet message to let me know that she's thinking about me. This small gesture makes me feel good and gets me through the night. And then when I get home, she might have a massage set up for me on a certain day and time. All of this is intimacy to me instead of the whole hugging, kissing and having sex thing.- **MALIK, 38**

Intimacy to me is being with someone sexually that I love or desire. When I think of intimacy, I think about going very slow, taking my time with a woman... just savoring her, soothing her, taking her all in from head to toe. It's a very slow and enjoyable moment in time. There are times when I like sex to be hot and heavy and fast and we're seizing the moment like two animals! This is all well and good but I'm the type of man who likes it slow. I want nice intimate slow sex where I can really just take her all in. - **RON, 39**

Intimacy to me is time. The most valuable assets that we have in life is time. Being able to spend quality, intimate time together trying to learn the other person and accepting the other person, whether we're talking or just laughing together, that's intimacy. It's spending time trying to elevate the relationship. - **CHUCK, 40**

Intimacy is a connection to someone. A personal connection where you can share things you like about yourself and that you don't like about yourself. It's having a sense of freedom to be able to open up the trust between the two of us, the good and the bad. I have a tendency to hide what I really feel because I don't want the woman to see my weaknesses out of fear that she may judge me and not like me as much. - **TYLER, 42**

Intimacy at the age of 41 varies from intimacy at the age of 18. There is no blueprint to what intimacy is. As a divorced father of two, I had to learn what intimacy is. Intimacy is personal. Intimacy is growth. Intimacy is transparency. Intimacy is vulnerability. So intimacy at this age of my life really means to me, transparency. One of my quotes for the year has been "intimacy breeds transparency". What I mean by this is, the more open I am with my partner, the closer I am to them. I don't ever want to not feel close to my partner because my partner is what makes me tick. So when I think about the relationship I have right now, it is probably the most intimate I've ever been with anybody because she deserves transparency. I also know what I want in a progressive relationship. The partner that I am with now has known me for over 20 years. We were friends and her presence in my life is such where she has seen the layers of me. So if I was being fraudulent, it would not make for an authentic relationship. By me being transparent and vulnerable to her, this breeds trust so that we can unlock and unveil our true selves, and this makes for a stronger relationship. Also, because my woman and I are friends, this makes us better lovers.- **WES, 42**

Intimacy to me is being vulnerable without knowing the outcome or being able to control the outcome. It's where I don't have the fear of being honest without retribution, so to speak. I have never had this type of intimacy with any woman, honestly, I don't know if it even exists. I don't think I've really ever come close to having it. I would like to have it. I think if we were able to create intimacy then we would be creating a different society of people because it is a different idea and a different consciousness, you know? I feel like now we are taught NOT to love, as opposed to love. Because we're angry all the time. We are so quick to judge and point the finger at each other. We are basing relationships on all this stuff that doesn't really matter. We are not taught to love and be intimate with each other. - **CHRISTOPHER, 42**

This is a good question, I never thought about it. Intimacy to me is being very comfortable with my partner, it's being open and understanding each other's *Love Language*. Being intimate with a woman opens up a level of trust, a level of understanding, because I feel if you are truly intimate with someone you fully understand them; emotionally, physically and mentally. - **KADEEM, 44**

Intimacy to me would be the openness one will give another without fear. I almost had intimacy with a woman, however I was apprehensive to give all of myself to her. I wanted to build intimacy with her but I was fearful in allowing myself to go there with her. I had this awareness that wouldn't allow me to give more of myself. In my mind I wanted to create intimacy but I had these instincts that stopped me from going there. I felt that she wasn't being consistent enough with the times that she was sharing and being open. I am completely open to being vulnerable and developing intimacy with women, however, they must be open to developing intimacy with me as well. I do not have any fear when it comes to building intimacy because I understand what it is. It's not that I am not wanting to share myself in this sense, and be in a vulnerable state with a woman, this is not a problem. I am mature enough now and more over-standing now to where I will express myself if it is being reciprocated from the other side. - **DOMINIC, 45**


Intimacy to me is when you spend quality time with someone, sharing personal things and views as you learn about that other person. It's about fellowship and doing things together, enjoying each other's company, and learning from one another. I think, depending on the circumstances and what I want, I've got to be that for the other person as well. If I want a woman to be vulnerable to me, I have to be vulnerable to her. If I truly want someone to understand me, I have to tell her the good, the bad, and the indifference. There are different circumstances with intimacy depending on the person I'm dealing with. There are different levels of intimacy as far as sharing information is concerned and the individual in front of you. - **GYNUINE, 47**


For me, intimacy has nothing to do with sex. It is the peace and solidarity I have with a woman. It's a certain look or an inside joke, it's me and that woman being 'one' and everyone else is outside of that. It's like an unspoken truth between the two of us that no one else has access to. I can probably count on one hand the number of girlfriends that I have had intimacy with, and I prefer it to be this way. I don't share this type of openness and vulnerability with many women. Also with intimacy, I have to start with myself. I make sure I give myself enough 'me-time'. This is the benefit of being a loner and not bringing somebody else into that intimacy. Everyone that comes in contact with me can kind of feel that this is the type of person that I am. I can honestly say that I haven't been totally as intimate with another person in the way that I have been to myself, this is probably why I'm still single. - **DEL, 47**

Intimacy is taking on and personalizing a shared space with somebody or something else. It's creating an intimate environment. It's about opening up my space, energy and attention in agreement with somebody else or something else in the same space and environment. What I do within this space and environment varies. For example, I am a poet and spoken word artist and I perform in small venues of about 15 to 20 people. During this time, because we are in a small, close space there is a level of intimacy that is created between us as we share our gift and craft together. And then of course the obvious way, intimacy is about sexual expression. With sexual expression I am literally allowing a woman to explore a part of me that is sacred, very sacred. So even if I open my sacred self up with my sexual expression, I am allowing myself to be shared with somebody else in an intimate moment. - **DI-AMEN, 47**

I think there are two types of intimacy that go into making a romantic relationship. Obviously there's physical intimacy but there's also an intellectual intimacy, which I think is far more important than the physical intimacy, it is how I really connect with my partner. Can we be emotionally honest with each other and can we have intellectual conversations with each other. Do we make each other laugh, is our interaction fun but also deep and meaningful. - **XAVIER, 50**

Intimacy to me is about communication, it's not always about sex. We're talking about our likes and dislikes, things that we can improve upon in our relationship. I've been married twice. I've dated 17 different women in my life, however I only found two women that I could be intimate with and share my feelings with. These two women filled a void within me. They understood me and when I talked, they sat back and listened. By them doing these things, they made me feel special and they made me feel like whatever I was talking about made sense. There are other females that just brushed me off and I didn't like the way this made me feel. If I feel a woman is not listening to me or if she doesn't care, then I'm not going to talk to her about my personal opinions about life, where I want to be in life, and other things. These two particular women I really vibed with and could talk to without judgment. - **WILLIAM, 50**

Intimacy to me involves a number of things. It encompasses the mind, body and spirit. I can be intimate in a very deep level of conversation where it expands into a whole genre of things. Because of this, it touches a space that I feel we are connecting on so many other levels, just really because we're speaking it. And as we're speaking it, it jives in my brain that we're sort of transcending to something and this itself is intimate. If I'm connected with someone on these two levels, then once we become physically intimate, it takes it to a whole other level because we've connected intimately in the mind and spirit. Also, I can get physical with a woman and sex is off-the-chain to where it created the feeling of euphoria. We are vibrating on all the right circuits. Our rhythms are to the point where we're losing our minds. But, what if we can't talk? Then all we have is the physical aspect of intimacy? - **DEION, 51**

I think intimacy is the nuances of relationships, the little things. The intention for well-being but this is done in a subtle way. For example, in my relationships I always liked cooking with the woman that I'm with. It's being in the kitchen, rubbing up against her on purpose, talking about food, feeding each other. Cooking together, to me this is teamwork, it's almost like a dance in a way. I watch my mate and observe the way she cuts things, the way she uses utensils, and the way she moves around the kitchen. These are the things that come to mind when I'm thinking about her or when I miss her. I am married now so it is very important for me, when it comes to intimacy, to find ways to display love for my wife. It is also important also for my children to see me engage with their mother in this way. I'm raising girls, so this is the standard I choose to set the standard for them. - **MAVERICK, 51**

The word intimacy is (into-me-I-see) and this to me means pretty much loving myself and having that self love. It's loving myself unconditionally and continually evolving. It's having those levels of love and empathy and caring for myself. When I have this kind of love and caring for myself, it's easier for me to love other people, really, on a soulful level. Knowing that I love myself and I know who I am, I am able to love my woman deeply and I have the ability to express that love. Doing intimate acts and sharing intimate moments, doing things just because I know that she likes certain things. Intimacy to me is making my woman feel that she's appreciated. Doing things that she likes when she least expects them. I do these things because I truly love her and I want to see her happy. - **ISAAC, 51**

Intimacy is mental foreplay, and what I mean by mental foreplay, it's mentally setting the mood. I may call my wife when she's at work and I will invite her on a date tonight. This will mentally stimulate her to the point where she's getting excited about being together later on that night. It doesn't matter how long we've been married, this can still mentally stimulate her. Like sending her flowers for no reason at all, writing her a sweet romantic card, or even having a warm bath prepared for her when she gets home with candles and soft music playing. - **GARY, 52**

This is a good question. Typically people associate the word intimacy with sex, however in my opinion, sex is just one part of intimacy. Intimacy to me is everything that encompasses being connected and close to my companion. It is everything that triggers those feelings that are associated with feeling good. It is creating an environment with my partner that cultivates those warm, fuzzy feelings all the time. There are different degrees of intimacy. For example, I consider walking in the park, cooking together, holding hands, and looking at the moon together to be intimate as well. Also, there are many non-physical things that I find to be intimate, such as, listening to my partner when she is sharing her feelings, or sharing anything that matters to her. Just being in the same space together and communicating is intimate. - **MICHAEL, 53**

Intimacy as it relates to relationships, I believe is being transparent and unmasked in my communication and in my empathy for my partner. I'm able to share feelings and emotions that go beyond the physical but really relate to how truthful and vulnerable I am to the other person. Intimacy without trust is impossible. My definition of intimacy changes as I get older.

What I thought was intimacy at age 23 I don't believe is the same thing at 43 and definitely not the same at 54. - **GREG, 54**

Intimacy is the open, free flowing, uninhibited exchange of feelings, thoughts, desires, likes, and dis-likes. It's important that a woman understands what's pleasurable, or what's not so enjoyable to me. I also want to make sure I understand that about her as well. Intimacy is developed by talking more and having intimate conversations. And what makes the conversation more intimate is if we are honest and uninhibited in what we are expressing. I haven't had real intimacy with a woman in quite some time. - **JORDON, 54**

Intimacy for me is in three stages: Stage 1 – Communication within intimacy. It's understanding the person's *Love Language* and paying attention as we communicate with each other accordingly. Communication for me is not always about talking. It's about action and the setting and the flow. This type of communicating comes from the heart vs from the mouth, and these things are more felt than actual words. With communication, it's not what you say, it's what you do. It's how you are, it's how you act.

Stage 2 - When I'm thinking about intimacy, it's all about the setting and setting the mood for intimacy. This type of setting is quiet, nurturing, and romantic. It's a warm and beautiful atmosphere with candles, dinner, lounging, and soft music. Creating a setting is the invitation into intimacy.

Stage 3 - Once I enter the act of intimacy, it's all about paying attention. Putting the phones down, looking each other in the eyes, listening to what the other person is saying rather than over talking over each other. Massaging my woman's feet or her neck while she is talking and entering into the realm of touch and feel. If I can do these things, then the intimacy part will be really really beautiful. It has nothing to do with sex. - **TRUSTIN, 54**

When I hear the word "intimacy" I automatically think that it is a physical connection, it's giving myself sexually to someone that's really important to me. When I hear the words "making love" or "falling in love" to me, that's more of a mental connection. Although these words can also be related to intimacy as well. It's like a mental connection where we are sharing personal things about ourselves that perhaps we've never told anyone else. It's talking about things we would like to do to each other sexually.... even thinking about this now, I'm starting to get aroused! Talking sexually is like making love to each other with actually being physical. - **STEPHAN, 55**

Prior to my adulthood or manhood, I did not know what intimacy meant, I thought intimacy was having sex with a girl. And I often wondered early on, why sex didn't satisfy me. As I grew up and started to mature and talk to women, they began to communicate to me what intimacy was. I had it totally wrong. When I made love to a woman, whether it was for 10 minutes or an hour, I thought that was intimacy, and it wasn't. To a woman, intimacy is a man understanding who she is deep inside. It is understanding her love language, because women have love languages. As I got older, sex was not satisfying for me without intimacy. I can be physical with my wife but after that's done, what kind of communication or interaction are we having in our home? I learned that intimacy goes beyond the bedroom, it is sharing other things in the home that makes my wife feel loved, appreciated and special. - **TARZAN, 56**

Intimacy to me is not always sex. It could be just touching, talking, caressing, and closeness. Intimacy is reserved for someone that I'm interested in. I don't want to open myself up like this to every woman that I come across. I think it is a waste of time and it leads to confusion between us. At this age, I don't want to waste my time building intimacy with a woman if it's not going to go anywhere further than that moment. I will only build intimacy with a woman that I am really interested in being with. - **ORLANDO, 56**

Intimacy to me, now, is different from when I was younger. Now intimacy is more about communication and me letting the woman know that I'm thinking about her. This could be either by calling, texting or sending her flowers, and I'm doing these things just because I'm thinking about her. It's letting myself go when I'm around her. It's hugging and holding hands. I also think pillow talk is intimate, I love pillow talk in the morning, it's a turn-on because it gives me this perspective that it's me and her against the world. - **MM, 56**

Being honest with a woman, letting my guard down and sharing closeness, is what intimacy is to me. It means being open with my feelings about her and other things that may come up in a conversation. Not feeling the need to be protective or macho for the sake of it. When I have real intimacy with a woman, it's a breath of fresh air to be able to be completely honest and open without worrying about being judged. It's being able to share openly, and this sometimes is hard to do because I was not conditioned or socialized to be so honest. I had a lot of fear letting my guard down, because I don't want to be judged. Also, I only seek to cultivate real intimacy with someone that I genuinely care about because I'm not going to let my guard down with just anybody, she has to be someone that I trust. It's about trust. - **DARRELL, 57**

Intimacy is definitely not sex. It's the quality time I would spend with my partner. Walking around, talking, holding hands... all that kind of stuff. Just the normal day to day routine of being in a relationship is intimacy to me. Going to the store, shopping, going to the movies, things that I can really do with a friend, actually. The only difference with intimacy between someone I was dating versus a friend would be the touching, hugging, kissing and having sex because I don't do this with friends. The words 'intimacy' and 'love' are almost like a gag word for me. When I hear this word, it makes me feel like the woman has read too many romance novels or she watches too much romance television. I don't think about the word intimacy, so when a woman puts that word in a conversation, it makes me feel uncomfortable. I just want to live and be happy without too many complications. I think thinking about intimacy and talking about intimacy makes relationships complicated. I don't think that the words intimacy and love need to define our actions. Whenever these words are tied to something it makes my whole interaction feel fake. - **DN, 58**

To me intimacy is that time that is shared with my partner that is secure. It's promoting the relationship, it is private, it is one-on-one. It is doing things with the woman that I am involved with that I would not do with anyone else. It could be holding hands, walking together, sharing a private moments like caressing, a gentle massage, having sex. These are things that I would just do with my mate and not with anyone else. There are certain aspects of intimacy that are secure in the sense that they are private and held totally within our circle, just between me and my mate. It's private in the sense that I'm not apt to go out and tell the world about what we share, I keep it secure and within the boundaries of my relationship. I think there are vulnerable moments of intimacy. I believe intimacy is to be kept within acceptable bounds and not be divulged to others. - **PILOT, 61**

Intimacy for me is the compatibility, the respect, and the honesty that the two parties, male and female, have for each other. When there is a true connection between the two parties both emotionally and physically, this creates great intimacy. When two people really like each other and they communicate these feelings, this creates intimacy. One of the greatest gifts two people can give each other is true intimacy. I want to get to know the person, enjoy the person and enjoy the moment with her. - **KEITH, 60**

When I was younger intimacy was a point of nakedness (physically) and I had sex with no intimacy. How I define it now has changed for me over the years, it's not just about sex, there is more to intimacy than the naked body. It also means revealing my inner most hopes, dreams, wishes and fears with a certain kind of vulnerability and nakedness also. Before I got married, there were only certain women that I could get naked with my inner thoughts. Now that I am married, with a wife and a family, what changed for me was that I no longer feel unconnected from my wife, like I had with the other women in the past. In the past I felt disconnected from anything that looked like family. - **ANTHONY, 62**

I think intimacy is spending time with the person who is special in my life. Spending time where there are no other distractions, just having that alone time together, one-on-one. It is when me and my significant other are giving each other our undivided attention regardless of what activity is taking place. - **PAUL, 66**

# *Chapter 2*

# WHEN MEN FEEL LOVE

I wanted to understand what love looked like to men. How do men feel about love? How do men behave when in love, what do they think about, what would they do for love, and how do they feel when that love ends? We don't often hear black men talk about their joy, happiness, pain, longing, discomfort or their emotional highs and lows when it comes to love. Most of the men I interviewed have felt love at some point in their lives. A few men have never felt it. Some have had big regrets and fleeting thoughts of suicide when their relationships ended. Love means different things to different people, and they experience it in various ways.

Yes, I was in love. That relationship lasted for about 1 ½ years. I fell in love with her because of her spirit, her laugh, the way she treated me, her intellectual capacity, and the way she carried herself. I took her virginity so it was a little more special for me. We were young, we were in college together, we were so honest with each other. She actually ended up cheating on me and this broke my heart, I never cried so hard over a female in my life. I do honestly miss her and I look for her in a lot of women, but I can't find that same love. - **JOSHUA, 25**

My longest relationship was about 1½ years. I cared a lot about her and wanted the best for her. I feel like if our situations were different then maybe I could have loved her. So if I can't envision myself spending the rest of my life with a woman then it's hard for me to say that I love them. It was a long distance relationship so it was a bit of a drive between us. There were times when she needed someone there for her and I couldn't always be that person. I didn't want to hold her back or anything so I broke it off with her. - **SHAUN, 25**

Yes, I think I was in love with my wife in the beginning of our relationship. Looking back now, it was just the honeymoon stage where everything was good. We hadn't really gone through enough life together. This honeymoon phase lasted for about two years. I was cheated on by my wife. When I found out, it hurt! I really hurt like on a whole other level! In our relationship, I held myself to a higher standard and felt as though it was my responsibility to take the lead. So when I found out my wife was sleeping with someone else it was like, damn! I didn't understand what more she needed. I was in the Navy and I was on deployment when it happened. All the money that I was earning was being sent home to her and then I found out that she was spending it on other things, this was really hard to take. - **LAWRENCE, 26**

Yes, I've been in love a few times. I knew I was in love because I was able to open myself up and I felt free to be myself and say whatever I wanted or needed to say. They say 'men don't cry' but I do cry and the fact that I am able to express these emotions to my woman, confirms that this is love to me. I trust her, she has my back and we don't fight much, and if we do have a disagreement, we are able to come to a conclusion and settle it. We support each other and lift each other up. This is how I know I'm in love with my lady. - **LOGAN, 28**

I knew that I love her because of how genuine and pure of heart she was. I felt like I could trust her and that I could be myself around her. It was very important for me to be myself around her because I think that a lot of women don't get this from men these days, they don't really get to see men authentically. A lot of relationships are filled with guys trying to be the way that they think a woman wants them to be. Or men are trying to portray themselves to be something they think that particular woman wants. By doing this, men lose a little bit of who they are and they don't let women see the genuine side of them. - **DAMIAN, 30**

Yes, I've been in love. Love has so many different levels to it. You can have love for somebody. You can be in love with somebody. Or she can be that soul mate. I've been there before with my ex-fiance. When I was with her, I felt she had everything that I was looking for. We broke up because of my ego. When I was with her I was preparing for my first body-building contest. During that time I had to eliminate stress, I had to make sure I was on point with my meals and everything. So during this time there was a woman on my social media that she didn't like and I wouldn't block this woman. Even though my ex-fiance at the time had my password, she was stressing me about it. So instead of me dealing with it and talking about it, I left her and broke up because I wasn't going to keep dealing with that. To this day I honestly regret that this happened. I miss her and want her back. I have told her that I'm sorry for what I did but I can tell that she's scared and she thinks that I may run off on her again. - **GIANNI, 31**

I have never really been in love. I thought I was in love, but when I think about it now, our relationship was really just based on sex and having fun. We did not talk about things that would make us grow stronger as a couple. We drank, fucked, smoked weed, hung out and partied. Although the sex was great, we never went deeper with each other. Also, as time went on, I began to see that everything was about her, she did not want to compromise on anything and after a while this became frustrating. I realize, love, true love takes work on both parts. And the only way for me to truly love a woman is to know all parts of who she is, and accept her for who she is completely. - **HUGH, 32**

I'm a very non-traditional man and so is my lady, she's is my Wisdom. We share a lot of the same creative ventures and this is huge for me to have a partner like this. We actually met on Twitter. A few weeks afterwards, we met in person, and we've been together ever since. I knew my woman was the woman for me when I didn't want to control the relationship. My fiance listens to me. She's considerate. She pushes me as a Black man, and I need this. So, with her being a Black woman and having an understanding of me, she can do that. I can't get upset when she holds me accountable, this is one of the reasons why I love her. - **ANDRE, 33**

Yes, I feel like I've been in love three times. And the reason I felt like I was in love because I had a willingness to do almost anything for these women, that was the deciding factor for me. It wasn't about seeing a future with them, like getting married or having kids. It was more like I'd do anything for them. To me that loyalty and that trust is almost more important than the love. Telling someone that "I trust you", to me, means more than saying, "I love you". If I really love somebody, it is freedom, there are no conditions in which they can do wrong and I think this feeling should go both ways. - **ISAIAH, 35**

I've only been in love once when I was 26 years old. I always had a crush on her since high school. We talked about everything. We knew each other's backgrounds and each other's family, so we always had a connection between us, we just never made anything happen. Our friendship grew into love, we had this unbreakable bond. We loved each other. We kept it 100 with each other talking about everything that was going on. We were in a long distance relationship, I was in Atlanta and she was in Wisconsin. Over time, things began to change between us. We talked everyday, laughing and joking... everything was great. The intimacy was growing between us. But the long distance no longer worked for her because I wasn't there when she needed and wanted me.- **RL, 36**

No, I have never been in love. I've been close in what I thought was love, but it wasn't really. But now that I am older I can say I was really at a point where I wanted to open myself up to somebody, but it really wasn't love. Love, for me, would be a really good balance within union. This comes with time. I would say it is what builds as two people get to know each other over time. Within all that we do, we would both be in the same frame of mind but balance would be the thing that builds the love between us two. - **DOMINIC, 45**

I can't say that I've actually never been in love nor have I had 'real intimacy' before with women that I've dated. I had to realize that this all stems with me, with myself, and I had to take a look at how my ego plays into this. I am seeking something special. I've been in relationships where I felt I like I deserved better than this. Most people accept the love that they think they deserve. For me, growing up poor, I had some insecurities about that. I always operated from the standpoint that this is the way things should be. My intimacy came from my friends, I always had and still have a few close male friends. I learned early on that the coolest thing I could ever be is myself. Unfortunately, the women that I've dated have never matched up to this. It's crazy because I want love, but not at the expense of my peace. Because I'm completely content with who I am, it allows me to accept people totally for who they are. - **DEL, 47**

I think I've been in love. I was in my late 20's and I had been dating this young lady and she basically used me. The reason I knew I was in love is because I wanted to kill myself because of the pain I felt after we broke up. This thought only lasted for about 30 seconds though. I knew it was love because of that feeling I had not being with her, I couldn't sleep. It took me about a year and a half to get over her. We never had any closure. It was frustrating to think I had those thoughts of killing myself because it's so cowardly. - **GYNUINE, 47**

When I'm with a woman that I care a lot about, I don't define it as 'love', I define it as an experience. And within this experience, we are acknowledging love. This is the intention I bring into the relationship when I'm with someone I want to share my life with. The intention is to discover our agreement in love first. Love always defines the level and the quality of our relationship. It always does. The way that people say, "being in love or falling in love", these words or this mindset doesn't exist for me. Mainly because 'love' itself takes an act of intimacy to open up and acknowledge love in an agreement with somebody else. What I call, 'falling in love' as other people see it, is nothing more than infatuation and it's self gratifying. It doesn't really fall into the constraint of what love truly is. It's all about what the other person is doing for you, how the other person is making you feel. So it is extremely selfish. When in actuality, love is selfless. This is why I say that love doesn't exist. And for us to keep thinking in this way we will continue to have problems that we have amongst one another. Currently, I am just looking to live out love and acknowledge love with someone. In my spiritual system, we describe love as 'Maat'. - **DI-AMEN, 47**

I was in love twice. I was able to sit down and talk to them to the point where we were really feeling each other. She had my back and I had hers. We were friends and I felt like I could tell them anything... This is what love is to me. It doesn't even matter how she looks. It's about vibing together and understanding each other. I feel the most loved when I am able to freely express myself, and she is able to do the same with me. I saw a lot of love around me growing up, and this was pretty exciting to see my parents loving each other. One minute I would see them argue and 15 minutes later, it was like it never happened and they were back in love. What this taught me was to not let the argument persist. Just go on and deal with the situation; shake hands, make love, kiss or hug, and move on. I've been with some women where we would go to bed mad at each other and we wake up and we're still arguing. This isn't for me. At that point it was time to go, the relationship was over. - **WILLIAM, 50**

I've been in love twice. First with my ex-wife and now with the woman that I am dating. My ex-wife grew out of love. I still have love for her in terms of wanting her to be happy and I care for her wellbeing. She's the mother of my child so I want the best for her. I am in love now with the woman that I'm dating, and what I love about her is the fact that she cares authentically from her heart. She loves me unconditionally. It is really hard to find somebody who loves unconditionally. She's very intelligent; we have great conversations; we have a lot in common; we laugh and can be silly together;

we accept each other for who we are; we support each other and try to push each other to be our best; and we hold up a mirror to each other as well.
- **ISAAC, 51**


For me, being in love feels very much like I'm satiated, like I'm good. There is no more sneaking. There's no more feeling like something is missing, everything's in its place. It's crazy because I've been in love with women that I knew I could not be with. The reason why I could not be with them was because of the person they brought out in me, I did not like that person. Love is different now because everything that I thought love was going to provide for me, I have now gotten to the point where I can provide it for myself. I don't look for love to provide things that are not capable of providing. The things that I thought I would find or that love would provide for me, once I found love I found that I could provide for myself. It's like that feeling that I have when I'm really into someone, I have this air of confidence. My heart feels settled and I feel solid. I feel this way now, regardless if I'm in a relationship or not. I don't need a relationship for this to happen. I took the onus off of 'love' to provide this for me and I found love in myself in other ways. I don't need my wife to tap me on my head, pat me on my butt or to put the battery in my back because I already have my battery. So if she fails to do this, then I don't look at her and begrudge her for not supporting me. Now, I alleviate my excuses for falling out of love with my wife by providing certain things for myself. - **MAVERICK, 51**


I struggle with saying I've been in love because I don't know what it feels like. I'm kind of hard on emotions, I'm not an emotional person. If I had to rate my Love Language, it would definitely be acts of service. I show my love by doing things. I show my love by giving things. If my significant other was asking me for words of affirmation, I am not very good at that. So I say this about myself in expressing or feeling love. If a woman tells me that she loves me. I know that she cares for my well being. But for me, I wouldn't do these things for her unless I loved her. - **DEION, 51**


Yes, I've been in love once. I was around 19 years old, she was my son's mom. I knew I was in love because I started developing feelings that I never knew about. I grew up in the streets and I didn't know how to handle my feelings or express them or even have a conversation about them. I was never taught how to love, to receive love or how to get love. We broke up because she ended up fooling around with other men. All I knew about being in a relationship was taking her to dinner, then to a motel and dropping her back off at home. If she got out of line, I would yell at her and cuss her out. I had no real role models when it came to how to treat a lady. I learned from watching the drug-dealer on my block and seeing how he treated women. - **GARY, 52**

I've been in love many times. I've been married twice and in love with both of these women, however, I've only been deeply, deeply in love once and that was with my fiance. My relationship with my fiance lasted a little over four years and she passed away due to an illness. This was over a year ago and I'm still in love with her today. Although I am still in love with her, I believe I can still open myself up to love someone else. The things that I learned in that relationship really helped me to become the person that I am now in terms of understanding what real intimacy is, what real commitment is and what real companionship is. So I believe that I am prepared for the next relationship and I'm in a better position than I was from a maturation perspective. I am a person that seeks intimacy and at this point in my life I definitely understand it more. - **MICHAEL, 53**

I have been truly in love three times in my life. The last relationship that ended because of a lack of trust, honor and respect. My ex-wife was not truthful, she did not honor our marriage or respect me and this was lost by actions that were repeated over and over again, that were not necessary. - **TRUSTIN, 54**

I was in love twice. The first woman that I love, she had been married before and had been through a lot in her life personally. I underestimated the impact that those experiences had on her and would have on our relationship. I don't do well with jealous and insecure types. Despite the fact that she was an absolutely gorgeous woman and I was a faithful boyfriend, she had been cheated on in her previous marriage and this just made her think that every guy was that way. So despite the fact that I was blindly in love with her, I broke up with her because I couldn't deal with her behavior anymore. - **JORDON, 54**

I've been in love on occasion with women that I connected with in between my marriages and sometimes while I was married. Towards the end of my marriages when things were really bad and I was just holding on, I met a few women that I can definitely say I was in love with. Even though I was in love with these women, the timing was not right. - **GREG, 54**

I've been in love twice in my life, and the variation of both these loves were different. The first love was a destructive love where it is more of a controlling situation. When I was younger and in love, it was more of that control saying, "Hey, this is MY girl!" and she should be acting according. I tried to keep her attention as much as possible by acting stupid or being the way I thought she wanted me to be. So in doing this, I did too much and she didn't understand me. In a woman's mind, she always has the illusion of how she thinks the relationship should be. Whatever she was taught at home is the way she thinks it should be. So when I was doing too much and it went outside the lines of what she believed, then she didn't understand me or have an appreciation for me. I was vulnerable and I probably looked weak and insecure to her. I was no longer cool to her and once she felt that way I did not know how to pull this back. I cared about her more than she cared about me and I could never get her to understand how much I cared. Now my variation of love in my 50's, it's hard... it is still hard. A woman has to like me more than I like her, and I honestly believe this. - **MM, 56**

I've been in love three times to the point where I was head over heels for these women. The first time I was in love, I was in high school and we were together for about five years. She was always around. I enjoyed her company and always looked forward to seeing her. We talked about our hopes and dreams and our future together. I actually thought that we would be together the rest of our lives. We broke up during our first year of college when I caught her out at a party with another guy. It actually took me about two years to get over her. I wouldn't let another woman get close to me after that because I kept thinking I could get her back. I didn't want to waste time

on someone else because I was trying to get her back, I wanted to be with her. I thought it would be unfair to someone else if I started to develop a relationship with them, knowing that my heart was with someone else.
- **ORLANDO, 56**

I've been in love several times, but there was one woman that I was really in love with. We dated for a couple of years. At the time, I was afraid that she was too young for me and I couldn't allow myself to accept the relationship because I was 28 years old and she was 18. It just felt too off balance. In retrospect I should have just gone for it because she was all the things that I wanted in a woman, but in my mind I was thinking that she was just too young. - **DARRELL, 57**

Yes, I was in love once and it was almost complete misery. I was so consumed by her that I felt sick when she was away. She was on my mind all the time, regardless of what I was doing, it was just way too much emotionally. When we broke up, it gave me a sense of relief. The thing about love, I don't think it ever ends, it becomes edged into the heart and this is an issue. I can't expect a certain kind of love, I can only accept the love she gives me. There's no such thing as, 'I'm not getting enough love' or 'she's not loving me the way I want her too', because I don't know how she perceives love to be in her own mind. So all the stuff she gives me I accept it. If I can't deal with what she gives me then this is when the relationship starts to fall apart. - **DN, 58**

I've been in love three times in my life, and the love I had for each of those women was different. Real love to me, takes on the characteristics where I'm thinking about her a lot. Throughout the day and night, when we are apart, I don't feel complete without her. When she calls and when I see her, there is a certain feeling of joy that comes over me. I feel totally content where I block out the rest of the world. It's almost as if the rest of the world doesn't exist. Any problem that we may have gets put in the background. Everything that does not relate to that woman becomes secondary to me. It's almost like we establish a spiritual connection. I stop whatever I'm doing to make sure the connection is as strong as possible. I'm putting all my attention into maintaining my connection with her. - **PILOT, 61**

The love I have for my wife is different from any other love that I've had before her. Honestly, nobody can convince me to put myself in a situation where my marriage could be jeopardized. This was never true before with any other woman that I dated. Before, I could have been in love, but not really afraid of any consequences of my own actions with another woman that came along that I may have been interested in. In the past I could have been dating somebody, even living with her, and if another woman came along that I was interested in or attracted to, even if it was just for one night, I may have explored that. I didn't feel that it would impact the love relationship that I was in at the time. - **ANTHONY, 62**

Yes, I've been in love and in a lot of ways I still love this woman. We were together for seven years. We broke up and went our separate ways for several reasons, but it doesn't mean I don't still love her. We broke up because of my vocation, I'm a musician, and she was insecure and had poor self-esteem. Although I still love her, we can't reconcile our differences and I don't take any backward steps. I learn from my mistakes and don't want to repeat them. I would not revisit that situation. - **PAUL, 66**

# Chapter 3

# WHAT MEN FIND ATTRACTIVE
# IN WOMEN

Black men come in all shades, shapes, and sizes. Each one has his own unique interests and preferences. I wanted to know what qualities they find attractive in a woman, as well as how these qualities will help build a strong, passionate and intimate bond with her. What they find attractive is based on their life experiences and what they deem to be important to them at this time in their lives.

When I asked this question, most of the men immediately talked about the physical attributes of a woman. I had to reel them back in and restate the question to get them to look beyond physical attractiveness and focus on more innate qualities. Some men have never thought about their attraction to a woman's heart, mind, and spirit. They pondered over the question prior to answering. Other men were very clear about the qualities they sought in a woman. I discovered the emotional and intellectual qualities men find attractive, aside from physical appearance, are just as individual as each man himself.

- I love a woman with intellect, this really turns me on. I don't like women who are air-headed or materialistic. Being intelligent to me means knowing about the world and knowing about herself. She is able to teach me things that I didn't know relating to spirituality or meditation. She can open my mind on different horizons by simply giving me a book to read so that I can learn about other things and enhance myself as a man.

- I like a woman who is down to earth and practical. She has no illusions about things and she's not pretentious.

- I like a woman who has sex appeal. Sex appeal to me is the way she looks at me, the way she talks to me and the tone of her voice; her eyes; the way she twirls her hair; the way she walks away from me. A woman who is confident with her sexuality and doesn't exploit it. - **JOSHUA, 25**


- This is a heavy question because I never really thought about what I found attractive in a woman. The first thing I would say would be kindness. Kindness to me means not always thinking about oneself, but thinking about others as well. How she acts towards other people in her life and in her community, and how much she considers other people is pretty important to me personally.

- A second quality would be a certain level of self-sufficiency, where she is able to take care of herself and doesn't need or isn't dependent on someone else. She has her own goals and aspirations. She's her own person and has her own mind and has the will power to achieve her goals on her own.

- The third quality would be a woman who takes care of her body and keeps herself healthy. She takes the time and the effort to take care of her 'meat-suit'. I'm certainly not the healthiest person ever, but I personally find excessive unhealthy habits unattractive. I never dated a woman that smoked cigarettes. - **SHAUN, 25**


- The first quality would be her personality, mainly her having a positive attitude and a positive outlook on life and anything in her life. I find that when I'm in a relationship, a woman's attitude may start out great but eventually her negative attitude comes out and this leads to conflict.

- Secondly, I also find independent women to be attractive as well. And what I mean by independence is that she can think for herself to determine what it is she wants. In my generation so many women are influenced by social media and their actions go far beyond what I can understand. I feel that if she is influenced by social media then this can produce problems in our relationship by setting standards far beyond her reach. A woman may want what someone else has, which may not be within her reach, and this becomes a distraction in our relationship.

- The third most attractive thing to me would be her ability to communicate to understand me, not to defend herself. When I get into a new relationship I go into it with the possibility of having a life with her. So in this case, we have to try to understand one another because at the end of the day, when it comes down to it, we may be all each other has when everything else in our lives is gone. - **LAWRENCE, 26**


- The first thing I notice about a woman of course are her features, A woman's eyes show a lot about her character and who she is. There is a certain vibe a woman gives off through her eyes.

- I like to see a woman smile. I don't like when they frown or have a straight face, this is a turn-off for me. When a woman smiles she radiates happiness and joy and it shows another level of affection.

- A positive personality is attractive. Personally, I'm a very positive person, I don't think negatively. In a lot of situations I think of positive outcomes. If she has a positive outlook on life and other things, even if she comes from a negative place, she will attract more positive things into her life. - **LOGAN, 28**


- Her ability to be nurturing is something that I look for when I'm thinking about a potential wife. This is something that I was able to experience as a child growing up and I definitely want my children to understand what it's like to be nurtured and to be loved.

- A woman that is financially aware. I've experienced women who were not financially responsible and it is definitely a turn-off for me. It is attractive to me when a woman is responsible about her money and life. It's attractive when she has the mindset of wanting to be financially stable and secure. She wants to take care of herself and not be dependent on someone else.

- A woman who is comfortable with who she is as a woman because when a woman is this way, this breeds confidence. She experiences things in her life that makes her want to appreciate herself. I've been in relationships where women didn't appreciate themselves or their bodies and this came from them not being comfortable with who they are. Her discomfort and insecurity had a huge impact on our relationship. - **DAMIAN, 30**

- Spirituality is number one, she has to have a prayer life. When she gives herself to God, that's beautiful because there are a lot of women out here that don't even know what God is. They're out here running around with loose morals and all kinds of stuff... that's so unattractive. This whole thing with "Hot Girl Summer" diluted a lot of these women's best qualities.

- She has to have a sense of humor. If I can laugh with her and be open with her jokingly, then she has a place in my heart.

- I also love a woman that can be a woman. She's not out here trying to get the attention of 1,000 men. Being a woman is someone who is morally sound. She can look sexy without being loose out here in these streets. Someone who wears her head on her shoulders and never looks down. - **GIANNI, 31**

- A woman who is self-aware and she is able to talk about her feelings. She is able to understand why she does the things she does and can express herself freely.

- A woman who is a nurturer is attractive. She is thoughtful and is able to understand other people and support them in their development. This quality should be innate in her and not forced. It just flows naturally.

- A woman who is confident and has the ability to do many things. She doesn't need me to do things for her, but she appreciates when I do. - **JAMAR, 32**

- A woman who is a good communicator. She has to be able to express herself in all areas of her life. I want to know what she is thinking about life. I want to know what gets her excited and what makes her sad. Some women have a hard time talking about themselves authentically. They think as men we should just know certain things. I'm not a mind reader, if she doesn't tell me then how will I know?

- A woman who can handle her finances and does not try to keep up with the Jones. There are some women who have a compulsion to spend money on things they don't even need. I remember dating this woman who had a closet full of clothes still with the tags on them. She said she brought them on sale and some of the dresses have been in her closet for two years and had never been worn. This is wasteful to me. She could have put that money into investments instead.

- A woman who has a happy spirit and loves to laugh! A beautiful smile and a twinkle in her eyes will get me every time. - **HUGH, 32**


- Creativity, a woman who is creative is very attractive because to me it shows brilliance. There is a difference between knowledge, wisdom and understanding. When a woman can manipulate something that she understands for herself and is able to cultivate it, nurture it and love it to what she wants it to be, this is a sign of genius, and I respect it as such.

- A strong-willed woman with resilience, she doesn't give up. I come from a family of strong women, a village of them, my mother being one of the strongest. I've seen my mother work three jobs, sometimes working until two-o'clock in the morning. She'd cook meals for the entire family and do so many other things... she was just strong! But then again, this is the essence of a Black woman. A woman who doesn't break when it comes to her morals and her abilities.

- A woman with intellect is very sexy. If she captures my mind, then she captures my heart. This is hard to do because the way most people think is monotonous to me in this day and age. Right now, in this present day, most people would rather be entertained then to produce something or be productive. - **ANDRE, 33**

- I like women who are nurturing. Seeing a woman actually care for someone is selfless, and this to me, is a turn-on. It's a very attractive thing. I can't really explain it. It's seeing her in her natural element, it's her being herself. It's like she's doing this but it's not something that she's forced to do or doing it out of obligation. She's just naturally doing it, and she's happy doing it. For me, I like to sit back, watch, and appreciate her being happy in her element.

- A woman who can just be herself where she's not worried about what another person thinks or what they feel, I mean she'll take those into consideration, but for the most part she's just being herself. There are so many women out here just focusing on the social standards and they think this is what the norm is supposed to be. They feel like they have to live into society's expectations. So a woman who can think on her own and be her own person, this is attractive.

- A woman who is a good listener is attractive. For example, if I'm going through something and I want to vent or get her opinion on something, she can hear what I am saying. She tries to understand where I'm coming from and she gives me her opinion. Not just telling me what she thinks I want to hear but what she really believes, what she really thinks and what she really feels. - **ALONZO, 34**

- I love when a woman is innately maternal. When she is caring, wants to protect me, makes sure I'm good, and anticipates my needs.

- I like curvy women, a more modern curvaceous woman. I'm from the South so I like a little bit of thickness.

- Women are the bearers of life, this is phenomenal and very attractive. It's like she's Mother Earth. Having the ability to grow and change and bear children. It's fascinating to see all the changes going on in her body. - **KING, 34**

- I am attracted to a woman's mouth, for some reason this just always turned me on. I don't even know if it's really sexual, I think it's more of the intimacy thing. Then on the sex side, I'm not thinking about her giving me head or anything when I see her mouth. It's not even about the shape of her mouth, it's more so, is her mouth appeasing? Braces or no braces, pouty or not pouty. Thin lips or thick lips. Are her teeth pretty? It's not a particular thing, I can't really define it.

- Secondly, I am continually growing myself, so I'm really into somebody that's a consistent grower, this really is a turn on for me. A woman who is looking to become better at all moments in whatever way that she can. So obviously if she's somebody who reads a lot and likes talking about books or finances, investments or business and other things that she's doing, this is really attractive to me. I know that even if we become stagnant in a relationship, we won't be stagnant people. We'll be consistently growing and if we are always growing, we will be communicating and connecting on a different level and there is always hope for the relationship.

- Lastly, I think this may be real shallow, but the third would be her physical looks. I like a certain type of girl. She doesn't necessarily have to be African or Asian or Latina, I just like an actual pretty woman. I don't really have a type so the physical attributes aren't going to matter. She could have small breast or large breasts, big butt or small butt… it really doesn't matter as long as that woman is an attractive woman to me. I can't put my finger on it, I just love the energy of a woman. - **ISAIAH, 35**

- Empathy is important because a lot of people will say nice things or they think that they are saying nice things. A woman who understands what works for me and she knows how to handle me by showing empathy. She is able to affectionately put herself in my shoes to recognize what I am going through. She may not completely understand the feelings and the emotions that I'm going through (the hurt, the pain, the embarrassment, or the anxiety) but whatever it is, she knows what these feelings are.

- High emotional IQ is important where she can understand when I'm going through something and she knows how to manage me and the situation.

- A woman that is a good hearted and a good natured person. I'm going to need a woman to apply that softness to help balance me. I like her to be nurturing and direct. - **BRYCE, 35**

- I find women who can communicate and have conversations very attractive. If she can make me think and challenge my brain, this is sexy to me.

- A woman who is honest and real and can keep things 100, would be the second thing. I let her know what I'm getting into and she lets me know what she's getting into, we're honest and we can go from there. These days, it's hard to find women who are honest, it seems like nobody's honest anymore. Nowadays, men and women try not to be honest anymore because they don't want the other person to feel some type of way, which I get. But, if we're starting something and we're going somewhere, then let me know what I'm getting into and I'll let you know the same. She just needs to be honest if she's talking to somebody else. Then this will give me the choice to decide if I want to stay and see where this could go with her or to let her finish that situation and then come back and talk to me.

- Her smile will catch my attention more than her ass or titties because it tells me the type of energy she's bringing. If her smile can brighten up my day and make me look at her and say, "wow, this woman is beautiful! She got all her teeth and they're clean!". This is a beautiful thing. - **RL, 36**

- The first thing that made me fall in love with my wife was a conversation we had one day and I just said, "Man, I just love your brain! I love the way you talk and the way you put things together." When she speaks, the way she speaks and the way the words flow just made me fall in love, or grow in love with her even more.

- Number two - is her body... she's fine!!! My wife is like 6' tall and I'm short. I've always been fascinated with tall women since I found out what an Amazon was, and in my whole life I was like "Man I gotta get one!"

- And number three would be her spirit. My wife and I connect on such different levels. We meditate together. We read a lot of books together on a metaphysical level that makes us become closer. There are certain things that we do that makes me more attracted to her. She's into some other stuff that I didn't even know about like Reiki energy healing, she's got me into it. Just my wife being herself makes me more and more attracted to her every day. - **MALIK, 38**

- A woman who is open to learning new things is attractive to me because as I get older I am set in my ways. I am set in my ways due to the systems that are in place in my life. If a woman is open to learning new things then she is open to figuring out different ways to enhance our relationship. If she has these thoughts then she's looking for ways to make our relationship better. This way we can both continue to grow together.

- A sense of understanding. She understands who I am and what my life is like as a Black man in this world. We get each other and the way we ebb and flow as Black people together. Black people get killed over bullshit. Being a professional Black man is not always easy. I have been racially profiled by the police on a few occasions and a woman who understands this is attractive to me.

- She is interested in making our time together exciting. As a professional man, I am constantly going from zero to sixty, meaning I hit the ground running and taking care of business for my family. And if we are both in professional situations, then the same energy has to be put into our intimacy. If my wife doesn't put this same energy and time into enhancing our intimacy then it appears that she would rather be with her work husband. - **CHUCK, 40**


- I see with my eyes first so I would say the physical attraction leads the way. I'm really big on her eyes and her smile. There is nothing like seeing a smile from my partner in a crowded room. There is an energy in a person with eyes that are expressive and a smile that warms me up. A woman can say a lot with her eyes, without saying a word.

- Next would be her personality. If she and I can't vibe then I just can't fuck with her, no matter how beautiful she is. She would have to be easy going and not complicated. I've dated several beautiful women, but there was one woman in particular who was probably one of the most petty women that I have ever met in my life. She was beautiful, she was a business woman, but her pettiness was very off putting to me and I couldn't see myself being in a long term relationship with her.

- And thirdly would be her spirituality. Having a woman who can pray for me and has that faith is very important. Somebody who believes in God.

Somebody who is a Christian. Somebody who prays on a regular basis and she has a sense of peace. - **WES, 42**

- I find intelligence very attractive in a woman. This is the ability for her to think outside of the norm. For example, is she is able to have a conversation about philosophy and different thought processes and how people learn, absorb, and create.

- The second quality would be a woman that is okay with being herself. And what I mean by that is, some women think they have to be like somebody else or look like somebody else or sound like somebody else instead of who they are. Many women are looking for answers in a book about who they are and most of the times the answer is right there within them. She has to be her authentic self, you know? She has to be true to who she is and the choices she makes without guilt, shame of excuses.

- Lastly, she has to have genuine parts, no fake nothing. No fake booty, no fake titties, no fake hair... she's genuine... I want the REAL thang! - **CHRISTOPHER, 42**

- Intelligence is a must. She has to be able to hold a conversation outside of social media and be able to talk about things like world events, finances, and astrology per se. She is able to have a thought provoking conversation that doesn't include gossip.

- I am attracted to a woman's eyes. Eyes tell a lot like if she's being forthcoming and up front. Her eyes can also express if she is in tune with herself and how she cares for her body and her health. Also hazel, light grey or unique color eyes are a turn on to me.

- The third thing I find attractive is a woman with nice hips and butt, aesthetically this turns me on, a slim waist and juicy booty. - **KADEEM, 44**

- My first quality that would attract me to a woman would be if her spirit is balanced. And what I mean by her balance is does she feel okay about herself spiritually without the baggage. Relationships for me are not always caught by the physical, it's always spiritual first. She may not know it, but I know it. Being spiritual is a feeling. It is something that was taught to me as a child with my mother and grandfather. I came up in a different type of home where I was taught to feel first. Most people learn by watching, I learned by feeling. When you learn by "feeling" this becomes part of your safety in any situation.

- Confidence would be the second quality, but not arrogance or aggressiveness. Confidence is knowing who you are and the abilities that you possess. A woman who is confident has the ability to help, to love, to nurture, to care for other people. With confidence a woman would really have to have the ability to allow her spirit side to show.

- The third quality, I would call extra credit, and this would be her physical make up and how she cares for herself. This means she would have good health, she would have a glow. If she is healthy inside she will carry a certain type of frequency, or aura. - **DOMINIC, 45**

- I like a woman who is independent and self-sufficient. She understands the value of a dollar. She knows how to take care of herself, shes not looking for a man to take care of her. I was raised by a woman, there was never a man around, this isn't an excuse, it's just an explanation. If I meet a woman in her 40's, she should be independent and self-sufficient. She should know how to pay bills, have a place to stay, and build her own reputation. She should know how to provide for herself and maneuver throughout the world as an adult. Just because she gets in a relationship, it shouldn't change. Being in a relationship should only make it better. If one of us comes up, we both should come up.

- I like a woman who is a 'giver' because I like to receive, I just found out this is my *Love Language*. I don't want to say women are narcissistic, but I believe I'm meeting women who are selfish and self-centered, it's all about what I can do for them. They want me to prove myself first. They want me to take them out on 10 dates before they finally treat me to fast food on one date. Women will hold me to a higher standard, where to me, if we like each other we treat each other. I'm all for the courtship phase. If I'm dating you I'll take you out, but at the same time, I'm important too. I want to know that she likes me enough to spend her money. I also want to know that it's not all about the money. I want to know that she's just as good with going for a walk in the park as opposed to me taking her to Ruth Chris Steak House.

- I like a woman who likes to look good. For example, if someone were to ask me, "What's my type", I try to give this analogy of Meagan Good in the movie Stomp the Yard. She was sexy no matter what she had on, whatever she wore, whether it was Timberland boots and shorts or a jogging suit, it was sexy. So I like a woman who just likes to look good. Some women have these excuses where they only want to look good when they're trying to meet someone, but when they go to pay bills they look a mess. My thing is if you stay ready, you don't have to get ready. - **GYNUINE, 47**

- Honesty is very important, and what I mean is being honest with little things in terms of how she feels and sharing her true opinions with me. I need to know who she really is. This is one of the main reasons why I hesitate with building intimacy, it's discovering that some women are not who they really say they are. Honesty is so much more than just saying the words.

- I like a woman who is adventurous because I like to be inspired. I work from home so I don't get out a lot, so for me it's important to date a woman who is open to getting out and bike riding or traveling over the weekend or going to events or different shows.

- Women who workout and eat well are attractive to me. These things really matter to me because these are things that I like to do. At this point in my life, we need to have similar things in common that we both like, I don't want to make concessions. Making concessions has never worked out for me from a dating standpoint. Now it's really important for me to be deliberate and to be okay with being completely alone, if she is not what I want. I'm okay with dating casually if the relationship is not what I want. Sex is important, but to me if she is honest, that's sexy; if she is adventurous, that's sexy; and if she takes care of herself, that's sexy. - **DEL, 47**

- The first and foremost thing I find attractive in a woman is the quality of self-knowledge, how much she knows who she truly is. The reason why this is so important to me because I have purpose in everything that I do.

I'm also looking to evolve to live out that purpose, so I'm trying to grow into that purpose. So for me to bring a woman into my life to share the rest of my life with, if she knows who she is, then I know that I will evolve. I know that I'm going to become a better person. My vibration is going to go up if she knows who she is. She can assist with that because if she knows who she is then I don't have to wonder if she knows who I am. This is why self-knowledge is the most important quality to me. If we are in agreement with our identities  then there is a whole level of respect that comes with that.  We should never have to ask for respect, it will automatically be given.

- The second quality is her ability and her zeal of self-care. When she cares for herself, there is love being acknowledged on that individual level. And when she gives this love to herself, she should never have to ask anybody else for.  What I'm really talking about is self-esteem. Do you know how attractive and sexy a woman is who not only knows herself, but she loves herself enough to take care of herself.

- The last thing I find attractive is a woman who is selfless. She is able to open herself up and consider other folks. She has a level of compassion for other people and everything around her. When she is selfless she is always looking to bring balance to her situation. Not dominate, not overthrow, but bring balance because she recognizes herself in everything and everyone around her. This brings me to tears when I even think about it because it is so attractive. - **DI-AMEN, 47**


- I like when a woman is athletic and likes to be active. She likes to get out and take a walk. If I have to take off running and she's back there breathing hard, she's going to slow me down... LOL!

- She needs to know how to mix and mingle with different types of people. She's polished with a little bit of 'thug' in her. She can assimilate in all types of situations if she's respectful to all people.

- Lastly, she enjoys her life. She is comfortable with her decisions and her chosen profession. She has that mentality that whatever she does, she does her best. This will make her happy. When she is happy, she shines and when she shines, this makes me happy. - **WILLIAM, 50**

- Cleanliness is important to me because I think that cleanliness is a sign of self-love and self-care. If a woman doesn't love herself then how is she going to love me?

- The language she uses and how she speaks is important to me. I passed on the opportunity to be with many beautiful women because of the way they spoke, they murdered the English language. For me, this is birth control. It bothers me when women misuse words and conjugations.

- I like when women are inquisitive and they genuinely want to know about stuff. This means that there is always a possibility for self-improvement. The most important thing that any of us can do is self-evolve. - **MAVERICK, 51**

- The first quality for me would be intelligence. A woman that I can have a great conversation with is sexy. The mind is a terrible thing to waste and most people waste their minds on garbage... garbage in is garbage out. So when I come across a woman that actually takes the time out to educate herself and is knowledgeable about herself and the world, it's really great to connect with her on this level.

- Inner beauty is attractive to me. And what I mean by inner beauty is her ability to express herself creatively, the way she keeps her house, and the way she treats other human beings... This is sexy to me, when she is beautiful inside and out.

- The third quality, would be if she is caring. Caring for herself and caring for other individuals. If she doesn't care for herself then she doesn't value herself. And if she doesn't value herself, then she can't value me, as a man or value a relationship. - **ISAAC, 51**

- The old additive is great for me man! Brains, beauty and drive, and I list the qualities in this order. She's got to be smart, read a book and articulate some things. I am turned on by sapiophiles. She needs to be a little smart and able to talk about a lot of things and then be able to share that.

- I know this might be shallow, but she has to be physically attractive with natural curves. If she has the body of a Black woman, meaning a phat ass, small waist and beautiful legs, and then you apply every color that a Black woman comes in from light to dark, to that physical frame, this is very attractive to me. I'm also turned on by 'tiger stripes' (stretch marks) because this means she's actually got a little seasoning on her.

- She also has to have a drive where we both want to work towards something if we are going to be a couple. She has a career, she has her own thing materially, she has her own friends, and she has other things in her life that she likes to do. She is a happy individual and can do her own thing and I'm a happy individual doing my thing so then when we come together it's a great thing. - **DEION, 51**

- For me, she has to be a believer and love God first, this is a true turn-on for me! How can she love me if she doesn't know or love God? If she doesn't, it ain't going to work between us. Believing in God is a consistent growth process. She fears God, reverences God and respects God. She prays with me and allows me to stand with her and be the head of the relationship and not the dictator. This type of woman would be evenly yoked with me.

- I like a woman who is about her business, she's a true player of this worldly game. She's about her education, she's about her job and her career. She can handle herself and she knows how to have a conversation.

- Lastly, a woman who takes care of herself, hygiene wise. She doesn't have to look like Miss America, she just has to be beautiful inside and out. She should be comfortable wearing a little bit of makeup, I don't like a woman to wear a lot of makeup. - **GARY, 52**

- A woman that is not antagonistic, or argumentative, she's more of a peacemaker, and is more interested in having harmony rather than being combative. This is a big quality for me. I'm past the arguing stage, I've done a lot of it myself. So I realize the pitfalls of that and it never ends good.

- Secondly, her appearance is a huge, huge quality for me and one that I really admire. I like a woman that is well kept. She is groomed well and shows some concern and pride in her appearance.

- And the last quality I would say is a woman who shows a natural affection for the people around her and she is nice. I do a lot of work in the public eye and I'm talking to people all the time. It is great to have a woman who reflects this quality as I do. I would be enamored by this attribute in her.
  **- MICHAEL, 53**

- I love a woman who is very intelligent and worldly. She has presence and she knows that she is a force to be reckoned with, this is a beautiful turn-on for me. When a woman understands her power in the world, she knows how to be able to command a conversation and she knows how to utilize her resources around her to make things happen. It's not about being forceful and it's not about ego, it's just a beautiful essence that she has inside of herself.

- She knows that she's a diva; she knows that she's strong; she knows that she's beautiful; she knows that she's humble; and you can see this presence in a woman who understands this.

- I love a beautiful woman in the way that she carries herself physically, and a woman who can smile which resonates from her face and her heart. It's not so much about her physical look but the beauty that resonates from inside of her. **- TRUSTIN, 54**

- For me, honesty is very appealing, and maybe because I've had such bad experiences with women and dishonesty in the past, so when I encounter women like this, it appeals to me a lot.

- Since I am into health and fitness, I find a woman who takes care of herself physically very attractive. I'm not attracted to someone who is excessively overweight, this would be a problem for me.

- A woman who is confident not arrogant, but someone who is secure, trusting and a realist, is attractive. Maybe she's been through some things and she doesn't take that out on the next person that comes along.
  **- JORDON, 54**

- A woman who knows herself is very attractive. She is self-aware in her sexuality, her spirituality, her career path, her womanhood, her self-esteem, and her sense of self. In her black skin, her caramel skin, in her thick thighs or lack thereof, her small titties or huge ones, her long hair, no hair or medium length hair. She stands for herself and is able to say, "This is who I am and I stand unequivocally in this space. If you want me, this is what you get and I'm delivering the best version of myself". This is self-awareness. She's not arrogant, she has a sense of peace and she radiates that.

- The second thing that is attractive is a woman who pursues peace. Many women like drama. They want to argue and they want to debate, I'm not talking about a friendly debate. I'm talking about the absence of drama that makes them uncomfortable because for whatever the reason, they like stirring up shit. These types of women are not at peace with their girlfriends or their mothers, or their boss. This type of conflict makes a woman extremely unattractive because now I've got to put up with her bullshit!

- The third quality I find attractive is a woman's ability to communicate effectively and use her words in order to get results. So a woman who doesn't have a command of the English language, I don't care how phat her ass is, I consider her to be a liability and not a help mate. - **GREG, 54**

- Definitely having intelligence. I know it's cliché but I like a woman who is independent and thinks independently and she doesn't let anybody influence the way she thinks. I even like when she is open and forward enough to tell me when things are not right because some of us men can be very dumb.

- I love a woman with a sense of humor where we can just sit, talk and laugh... I just love this!

- And lastly, a woman has got to look good, physically keeping herself together and taking care of herself. I like a woman who is well portioned, she does not have to have a big ass or big breasts, I'm not into all that. I don't want an overweight woman because that's not healthy. I would not start a relationship with a woman that I'm not physically attracted to and then later on go out and cheat because of that reason. - **STEPHAN, 55**

- How a woman takes care of herself is first and foremost for me. Her presentation, meaning her style, her body language, and her conversation is very attractive.

- Communication for me is key, and how she handles me with her words. For example, I remember dating this girl and she said to me, "I know you're being a jerk, but in-spite of yourself, I still care for you". This was a big statement for me because she recognized that I'm not perfect and that I may not always be exactly 100%. This was a turn-on for me because she understood me and she didn't put any expectations on me. I don't have to be anybody but myself, she just told me this upfront. This was an instant turn-on for me because she accepted me for me. I felt like I didn't want to lose her because she's one of the few people that understands me and she was ok with who I am.

- I love when is woman is willing to do whatever it takes to do something. I like ride-or-die women. She has my back, no questions asked. Is she down or not? When a woman asks me a lot of questions, this drives me crazy... what the fuck! - **M.M., 56**


- A woman who is compassionate is very attractive to me. It's important that she is understanding and caring about things, especially if it's an issue with me. If I'm involved with her and if she's having an issue, then that's going to be an issue for me too.

- A sense of humor is also attractive because I don't like when women are so serious and emotional all the time. I've dated women in the past where everything was so serious, and life ain't always that serious. This is a turn-off for me.

- I know this is going to sound like a cliché but honesty is important. I find a woman who is deceitful very unattractive. I don't want to find out that a woman has been lying to me in a round-about way. Once I catch her lying I begin to wonder, what else has she been lying to me about? Now this has created an air of distrust and I'm never going to be happy with her, nor will I ever believe her. This doesn't make for a good relationship. - **ORLANDO, 56**

- I love a highly intelligent woman. A woman who is able to have stimulating conversations and healthy debates about many topics.

- A woman who is ambitious and who is like me in a lot of ways is attractive. I think I bring a lot to the table and it's hard often to find a woman that brings the same. I don't want to be the one that's bringing all the goodies and she's just reaping all the benefits.

- Lastly, I like a beautiful woman who is physically appealing. It's hard to explain what I mean by this because I don't have a set type really, it's just the way she puts herself together, and how all the pieces fit. - **DARRELL, 57**

- A woman's ability to laugh, have fun and smile is most attractive to me. This is important because most ladies that I meet have a frowny, pissy attitude. I don't know what it is or why it is, it could be a defense mechanism that they build up because men are always bothering them or picking at them or trying to go out with them. So women take on this kind of attitude, probably just for survival.

- I also find a woman that is not too needy attractive. When a woman is always asking me to do something and acting like she can't do anything because she thinks that's what a man wants to hear, this is a turn-off for me. I want to know that if I ever needed help or assistance with something that she is able to help me as well. I don't want to feel as though the woman is not capable of reciprocating the ability to help me when needed.

- Also, a woman who has the ability to talk and debate about thing without have an emotion attachment to it. As soon as she becomes emotionally attached, it is no longer a debate but an emotional response. She should have the ability to remove herself from her own mental construct and be able to discuss many things. She should be able to disconnect herself from her own personal biases. I've only met a few women in my life who have the ability to do this. - **DN, 58**

- The three qualities I find most attractive in a woman have changed for me over the years. Now, at this point in my life a woman who is comfortable in her own skin is first and foremost. We all have issues, but if a woman is happy with herself and she doesn't allow those issues to dictate her personality then this is great.

- A woman who has a sense of humor is important because life is too stressful as it is and if she can't laugh then this is a problem. She is able to see the humor in things that make life enjoyable. The last thing I want when I come home from a hard day at work is to see my woman moping around and angry or she wants to fight all the time. A lesbian doesn't even want to come home to all this nonsense, LOL!

- A willingness to learn would be the third thing that is important to me because people get stagnant in life. I'm big on going to museums, learning about history and different things. When we learn new things it stimulates the brain. It makes us inquisitive to want to know how things work and how things happen. There a women who are stuck in reality TV or gossip and this doesn't do anything to stimulate the brain. As a matter of fact it takes them backwards because when you look at nonsense, you become nonsense.- **KEITH, 60**


- How a woman thinks and problem-solves is very attractive to me. Intimacy to me is not just based on the physical. What really highlights the intimacy is the intelligence level of the woman that I'm involved with. It seems as if I accomplish more if I'm with a woman who thinks clearly and logically and if she has a good head on her shoulders. The higher degree of intelligence corresponds to me with the higher level of intimacy.

- How she takes care of herself is attractive. Does she workout to keep her body toned? Does she pay attention to her outside appearance? Does she ascend towards the higher things in life in terms of how she dresses and how she carries herself? If she loves herself with a high degree of care, then I feel that she has the ability to love me with the same quality and intensity.

- A woman's spirituality is important because it shows her ability to love something other than herself. I think that if I am able to exhibit some of those characteristics that she loves, then she could extend her love to me also. - **PILOT, 61**

- Intelligence is attractive because I feel like I'm a nerd and I can speak about a wide variety of things across race, gender, and international boundaries. I need to be able to indulge in those conversations with my partner.

- Humor and playfulness is attractive because as people, we can be sensitive to a lot of things. Humor can help to reveal truths and with the truth, we're better armed to present ourselves to each other. For example, the age old question, "Baby does my butt look big in these pants?" I could jokingly say, "Baby you got too much butt back there!" She can either laugh along with me or she will become devastated over my comment.

- Trust would be the third quality. If I look at a lot of Hollywood couplings, I see that there are high divorce rates. I travel a lot, sometimes up to two to four months at a time, and I need a certain amount of trust in my legacy and in my home. I need to know whatever commitment my wife and I made together would be honored. So trust in the relationship is very very high for me. - **ANTHONY, 62**


- I am attracted to the physical aspect of a woman, meaning how she's built. I like a very curvy, full figured woman with thick thighs. I like my woman to be thicker than a Snicker.

- A woman who is independent is also pretty attractive to me. If she is independent that means she is not needy and she doesn't depend on me every waking minute of her day. She doesn't need to talk to me every minute, she doesn't need to hear from me several times a day, or even every day. She is independent and has her own stuff to do.

- And lastly, a woman who is private and knows how to keep her business to herself. This is important to me. - **PAUL, 66**

# Chapter 4

# MEN AND MARRIAGE

One of the most important social changes unfolding in the United States over the past half-century has been the decline of the institution of marriage. According to BlackDemographics.com, marriage has been a declining institution among all Americans and this decline is even more evident in the Black community. In 2016 only 29% of African Americans were married compared to 48% of all Americans. Half or 50% of African Americans have never been married compared to 33% of all Americans. Marriage has historically provided many benefits for individuals such as better physical and mental health, more social ties, higher household incomes, and the accumulation of wealth. And still, so many marriages end in divorce.

Do Black men really want to get married and do they see the benefits of marriage?

In this chapter, men share what their marriages are like, why they got married or why they are still single, and what are the pros and cons of marriage. They all have various reasons for the way they feel about tying the knot and everything associated with this institution.

I've never been married, but I've been engaged for about 1 ½ years. She was 10 years older than I was and she was trying to change me and control me. As I grew up in the relationship I began to realize what I want and don't want in my future wife and the mother of my children. I fell out of love with her. What was crazy about this is that we met and had a one night stand and a month later she told me she was pregnant. Two months after that she had a miscarriage and I didn't want to be one of those dudes who says, "Oh you're not pregnant anymore so I don't want to be with you". I took it upon myself to make it work because I know how difficult it could be mentally and physically on a woman when she has a miscarriage. I was trying to do the right thing. And what's crazy is, after the relationship was over I found out so much about her that I didn't know. - **JOSHUA, 25**

I want to get married one day, it's one of my life goals. There are so many good things about marriage, including working as a team together, celebrating life events, and having children. Other pros for me are being able to wake up every morning next to the woman that I love, my best friend, watching our children grow, sharing ourselves both positively and negatively, and coming together as one. The cons are that you get bored after a while and sometimes couples try to live their lives beyond their means. Also being monitored for everything that I do can become annoying and dealing with her jealousy or envy of women. She may nag me about things when I'm trying to get my life together or if our financial situation changes. I have an ego and I have pride. All I want to do is be able to take care of my wife and my kids and not stress about it. If I were not able to do this and provide financially for my family, it becomes stressful, it may make me feel like I want to break down and cry. I would not want to have to ask anyone for help financially, this would really hurt my ego. - **JOSHUA, 25**

Marriage is all about having someone to build with, in every way. Building a family, building a legacy and building a deep connection with that person. Men and women need each other. People need other people. We should be building connections that make us stronger together. I would like to find a woman that I can build a strong connection with. I think it's much better than dying alone. The cons of being married are not being able to take a break from someone when I need to, especially being married too early in a relationship. - **LAWRENCE, 26**

I read an article a few weeks ago that said there is a surge in divorce. A lot of people are stuck in the house due to the Covid-19 pandemic, and they are being forced to examine what they have created. They are starting to realize that they don't like what they see in their spouse and their relationship. When people get married sometimes they get so caught up planning the wedding day and not the actual marriage itself. So when the reality hits they realize they don't really even like each other. They don't focus on ways to strengthen their relationship. Maybe they just don't know any better. Maybe they are too afraid to ask for help. We are so busy with the external things going on in our lives, we don't take the time to cultivate the marriage. Couples have to fight for their marriages. Women think men are going to whisk them off their feet and men think women are going to cater to them. This is not true. - **DONNIE, 27**

Marriage for me is partnership because I believe in having a true partner in my life. Somebody that I can share responsibilities with, share my burdens and mental and physical loads with, and to raise a child who is going to be bigger than us one day, hopefully. Also, another pro for me would be having sexual freedom. I've been in relationships that were stifled sexually because we weren't on the same plane sexually. I don't know if she enjoyed sex in the way that I did or as much as I do. She had boundaries, spiritually. She felt bad and wasn't able to fully enjoy sex because of what she believed in versus what she physically enjoyed. This caused a bit of a rift between us. It's not that I didn't appreciate her decision and it's not that I didn't support her decision, this is what made it tough for me. We just looked for the happy mediums like having oral sex, instead of full-on intercourse. Things just didn't seem reciprocated equally and this caused a lot of issues for me. I'm big on reciprocity. I've been in relationships that didn't feel like true partnerships, either financially or sexually. - **DAMIAN, 30**

I think one of the cons to marriage may be an added level of sensitivity. And what I mean by this is how husbands and wives react to some of the things the other person does. These are things that may not have bothered us in a dating capacity or in a relationship that was not leaning toward marriage per se. Our tolerance and sensitivity to things that we do and don't like are going to change. Being with the same person for the rest of my life and potentially every day, this is a high commitment. It's very easy to be in a relationship and become comfortable being around the same person all the time. You can become irritable or less tolerable of things that you may not like about your spouse. Some people get married and they don't see their spouse as perfect, they just tolerate them. Sometimes we can lose sight of our friendships and our social life outside of the relationship and outside of our spouse. - **DAMIAN, 30**

When I think about marriage, I think about being a power couple! It's like the two of us coming together to build our lives. I think for me, being married would make me buckle down, be more focused on my career, and be more resourceful. Now on the other hand, I think that marriage is a man-made concept. I don't think marriage is a necessity. In 2020, and the way we live our lives now, marriage is just a document. I don't need a document when we've already come together as one. Why do I need a piece of paper to prove this? I've seen many marriages fall apart, and I've been told that it's hard for people to really see themselves with the same person for many years down the line. - **JAMAR, 32**

I was engaged to be married at 25 years old. We had been dating for two years. I thought I could build a future with her, although everything between us wasn't perfect. I thought I could fix the imperfections once we were married. The reason I didn't marry her was because, to be honest, our sex life wasn't great. We really weren't sexually compatible, sex was good but it wasn't great. We both wanted children and I thought she would be a good mother. I pulled out of the marriage due to the uncertainty of our future together.

The pros to marriage is building a legacy together, raising children and building wealth. It's forming a partnership and taking on life's challenges

together. It's having each other's back. It's growing together mentally, physically and spiritually. The cons to marriage is when the boredom sets in. It's taking on the challenges when things are not going well. People say that sex stops once you get married, this is not cool. I am not ok with this.
- **HUGH, 32**

I was engaged when I was younger. I was dating this lady and we got in a fight. I became vengeful and I reopened communication with one of my exes and I cheated on my girlfriend with my ex. We ended up resolving our fight and I asked her to marry me, and she said 'yes'. During this time I got notification that I was going to be a father. I told my girlfriend that I impregnated another woman and we called off the engagement.

There have been very few examples growing up of what I would call a good marriage. I've seen some good marriages now, but I'm still trying to figure out what that looks like. Thinking about the pros and cons of marriage, I would say being open and transparent with my spouse and to not give up on the relationship, is a pro. My fiancé is my best friend, we really enjoy spending time together. My relationship with her is not about being in love, it's about appreciating her. My appreciation of her is so deep because we allow each other the space to just to be ourselves with no conditions.

I am very non-traditional so the cons to marriage for me would be that I do not want to give any type of sanctions to the United States Government over something that only God can create. I am so against getting a marriage certificate. It took me a while to get to this place because I don't believe in traditional ways of marriage where everything seems to be tied to money. As soon as the focus of marriage is on money, it's like a black dye that lingers, spreads and takes over. Another con is outside opinions of other people. Automatically people (family members and friends) feel like they are entitled to give their opinion when it comes to marriage. This is crazy and it's nobody's business how we structure and live within our marriage. I don't want to be put in a box with people telling me what my marriage should look like, or how we should live, move or think. Nobody questions the so-called rules to marriage. Why do I have to live this way? I believe marriage is what you make it. - **ANDRE, 33**

I knew I loved my wife, when I woke up one random night in the middle of the night and I just noticed her cleaning. She was staying over at my place and she just randomly started doing this. I had never been that close to any woman before. With the other women it was like, "Alright, good night!" and they would leave. But with her, she stayed the night and I was comfortable with her. I remember there was this one time when she finished cleaning up and we were watching movies and eating pizza, and I said to myself, "I can see myself marrying her. We have a great connection. I could see myself being comfortable around her".

The pros are knowing that I can come home to my wife. She's someone that I can talk to, we enjoy ourselves together, and she's someone who's got me... my authentic me. Cons are sometimes needing a break from each other. Being around each other too much and sometimes we need that space. Yes, divorce has crossed my mind and I'm sure it crossed my wife's as well. One of the most important things we are doing right now is actively spending more time together and focusing on each other more. I try to be more understanding when she's upset about things. I'm not going to lie, there was a point in my marriage where my wife and I were becoming distant from each other and my wife and I did get bored in the relationship. We have our highs and lows. What's important is how we come out of these dark places and start connecting again. We are really good now. - **ALONZO, 34**

Yes, I would marry a woman if she was cool with me being bi-sexual. We would have to be swingers and she would need to be bi-sexual too. This way we wouldn't cheat on each other and we would only mess around together, you know what I'm saying? So there wouldn't be any type of infidelities in the relationship. This way she knows what I'm doing, I know what she's doing and there wouldn't be any trust issues, we would trust each other.

The pros of marriage are having someone that you can confide in and know that they're going to have your back, no matter what. No matter how hard your day was, you can go home to the person who's going to turn your day around and make you laugh and hold you when you cry. When you feel defeated and your confidence is low, your spouse is the person that's going to build you back up. - **KING, 34**

I've never been married and honestly I don't know if I want to get married anymore. I don't think that I'm going to find 'her' and I don't feel like it's worth the headache. I'm in a situation now, where I'm not with the mother of my child, and it is like the worst headache ever. We're not making love, we have no reason to fight, whatsoever, so I don't understand why we argue so much. It's such a headache that I'm kind of turned off by the whole idea of being with somebody for life. I almost don't believe in marriage anymore. I get the marketing ploy around it, but the idea of one person for life? I don't want to be alone when I get older, but I don't know if I want one person anymore. I'm not afraid of commitment, I can be committed. I just don't think I will find that one person that I want to be with. What's the chances of that happening? Ya know? - **ISAIAH, 35**

I would like to get married. I've never been married, but I was engaged a few months ago. I've known this woman since high school and we reconnected years later. We both grew up in New York. We got along really well and we liked a lot of the same things. She was empathetic to me, she got me as a man, and she was supportive of me. She was down with what I had going on and she was cool with my transitions in life. I proposed to her eight months into the relationship and we moved in together, this is when the relationship started to unravel. We started to deal with child custody for her son and dealing with issues with her son's father. I also started to find out more about her. She was on medication and never told me she was bi-polar. She would get frustrated and would shut down, turning her phone off and not talking about it. After a while we broke apart and called off the wedding.

Pros of being married are being able to finally create my own family unit and to experience a healthy material family (husband, wife, children). I can create an environment where I don't not pass along the same generational trauma that I had experienced. I don't want to have children and have them struggle the same way I did growing up. I want to be able to take my wealth of experience and knowledge, and set my family up to be better off than I was. Also, I want to be able to help my wife grow beyond her limitations as well. Growing together, we can both pass down parts of our family legacy. There are economic benefits to marriage as well. Two functional adults are better than one. We can start building wealth through home ownership, investments, and businesses. Also, just having someone to enjoy life with and to spend intimate moments with and knowing at the end of the day my spouse has got me.

The cons are knowing that I'm now on the hook for being responsible for someone else and her emotional states, and her ups and downs. I am responsible for someone. My life isn't just about me anymore. These are things that I have to pay attention to. It is an enhanced level of responsibility that I have to be prepared for mentally and definitely financially, on a certain level. - **BRYCE, 35**

I never put a time frame on when I would get married. But honestly, I did think that I would have a woman who would stick around long enough or be there long enough for us to be married. I've dated women who were not keeping it real or telling the truth. I've been in situations where I'm talking to a woman and I think everything is going great and then, BAM! I find out she's got somebody else that she's dealing with.

I've never been married but I would definitely love to be married. The pros of marriage are that I would have that one person that always has my back. I'd have that woman that I can raise kids with. A wife that I can always go home to after a long day at work and have a conversation with. I can be silly with her, travel with her, make memories with her, and we can pray over each other. I want to be loved by that one woman, you know what I'm saying?

As a kid I grew up with the hope that I'm gonna have a wife someday and I still think like this today. As I get older, I see people giving up on love. What happened to that 'real love'? What happened to that type of love where couples stay married 25, 35, or 45 plus years? This is the type of love that I've always wanted and the type of love that I'd rather have. I don't want a situation where we've been together for five years, married for two years and then we get divorced. I want that love that sticks around. I want that love that no matter what we're going through we can stick it out, we got each other's back. We don't dog each other out if we're going through something. I want that type of love where we pray about it together. - **RL, 36**

I've been married for 14 years. I married her because she is extremely smart and attractive, and I loved her. One major pro to marriage is having stability. Having stability is very important to me because I am scared of these folks out here running around who may have diseases and what not. There are folks out here knowing they have HIV/AIDS. They are taking medication and claiming to be undetectable. When I was growing up and HIV hit the scene, we shut it down. I think people get married, for the most part, because of convenience. However, if we are both confident in the marriage and confident in each other then there is a lot of good that comes out of being married.

Marriage also represents status, and there are expectations that people have for status. This status looks like being a member in country clubs and churches. It's being around like-minded couples who are also acquiring a finer way of living. The cons of marriage is that it's a contract and a lot of people don't understand contracts. If the relationship does not work out and couples get a divorce, the legal ramifications can be devastating. You don't always get everything that you want and even need from a marriage, but sometimes you can look at it as the lesser of two evils. - **CHUCK, 40**


I was married for five years. We got divorced over miscommunication about money, career goals and children....we had a total disconnect. We were two very stubborn people who didn't have a real reason to divorce, we just never tried to connect. And what's so crazy about this is that after the divorce we began communicating differently about the things that split us up in the first place. The good thing about marriage is that two people working together are better than one. You have each other's back in a marriage. Black women are good elevators, they see things we Black men don't see. If you have a good Black woman, she may nag you to death when you are not doing something right. I had to get it out of my head that she is always trying to change me, however, she still loves me.

The bad thing about marriage is that you get used to each other sexually and you begin to get bored, especially if you're not with someone who wants to spice it up. After a while people fall into a routine and things slow down. Sex is not as adventurous a lot of the time. I am a very sexual person and I like trying different things all the time. I met my wife when we were in college, we were fucking all the time - in the movie theater, in the back seat of the car, everywhere. Once we were married she was like "Stop, get your dick out of my face!" I was like, "Damn, I had the same sexual appetite since college". Instead she wants me to hold her. "Hold her! Can't I hold you after sex?" - **TYLER, 42**

I was married at the age of 31 and was married for 7 years. I found that when I was married I had to shed my old self, and that was very challenging to do. I should have gotten counseling before I got married in order to make the marriage work, and the same for her. We would have had to make peace with our demons before we got together. This way, we would not have fought so much with each other. It wasn't the relationship that was broken, we both were broken. There were times when she was a yeller and I was too soft. Other times I was aggressive and she was too soft. She had daddy issues and she saw my love as too much. In actuality, it wasn't the way I showed love, it was the way that she interpreted my love. - **CHRISTOPHER, 42**

I was married for 10 years. I did not love her when I married her, I married her for several other reasons. #1 - Because she was pregnant; #2 - Because we had a good story to tell. We were both from big families and our families knew each other and #3 - I got married at 28 years old, but I had wanted to be married at 25, so the time frame for me wanting to get married was just right. I figured, there isn't necessarily a blue print on being married, so fuck it! I'll work on it as it goes. Unfortunately, I had to go through growing pains. Being married at such a young age with two children at the time, was literally on the job training. Hindsight is 20/20. If I knew then what I know now, I would not have gotten married. I would have had a baby mama because honestly, I wasn't prepared. I wasn't prepared financially, emotionally, or mentally to lead a family nor another human being. I eventually learned to grow to love my ex-wife because when I got married I wasn't in love with her. I loved her, don't get me wrong but I was never in love with her.

The window of me being in love with my ex-wife was very small. There were so many different dynamics that played in and around that relationship. She's the mother of my children, she is a very good mom, however, she and I were not friends. Also when I got married, I was not smart financially and she was worse than I was. I did not have enough life experiences. If my ex-wife and I had an honest and intimate conversation before we got married, we would not have gotten married. And the ironic thing is, she had given me an out when she got pregnant. She said we don't have to get married, but my pride and my legacy were on the line. I said, "No I wasn't going to be another Black man with a baby-momma", so my pride got the best of me. A lot of marriages happen because pride is an issue. If I would have been honest with myself then and stuck to it, I shouldn't have gotten married. - **WES, 42**

I definitely love my wife. We've been together almost 15 years. I noticed however, that six years into our relationship, our love began to dissipate a little. Things were getting mundane and redundant all the time because we didn't change things up. The love is still there, it's just something is missing. We do not have the same type of intimacy and love from when we first met.

The pros to marriage are knowing my wife and I are creating a relationship where we're on the same frequency together. It's also being able to create and share a legacy with her by building our family and finances together. Another good thing about marriage is building loyalty together. However in today's world I'm not really sure how that's working. Both people have to be willing and agree to build their lives together.

The cons of marriage are sometimes you don't get sex when you want to. I guess this happens because once you're together with someone for so long and you're doing the same things over and over, it gets to the point where it just gets boring. When the sex stops that's a problem. I've spoken to many men who say they got more sex when they were just dating... this is real! Also, if the woman is not in the space of really understanding what a marriage is, then this is a problem. If she looks at the gender roles from the 1940s and 1950s, where the man is supposed to do everything, then her lack of non-support in the marriage is a definite con. In this day and age it doesn't work like that. - **KADEEM, 44**

I probably got married because I wanted to have a family. For me, I guess it was just something in my mind that I wanted to experience with this woman, because up to the point of us getting married, we had been dating for 13 years. There were break ups here and there and she would continually say that I needed to be more open. So during our breakup period I would reflect on certain things that she would tell me about myself and when we would get back together, I was the one to say, "Hey, let's sit down and talk". By the time we had gotten married, she admitted that she felt I was a real adult man. I was an introvert when it came to expressing feelings, like most guys.

My grandfather was the male figure that had the most influence on my life and he was gone, so there was no real role model in my life. I continually sought self-growth starting as a young man, up until now. When I got married it wasn't because I loved her, I really wanted some stability and I had known her for a long time. It was more of a doctor-patient relationship. And what I mean by doctor-patient is, my ex-wife had some really heavy situations that happened to her in her life. Although she never came out and told me, I just knew that something wasn't all the way right. I've dated a young lady in the past who had been molested so I recognized these same behaviors in her in certain areas where she would not discuss. So that caring side of me wanted to be there for her and the whole nine-yards. It was my savior-syndrome. I am open to get married again. I have no stained heart, nor do I have baggage from the past.- **DOMINIC, 45**

I married a woman straight out of high school, we were married for eight years and we were young and immature. I had a strict upbringing, so I didn't get to play the field, or have the 'sowing my oats' phase in life. My family was dysfunctional, so when I met her, I gravitated towards her. I never had that phase where I was out of the house so let me live a little, instead I choose to settle down. In hindsight, I should have just dated her and let it be because we weren't meant for each other. She was more street-wise and I wasn't. I was square as a pool table and twice as green. I should have just stayed single and lived a little. We got divorced because we were young and immature and we cheated on each other.

The pros of marriage are building a family and having a partner you can trust to have your back. It's sharing activities and our lives together and not feeling alone.

The cons would be the challenges of being committed. There will be times when you just don't like the person that you're with, you love them but you don't like them. Going through life's ups and downs and missing the newness of something different. If you meet someone that you're attracted to, because you're married, you have to put up these boundaries. You have to be careful of how you act with other women. - **GYNUINE, 47**

I've never been married but I know several people who have been. I would say the pros to marriage is that it is a partnership. There is nothing like a dual income. And not just a dual income, there is nothing like a duel strategy. We support each other to expand ourselves. It gives us something more in our lives. Nobody wants to die alone. Another great thing about marriage is just having a partner. I do pretty well financially. So to partner with somebody, we can kill the world together! You know what I mean?

I would say the cons to marriage are taking each other for granted. It is the worst to be in love with a woman who takes me for granted. Imagine being with somebody for so long and she is no longer attracted to me. I like the sanctity of marriage. I'm hurt when I see marriages go awry. - **DEL, 47**

I was married around the age of 29. We were married for a little over three years. What caused the divorce, in a nutshell, was my lack of self-knowledge and her lack of self-knowledge. My intention with her was to be the best father and the best husband that I could be. Because I didn't have an understanding of myself and I did not know my father, I had to try to mimic what I had been seeing when it came to relationships throughout the years. I did not have a good example so I tried to mimic the best of what I saw. The best of what I saw was the man who wanted the best for his family, taking the reins and leading. He was the leader and told everybody what to do, basically. This was the best of what I saw. I tried to lead this way in my household and what I ended up doing was ruling my household with an iron fist. Instead of inspiring mutual respect, what I was doing was inspiring fear. Not really knowing this because in my mind I had the absolute best intentions. The only thing is, I would enforce these rules very harshly. If they didn't do things the way I wanted them done, I would chew them out, raise my voice and whip their butts. I was very intimidating to our children when rules were broken.

I feel that marriage for me could be a hindrance if I'm not with the right person. I wake up and I live out purpose every single day. I interact with multiple people every day, of both sexes, and I can't be married to a woman who's jealous and who has a problem trusting. My lifestyle won't do her any good. She will need to give me that trust and get over her insecurities in order to be with me. I can't be married to someone who doesn't know how to bring harmony and balance into the household. There are some women who have a selfish agenda and I cannot marry a woman like that. It is not necessary for me to get married. I can live the rest of my life without being married. The only reason why I would get married now is really because she wants to. She also has to be in a place where she is worthy of that, and I also have to make sure that I'm worthy of her. - **DI-AMEN, 47**

I was married twice. The first marriage was nine years and the second was two and a half years. The good things about marriage to me were those intimate moments between me and my wives. Laughing together and having that close connection between us. When things were good, they were good! You know what I'm saying? We had each other's back for everything. The bad things about marriage were when we became disrespectful towards each other, when things were not going right. We strayed away from each other. I'm sleeping on one side of the bed, she's sleeping on the other. We should have been able to sit down together and discuss things, and talk about our problems and the things we needed to work on.

When my first wife got pregnant, I thought the baby was mine. I raised the baby for about three years and my dad said that the baby didn't look anything like me and that I should take a blood test. I took the blood test and found out this child wasn't mine. I put my feelings into this little boy and still to this day he calls me 'daddy'. The second marriage dissolved because my wife was having an affair. I found a picture in her phone of a man sitting on the couch with his 'goodies' in his hands and a bunch of text messages between them. I was very much in love with both of these women. - **WILLIAM, 50**

No, I've never been married. There were the two instances on emotional bases where I was deeply in love with these women enough to marry them. I'm not traditional in this way so it was never important to me. I grew up in a single parent household. My mom never got married. So I don't see marriage as the end all be all panacea to life. If we find a moment where it works in our life, then okay great! The only thing that will change will be our tax status and how society, family and external motherfuckers receive us. Marriage is just not my thing. I understand how society works and I understand that if me and my girlfriend walk into a place and I say "Hey, this is my girlfriend of five years", then the person will look at us differently than if I go into a place and say, "This is my wife of six months". People think that when you're married you made a different commitment in the eyes of God. I'm like dude fuck all that! The love wouldn't be any different if I'm married vs if I'm not married.

I'm not anti-marriage, but some of the cons are the two of us can become so intertwined in certain ways. This becomes troublesome if the relationship doesn't work out and we have to get out and go our separate ways. One thing that I always fear about marriage is settling for whatever goes on in the relationship. I'm not a 'yes dear', 'no dear' type of person who is just happy to have someone to sleep next to. Fuck that shit! I'll find someone to sleep next to me and then go home. I'm not going to be the one being bitch-slapped by his wife all the time. - **XAVIER, 50**


I was a single parent when I got married. The woman that I married was probably the first woman who was open to loving both me and my daughter. Other women weren't open to loving my daughter since she wasn't their child. My ex-wife and I never asked enough questions about who we were as people and what were our aspirations. We damn sure didn't know anything about Love Languages at the time, we were just young and didn't know any better. So fast forward years later, we realized that we really didn't know each other. This promotes the ideology of really asking the right questions up front, early. I don't think a man will ever prosper in life unless he has been married.

Marriage takes a man from living a selfish lifestyle to understanding that he has a greater purpose in taking care of his family and his woman. He cannot be selfish in marriage, he has to be selfless. Also, you're not alone. We all have this needed desire to be with someone, I don't give a damn what anyone says, it's bullshit when people say, "Oh I can be alone, I don't need anyone." We have a constant affinity towards something and someone to love and to be loved. I don't think we can exist without love. Ultimately we want that because love completes us, it completes me. I feel good when I am in a meaningful relationship.

One con to marriage is having that yearning desire towards another fine-ass woman that I may find attractive. Why do we have to live this monogamous life? Why can't we be polygamous? Well you can if you have a mate that is into it, however, the majority of Black women will not go for that. Most Black men will not be polygamous, sharing his woman with another man. There can only be one dick in the room. Another con to marriage is if one person is a vampire, this creates a lot of stress, because they are looking for the other person to make them happy all the time. - **DEION, 51**

After having my heart broken and dating several different women, I woke up one morning and didn't even know where I was. It was in this moment that I said to myself, "Wait a minute, I can't keep living like this, I have to get married!" I wanted to marry someone who was going to ground me and keep me from wild n' out. This is why I married my first wife. I loved my first wife, but I was not enamored by her. There were no fireworks or nothing like that going on. But I told her, if we are going to do this and get married, I need her to have three babies and she agreed. Six weeks later I was married. I thought marriage was going to help free me and make me free. I thought that by being in love, I would no longer be distracted by other women or unsettled with where I was in life. I thought that once I was in love that I would take my shit to the next level. And when this didn't happen, I said to myself that I was just going to let other people have love. I was just going to 'sport-fuck' and just work on my career. With my second marriage, it's a different kind of love now at 51 than it was when I was 31. I think the pros of being married is that it keeps me focused and by being focused, this allows me to focus on building a legacy, creating adventure, and building our agreed upon agendas. Outside of these, there are no other pros to marriage. The cons of being married are that it prevents me from having romantic adventures that may enhance the one life that I have here on this planet. Think about it... every major conflict between men and women, are all based on the same issue, since the beginning of time. And that conflict is either love unrequited, love denied, or love shared. - **MAVERICK, 51**


I was married in the past and I did love my ex-wife, but we grew out of love. I still have love for her in terms of wanting her to be happy and I care for her well-being. She's the mother of my child so I want the best for her. The cons to marriage are the rules and regulations that come with it. I think that most people when they get married, they think they own you, like you're a possession. Now I do think marriage is a beautiful institution because it builds character. You have to have a level of self-mastery because marriage is a very emotional and committed relationship. You have to be willing sometimes to put your emotions aside and really listen to your spouse. You have to learn to master your emotions because something your spouse says may set you off, and a lot of times that reaction comes from your own conditioning. So in marriage, you have to be aware of this and try to overcome this conditioning. If you're in a healthy marriage then all of this can happen and you can overcome your challenges and become more of who you are. You can appreciate life more because you're committed to somebody. - **ISAAC, 51**


I was married twice. My first marriage was when I lived in Los Angeles, it was a hustler's marriage. We were both in the 'game' with the same goals. I did not love her, I just needed a woman who was going to have my back. She was my "Cookie". I was deep in the dope game, selling drugs and making money. I started using drugs (rock-cocaine, marijuana, alcohol) and gang-banging, breaking into houses and doing stuff that I didn't need to be doing. I was moving a lot of dope and hanging around with the wrong people and clubbing every night. I started hanging out in "The Trap" with "Strawberries", women who would do anything for dope.

My second marriage, I'm still in it. I moved to Atlanta in 2010 to get cleaned up and start a new life for myself. I remember praying to God for better things. I knew that I needed a God-fearing woman, and a woman who was working. I wanted a woman that I could love, even though I didn't know how to love at that time. So I prayed that God would show me how to love. I had been looking for God throughout my life, off and on. My wife is my helpmate, she is by my side and I can confide in her about everything. "Seek ye first the Kingdom of God and the rest will be added on to you". I trust this woman with my life. We have no secrets, she's my safety. I had to first be married to God. I love God first, and then my wife. I truly understand this now.

The cons of marriage are the forces that come against me when my wife and I are going through bad times. Women will be there to challenge my commitment and I may think the grass is greener on the other side. I may have to resist temptation. Also, if there are things my wife and I do not have in common, like keeping the house clean, this can create a barrier between us. So we will have to understand each other and grow from this because we're not going to be exactly alike. - **GARY, 52**


I've been married three times and I was not in love with any of these women, my marriages were based on circumstances. I'm a fixer and a Preacher's kid. I grew up in holiness. I grew up Pentecostal. It was my belief that if I had sex with a woman I was supposed to be married to her. I had a traditional way of thinking about marriage. With my first marriage, I was 22 years old and looking for escapism. I think I was just trying to get away and build my own kingdom with my own set of rules, and to get out from under my father's expectations of me. As a musician and as a helper in ministry, I was trying to do my own thing. So really, marriage was my route out. I loved her but I wasn't in love with her and after 10 years we decided to go our separate ways.

With my second wife, we felt like the power couple. She was super smart and walked in her purpose. However, over time, I realized that she was trying to replace her father and I couldn't be that for her. Men will say, "You can call me Daddy, but I ain't your Daddy!" Seven years in I realized that this marriage wasn't working for me but I held on for another three years for good measure.

My third wife was an amazing individual. She was super anointed and talented as a singer. As a musician I was attracted to her and decided to give marriage a shot. Ultimately this didn't last because I realized I was not fully in love with her and she felt it. If I get married again, I've got to be able to look at her and feel that I can't live without her because I see marriage as a really dope partnership. It's a way to unite the kingdoms and a way to support each other and have each other's back. When children are involved, it's a way to provide support and protection and ensure that those children become healthy adults. Part-time (divorced) relationships don't really foster that.

The cons of marriage would be the control that each person inflicts on the other. Contextually the whole idea of marriage is about control in the sense that laws are set up based on property. When you partition the state for a marriage license, you unknowingly are bound by state laws and statues in terms of what you can and cannot do, what property taxes you owe, and what debt is assigned to the other person just as a result of association. There is a legal component to marriage in which the government decides what you can and cannot do. A lot of couples who are not really aware look at this as some type of protection, but is it really? There is also a perception and idea that you are MY wife and all things go through me. If I don't approve of it, you don't do it. And the same goes for women, he's MY man. So not only do we try to control our spouses from other people, we try to control our spouses from their natural inclinations and desires. I don't like this part of it, I don't like the unfree mind. It's a bad combination when you mix it with relationships. Unfortunately marriage brings out a lot of those bad ideals. - **GREG, 54**

I've been married twice. The first time I got married, and this is going to sound crazy, but I knew before I walked down the aisle that she was not a good mate for me. But because... and this is really stupid, but it's true... I was at a point in my life where I was ready to settle down so I got married. I was 33 years old and she just happened to be the person that I was dating at that time and I went into the marriage with the wrong attitude. I remember thinking to myself, "Oh well, if it doesn't work, we'll just get a divorce". We were together for 10 years and married for 7 years. I would not describe my relationship with her to be intimate at all because she was kind of subdued and apprehensive about being open and free sexually with her expressions. I tend to be a very positive person and she was the complete opposite of that. It got to the point where her energy was bringing me down.

The pros of marriage, if you're with the right person, is that this could be the best thing that ever happens to you, if you have a spouse that's really a partner in every sense. If my wife has my back and I can really trust her, then we'll go to the mat for each other. There's nothing like this kind of support! With my second wife, in the beginning I believed we were intimate and had a very good relationship, but once things started to go south, that just went out the window. She had been on her own and was very independent, so I think it was hard for her to adopt the mentality of having a partner when it came to making major decisions. There were trust issues on my part, I did not trust her. Once the trust was gone I really didn't care about the relationship. It got to the point where she lied so much I just didn't believe anything that she said. - **JORDON, 54**

The pros of marriage is having a union based on communication, trust, honor and love. When I have this in a marriage, it's very, very, very powerful! The thing is, you cannot let the ego take advantage of these things and separate them, because if this happens then you start to lose your grounding. These are the strengths I love about being married. I also love the fact that when we pull our financial resources together, we are able to be prosperous together. The most important thing for me is that we are able to spend quality time together, in all aspects - exercising, vacationing together, experiencing new environments together, meeting like-minded people who are evenly-yoked, and being able to do this with my partner is an amazing adventure! The cons of being married is the lack of respect. Just because my ex-wife and I had great sex, this was not enough to keep the marriage together. Our divorce had a lot to do with respect and honor. She disrespected me and did not honor our relationship. When this happened, it stopped the original love and the connections that brought us together in the first place, and it brings in the ego. Bringing in the ego is the number one issue, especially after an argument. People start to take a position and they become fearful. They start to get into protection mode, this is where the low vibration starts to get into the relationship. At first it affects the communication, then it affects the finances and then it affects the love-making and the intimacy. And once all of this is affected, you're done. - **TRUSTIN, 54**

The first time I was 21. We got married because our best friends got married, but within less than a year we got our marriage annulled because we realized we were just too young. Although we loved each other, we did it for the wrong reasons. Our annulment was mutual and we ended up staying in a relationship for about four years after that. The second time I got married, she was from Mexico and she asked me to marry her for her citizenship. We were really good friends and then one day she came out and asked me to marry her. I didn't have anything else going on so, I said, "What the hell, let's try this." We ended up getting married and during this time we became really close. After two years, she got sworn in and got her citizenship and we decided to continue to make the relationship work. We had become really close, she was my rock! Our downfall was that she was a Jehovah's Witness and her father was a preacher. She had fallen out of her faith during the time she was with me. Her father's influence was really strong on her and because I did not want to convert our marriage fell apart.

The pros of marriage are coming home to someone that I love, I can't wait to get home to see her! Having companionship. Someone to share my time with, to watch movies with, to talk about my day, to cook together. There are more pros than cons for me in a marriage. If there were any cons it would maybe be getting tired of seeing each other all the time. - **STEPHAN, 55**


I've been engaged twice but never married. The first time I was engaged I was around the age of 30 and it was a very toxic relationship. I felt like I needed to grow up and maybe all this energy is wrong because our communication was wrong. We had that love-hate relationship going on and I did not really accept this woman as my mate. My mindset was, 'fuck it, here's the ring, let's go through the motions'. There were red flags that came up but I just thought that I was being selfish, so I was going to throw myself in harm's way because I liked being around her but I couldn't stand her at the same time.

With the second engagement I was 40 years old. We dated off and on, and this woman was a 'boss woman' who was totally in charge of her whole program. Our personalities were so alike. She was used to being 'captain-save-a-nigga'. She was fly. The women were after her, the men were after her, and she was all over the place. So for me, I'm self-sufficient, so I didn't need all of that. Since I didn't need her like that, it became a very strained situation and we were butting heads all the time. However, when we were together, it was amazing! We were in a constant tug-of-war. It was like she was acting like a dude. So I decide to step away and end the engagement.

I don't care about the paperwork that comes with the institution of marriage. I think marriage is important and I think it is more important for older people than it is for younger people. Younger people are going through all these divorces, having kids, separating and going through all these things because that is what society is telling them to do. However, as an older person getting married, I know exactly why I'm doing it and we really like each other. We're pulling our finances together and we're good together. We want to be together, we're cool. As we get older our thought process starts to slow down. Our intimacy levels start to slow down and if sex slows down, I don't need to feel insecure or pressured to perform at the level that I was at 25 years old. When I have a partner that is there for me, I know that she really likes me. - **MM, 56**

Yes, I was married, but only for three months. We met when we were both actors in New York. She was a Black Canadian and she needed a green card so I married her just so she could get a green card and work in the states. I was in love with her, but I realized that she just wanted a green card. I was heartbroken. We got in a lot of arguments... it was just crazy, and we got divorced. I honestly don't know if I will ever find this again in a woman. I just have to believe that she is out there. I've always believed that whatever I want, I can have, no matter what that thing is. I've lived this way my whole life and it's worked for me. I've always gotten everything that I've wanted eventually. I just work hard and make it happen. So I believe that there is a woman out there that feels like me and she's waiting for that guy that has all these things that she can't find in most men. She's the one for me, exactly like I'm the one for her and we're looking for each other.

If I do not find this perfect woman for me then I feel like I'm married to my work. I get a lot of joy and satisfaction in producing and creating things. So I'm not terribly lonely. There is this woman that I date every now and then. She would be great, it's just that' she's a little ghetto for me. There are certain things that I really love and want in a woman. There are certain qualities that I crave and I require. This is hard to find because my expectations and my standards are really high compared to the average person. So if I marry somebody and she does not have all those things I require, then there's going to be that part of me that's missing some of these qualities. So I think subconsciously I may still be on the lookout for those things even though I'm happy with the woman that I am with. And if that thing shows up in another woman, I'm afraid that I might do something stupid like get with that person. So, I think because of that I don't want to be the kind of guy that cheats on his wife. And this is the reason I have not gotten married again. I don't want to be one of those guys, like 100% of my friends who are married and cheat on their wives. - **DARRELL, 57**

I've been married three times. One of the pros of marriage is that you're not alone, you have your buddy, your best friend there all the time that you can do stuff with. One of the cons in marriage are arguments that may occur. When you're with your best friend, you hardly ever argue, ever in life. But the moment the woman you're dating becomes your spouse, the arguments come and I think this happens because it's an ownership issue. The moment you get married there is an ownership component tied to the whole situation, meaning that your choices are not necessarily a choice any more, they're obligations.

Sexually there are differences in the way that sex is viewed when you're married versus when you're not married. When you're married you kind of feel obligated to have sex. When you're not married sex is spontaneous. When it's spontaneous you get in the mood and you do it. Whereas when you are married, you have to find time to do it like marking on the calendar and all this other kind of stuff. It's like when you're, dating having sex is almost on purpose, it's part of spending quality time together. When you're married, there is no purposefulness to anything because it already is. The quest is the key. If the quest goes away then everything else starts to drop off. - **DN, 58**

As a man, I was programmed from day one what I was supposed to do. Marry my high school sweetheart or my college sweetheart, have 2.5 children, a dog that looks like a rat on a string, and a home with a white picket fence. This was my programming. I realized after the fact that this was nothing but a fantasy put before me and in many cases it turns into a nightmare because it doesn't work out like that. I married my first wife because I was young and dumb. She was my college sweetheart. She was beautiful, she was intelligent, and I later found out that I didn't know a damn thing about her. I was not taught how to date or how to pick a spouse. My programming was to go to college, pick a spouse and then we will live happily ever after. People need to understand that they are coming from two different backgrounds and they need to do a little research and ask questions before they get married to find out if they like the same things. We did not talk about our goals and aspirations, instead we were just to going through the motions. Once we got married I learned she was a different person than I thought she was. Before we got married she was throwing the booty at me! Once we got married she shut it down, no more sex. After I got divorced I went on an extreme dry spell. I picked my next wife because I wanted babies and booty. We were married for 23 years and it ended because she stepped out and had an affair and got caught. This marriage turned out to be pure hell.

The pro about marriage is that it is a good family unit. This is a major thing for me because I always wanted kids and I wanted to be a part of developing them into great adults. I grew up not having this type of family unit, so to be able to develop this was something that I truly wanted. Also it's a joy to be able to have this when this type of unit is really working. If both people are on the same page financially and intellectually and they have the same goals and aspirations, then they can build wealth and a great relationship together. They have to have an understanding of each person's role in how to get there. But when one person is an asset and the other is a liability, that takes away from the person who is the asset and there is a lot of wasted energy. Couples should be using their energy to build the family unit to make the family better and to build wealth, or whatever it is they choose to do. When people rush into marriage and they don't do their investigative work first, then they have no idea what they're getting into. Now it's too late and divorce happens. - **KEITH, 60**

I've been legally married once and I shared a home with another woman for 10 years. I stayed with the woman that I was with for 10 years because of obligation. She became impregnated while I was in college and although we were dating and we had a good relationship, it wasn't my intent to marry her. When she became pregnant, out of obligation, I felt the need, as a young man to take care of her and my off-spring. I felt a certain responsibility to take care of her and our child, and I felt strongly about this. After a number of years had passed, I felt like I had lived up to the responsibility and I was not to be encumbered by that responsibility, then I felt freer to be able to leave her and go out into the world.

When I met the woman I eventually married, we got married after four months of dating. She wanted to wait at least nine months but I was eager, I was persuasive, and I convinced her that four months was more appropriate. My wife was 17 years younger than I was and she was still of child bearing age and I wanted to have children on my own terms. I wanted to embrace love on my own terms. So this was an opportunity to now do love and do marriage the way that I wanted to do it. Since I was 17 years older, I felt that I could also help mold her in a certain way because she had never really had what I would consider to be a real man in her life, based on what she told me about her history with men. I felt that I could provide a good example and re-engrave the image of a Black man who was responsible, attentive, adoring, and loving. I felt that I could do this for her. However, I found out the hard way that this could not be done, I was unsuccessful in changing the way she felt about men.

I think that marriage is God's will. When you read the Bible, there are areas of the Bible that talk about the marriage of men and women. And it is from these passages that I deduce that it is God's will and that He ordains marriage. We are not to be left alone being an island by ourselves. I believe that a man will not reach his maximum potential in life unless there is a woman that is his helpmate. With a helpmate, he can demonstrate mastery of family, mastery of raising children, and mastery of having a family that society will look up too. There are also the physical pleasures that marriage lends itself too. There is the fellowshipping of family and being able to share on many different levels.  It also displays a sense of non-selflessness when we are willing to share our lives together. These are all benefits. - **PILOT, 61**


I was married twice. My first wife, I married at the age of 31. We were only married for three years and it took us eight hellish years to finalize the divorce. We divorced because of incompatibility. She had a lot of insecurities and I had a lot of fantasy ideas of what our coupling could be. The reality was we weren't living up to each other's expectations. In all honesty, my wife was European and I needed a bit more cultural awareness from my woman.

What my second wife now provides is mutuality and a sense of spirituality. Even though I am not big on religion, it seems like a woman who has no religion has a different type of personality. There is also a certain trust I have with her. If I'm going to reveal myself to someone, standing in that certain nakedness, sharing my thoughts, hopes, wishes and dreams, it is great to trust that she won't go write a book about it. Most men get married because of a certain trust we have with a woman. I was also in my mid-40's when I met my wife and I wanted to have children. When I sat back and thought about the type of woman that I wanted to be with, my wife hit all the checkpoints for me. My wife met so much of my criteria. She basically had everything I was looking for in a wife. I have a partner in legacy. We are building something together and we are sharing these things together. Just being able to turn to my wife and acknowledge memorable times together, I feel like I'm centered. I feel like I'm doing the things that I do for a reason, rather than being selfish, and this is all expanded now because we have children.

The con to marriage is scapegoating. If there is a problem or if we touch on a problem area in the other person, then the conversation becomes one of blaming the other person for something that they don't do or have never done. Anybody who is married or in a relationship knows exactly what I mean. People blame each other for the internal stuff that they need to fix. So for married couples, there is a lot of this going on. Honestly, I think for anybody who's been married for a long time, their ability to communicate through those moments, are what keeps them together. The marriages that can't navigate through these moments, are the ones that get divorced.
- **ANTHONY, 62**


The pros of being married are that I belong to someone and she belongs to me. We are a team and we have each other's back. The cons of being married is that our relationship becomes routine and easily accessible, as a result of the routine. A lot of things that you would look forward to and day dream about don't happen anymore. When you're dating someone and you live in separate households, the element and anticipation of becoming physical with that person is heightened and is always something that you look forward to because you don't live together and it doesn't happen that often. The anticipation or urgency of sex is no longer a priority, we can always get to it tomorrow. I'm twice divorced and part of the problem I had in both those marriages was my zeal to compromise and please my partner and as a result denying the things that I really, really like. And as a man now who is not married, I do what I want to do and I'm not compromising. - **PAUL, 66**

# Chapter 5

# WHAT MEN ARE AFRAID OF IN RELATIONSHIPS

Many men fear going into relationships, especially if they've been hurt in the past.  Men don't often discuss their feelings, instead they move forward with caution.  For those men who have been cheated on or betrayed, the thought of opening up and trusting a woman again is not always an easy decision. They are afraid of giving all of themselves to a woman and not having those feelings reciprocated. These insecurities hold men back from fully investing in another relationship.

Men need intimacy and an emotional connection, just as much as women do. They also experience fear and insecurities around relationships, just as much as women do. They are afraid of failure when it comes to relationships. They don't want to repeat the mistakes of the past, nor do they want to fall in love and get their heart broken again. Men are also afraid of becoming bored, growing apart, declining sex, and losing everything that they've built with a woman. They understand that building intimacy is hard work, it's not always an easy journey.

I just broke up with a lady I dated since college. She was starting to become very insecure and controlling to the point where I had to check in with her every time I wanted to go somewhere, or do something with my friends. I felt like I was being suffocated. It was all about her wanting to be in control, she had no reason to mistrust me. This type of woman does not work well with me. If there is no trust, then what are we doing together? - **DONNIE, 27**

I'm fearful of losing everything that we have. It's like being together for years and then she leaves and we break up. A man will pretend that he's not hurt after a break up, but if he's in a long, intimate relationship with a woman, it's going to hurt. He will pretend that it doesn't hurt. But the reality is he just lost everything he built up over the years, and it hurts. - **LOGAN, 28**

Failure would be what I am afraid of. Not feeling like I am able to maintain a healthy relationship is to me a failure and it is something that I'm trying to get away from. It's getting this out of my mind that thinking the responsibility is all on me to make changes I should not have to be the one to adjust or to accommodate the other person. This is both people's responsibility. - **DAMIAN, 30**

My biggest fear being in a relationship is that we will stop growing together. I don't want to become complacent to the point where we get bored with each other. I get bored pretty quickly so the woman that I'm with will have to be adventurous and be open to adventure and trying new things, always. - **HUGH, 32**

My fear would be that we start to become distant from each other and get bored with each other. People are changing constantly and there is no way to tell if what excites us now will continue to excite us later on. There is no way of knowing. So I definitely fear the unknown. I also fear myself slacking in a relationship with things that I used to do that I'm not doing now or down the line. I want to be able to give the same commitment, energy and enthusiasm that I gave early on in the relationship. So it does frighten me that this won't always be there. - **JAMAR, 32**

I like to be able to move as much as I possibly can, I don't like being put into a corner. I have this saying, "I don't have a home, I'm homeless", one place can never be home to me. This whole earth is for me to live on it and to move freely as much as I want to, I believe this wholeheartedly. When it comes to being in a relationship, sometimes it's hard because the woman that I'm with may have things she wants me to do, and this can cause friction, because I am such a free person. This can be problematic to a degree. - **ANDRE, 33**

I have a very short attention span so I know, in general, I get bored quickly, very easily. In the past, I wasn't interested in being in a long term relationship with a lot of these women. When it got to the point where I didn't care about them anymore, I would leave. I used to wonder if I would always be this way, just discarding women. And will I find a woman that I really wanted to be with long term. I was hurt once and I don't want to be hurt again. - **ALONZO, 34**

I'm fearful of giving my all to someone that's not giving me their all back, this is a big fear of mine. This is a fear because this is what I was getting in my past relationships. This would be devastating to me if it happened again. - **KING, 34**

I don't want to be left in the cold. Applying all of my energy, all of my passion, working on the relationship, and opening myself to different levels of vulnerability, only to have these layers of intimacy unwrap and unravel towards that person. It's getting to the point where it's like, I'm not doing this anymore. This is why empathy, emotional IQ and nurturing are high on my list. I am cautious about opening up because this type of intimacy doesn't mean anything to some women, they are kind of dismissive to the point where they don't share in return. It's a deal breaker for me to be in a relationship with a woman who is not a talker. If she can't express herself then we will not work well together. I can't be the driver of every conversation. If we can't communicate, then how are we going to build a relationship together? She has to be comfortable with expressing herself. - **BRYCE, 35**

Sometimes I get discouraged because of the things that I want and how I expect my love life to go. The things that I want out of my love life and from my partner, I don't know if I'll have them. Women will ask me, "What can I bring to the table?" I'm going to be honest, I'm a king. I'm a God. I bring the table. Whatever she puts on the table, that's what we're going to roll with, but I'm going to bring the table. This is just how I was raised and we don't sustain relationships like this anymore. What happened to writing love notes? What happened to that 1990's type of love where we can take a walk in the park? This is what I want. With this new generation or "new love", people don't see it like this anymore. Marriage is going out of style, it's not sacred anymore. It's not a real thing. - **RL, 36**

To be honest with you, I do have fear going into relationships. The last two women I dated, those relationships didn't work out, it seemed they had different agendas. I found out one woman had been dating another guy the entire time we were together. When we broke up, she told me later that she was getting married to this other guy. I was pissed. There were no red flags or any indication that she was juggling two men at the same time. I recently broke up with a woman who wanted to have an open relationship, hell no! This shit ain't for me. I'm losing trust in women. Or maybe I'm just choosing the wrong women. - **RON, 39**

I have an issue with women when it comes to money. If you want to know if a woman really likes you, take away the money. I have been taken advantage of when it comes to money. Granted, every woman ain't out to get me and if I don't treat them the same then I can't expose the ones who are. My thing is, when I meet a woman, I'm trying to go to the park, or bowling, or to shoot pool, or go-cart racing. I'm trying to do everything that doesn't cost anything. As time goes on, if it's a special occasion, then yeah we can go ahead and I'll take her to Ruth Chris (steak house) or whatever. I want to know that she likes me for me and not because of what she thinks I'm doing for her. I want a woman to want me, not need me. I also don't want to feel like I'm buying her. My thing is, there are levels of getting in her panties and there are levels to getting into my wallet. - **GYNUINE, 47**

At this point I'm not afraid of anything when it comes to dating and being in relationships because I overcame my mountain of insecurities. The only issue that I have is with the quality of women that are around now-a-days. Where are the women who can really benefit from everything that I have and from what I can really give them? I know how to give and to bring a woman up to that level, but I'm not going to bang my head against the wall to do it. - **DEL 47**

There is absolutely nothing that I'm afraid of when it comes to relationships, in fact I love being in relationships. There is a certain level of security with partnering up and having two lives become one. It's now two people making an effort to make things happen. I love this idea, I'm cool with this, but at the same time I'm okay if this doesn't happen. I'm so self-sufficient, I'm actually good by myself, but I prefer to be with somebody because this means a little less energy coming from me to hold everything together. - **DI-AMEN, 47**

I'm afraid of mistrust. The last female that I was seeing could have been honest with me and told me that she still has feelings for this particular guy. She could have told me that she was still in a relationship with him, and if I still wanted to see her, then we can give it a try. She should have stepped to me like this. If it was me, I would have said, "Hey look, I'm in a relationship, however, I don't feel it's working out". I would have been honest with her about that. A lot of women are not honest. She didn't realize that whatever she was doing was going to come to light. - **WILLIAM, 50**

I think my fear about long term relationships is being with a woman for 20 years and only getting blowjobs on my birthday. I'm never going to be down for a situation where all of the sudden things that were done in the beginning now stop. - **XAVIER, 50**

I've been doing a lot of studying of the mind, and what I have come to realize is that everything is a reflection of me. So any fears that I project is a fear that's coming from me. I don't have any fears when it comes to relationships. - **ISAAC, 51**

I'm afraid of failure when it comes to relationships. Going down a path and spending a lot of time with a woman and things just don't work out. I think I just need to come to grips that if things are not working they just are not working and that's ok. Rather than focusing on the negative of it not working, I choose to focus on the positive and know that it's okay. I don't need to spend too much time investing in a relationship if it is not working. I also look at my life and say to myself, "Damn, I'm 51, I don't want to die alone!" I want to be in a long term committed relationship. I don't necessarily have to be married, I'm open to it. If we agree as two adults that we're going to move in together and live our lives together, this is perfectly fine for me. - **DEION, 51**

I used to be fearful of repeating the mistakes I made in the past, however, I'm not fearful of that anymore because I know I won't do that. So no matter what, if I don't feel like I'm compatible with somebody, I don't ignore red flags anymore like I used to. I met a woman who was into religion, and I'm not. She wanted to be with a man that would go to church with her and also have the same beliefs around religion. She said that she would pray for me that I would someday see the light and become a Christian. I am very comfortable with who I am spiritually and if it's her goal to be with a man who is Christian, then so be it. I definitely won't make this mistake of conforming to a woman's ideals if they are not my own. - **JORDON, 54**

I'm afraid of falling in love and getting my heart broken. I've been taught not to cry, to be strong and don't show any emotions. I take on a lot of stuff and I try to hide it, but at some point, the emotions come out. And if a woman doesn't understand my feelings or if she makes fun of how I'm expressing my feelings in my most vulnerable moment, then this becomes a fear for me. If I'm being open enough and letting her see me in this moment and she doesn't respond with compassion then I'm afraid to let her in. Because if I let her in and I let my guard down and she doesn't respect what I'm going through, then my guard is going to go up and it will be a long time before it comes back down again because I won't trust her. - **ORLANDO, 56**

In relationships, we will never know each other 100%. I don't give a damn what anybody says, we can be together until we die and never know that person completely. I'm an extremist so I'm either in a relationship or I'm out. I can't test stuff. Are we doing this or are we not? I haven't met too many women who are all in and because of this I often find myself on the side lines. A man's insecurity is being vulnerable to his woman. And if she accepts him for who he is, it is at that point that he realizes that he can unload on her. He is now her protection. They will now both bend over backwards for each other to make sure they're good and they can both do this without losing their individual identities. Most men are insecure and they will not bet on a woman who does not bring them to this level of comfortability. He will just look at her as someone to 'smash'. - **MM, 56**

At this point in my life I still fear rejection and I think it stems from being shy. It's some type of subconscious road block. I don't know if I'm getting meaner, I think I'm at the point where I really just don't give a shit! I've tried doing things that get either shut down or canceled out, so now I don't even try anymore. - **DN, 58**

I don't have any fear at this point in my life when it comes to relationships, I just don't have any motivation to be in one. I guess after two marriages and a lot of dating, I'm in a good space right now. Marriage is not on the menu for me neither is any relationship that is too serious. I'm enjoying my freedom to go and do what I want and when I want. Most of my adult life I've been married and I've got three beautiful kids. So I've checked these things off my list already and I really don't need to do these things again. At this point in my life I'm just not feeling it. - **KEITH, 60**

My fear is based on the uncertainty of how the relationship will turn out. When I look at forming a new marriage, a new relationship, or a new partnership, I have to contemplate what the outcome would be. Never would I have thought after proposing to my wife and after four years of wooing her and pursuing her until she said "yes", that we would end up getting divorced. - **PILOT, 61**

My biggest fear that I used to have is really just a fear that all men have and that is that another male can come along and dominate my sexual space with my lover. This used to freak me out. I would have a woman in my life that I am feeling, and somebody else can come along and she gets a whiff of him and suddenly she's out. This was a big fear back in the day. I had this fear too many times in my past. I was seeking women who didn't want a lot from me and I didn't want a lot from them. So having someone in my life who doesn't want a lot from me, this means she is also giving herself the freedom to love another man somewhere else. The lack of commitment was going both ways. - **ANTHONY, 62**

# Chapter 6

# MEN AND THEIR EMOTIONS

Today, more men are tapping into their emotions by choosing to express their pain, sadness and vulnerability. Men do feel deeply however, that they aren't always adept at expressing their feelings or showing any emotion, because they don't know how women will perceive them. They don't want to be judged, ridiculed or made to feel that being emotional is a weakness; and because of this, they struggle to find words to express their emotions. Men who deviate from the traditional masculine norms are reluctant to be exposed and only express themselves in small doses.

As children, men were taught not to show any emotion. They were socialized to shake off their pain and get tough. They grew up watching their fathers and the men around them refrain from expressing their feelings. These men were emotionally distant and rarely, if ever, cried or showed affection. Feelings of fear and sadness were stifled by messages like, "Be a man! Don't be a punk! Only sissies cry." Most of the men acknowledged that being apathetic is a coping mechanism to survive in this world.

I grew up without a dad and my mom passed away when I was nine years old, so I grew up with my aunties and my cousins. I was bullied a lot, so I always showed my emotions. I think more men should show their emotions and to show how much we really care. I don't think there is anything wrong with a man showing his emotions. However, on the flip-side, I feel like if I show too much emotion, then a woman will run away. - **JOSHUA, 25**

Definitely a lot of what I was taught was to 'man up', not to let my emotions get in the way of objectivity. It wasn't something that I rejected, this is something that I value and feel has helped me in my life to a certain degree. Although as much as I value communication, there are times when I feel that I am emotionally stunted, especially when it comes to showing emotions like sadness, sorrow, and anger. When I don't feel these emotions as much, I feel like I don't feel happiness, love and joy as much either. I feel like this has affected me somewhat throughout the years. Not being so emotional has helped me in a practical sense, but then I can say I'm not nearly as happy as I was as a child growing up. - **SHAUN, 25**

I was taught to not show my emotions to be a man, and 'man up'. I've been a quiet person most of my life and observed a lot of things going on around me. I use my ears more than my mouth. What I observed was that in order to have a successful relationship, I would need to be able to express anything with someone. However, because I was taught that men don't cry, I never put too much emotion into a relationship until I got married. - **LAWRENCE, 26**

I keep a lot of my emotions to myself. When I get emotional or I'm going through something, I don't reach out to anybody as much. I may talk about it when I'm ready to or I'll decide when I want to talk about it based on how I'm feeling at the time. There are times when I just wait for another situation to come up before I bring it up. I need that time to get my head together before I address the situation. - **LOGAN, 28**

I was definitely taught to love. I was able to have a friendship with my dad. I was able to be emotional around him and my mom. I didn't feel like I was being kept away from any level of intimacy with my parents. I think this impacted me in a different way as a man. I find this type of freedom through sexual expression, but I don't find this type of freedom when it comes to communicating verbally. Sex is one thing that drives my vulnerability to communication. So I'm a lot more open and free after having sex once I've shared that connection with my significant other. It's this connection or bridge that is built from her emotions to mine. - **DAMIAN, 30**

I grew up running the streets, so with running the streets, the main thing that we were taught was, "Man, fuck these hoes! Fuck her, fuck her friend, fuck her mama, fuck her sister, and fuck her auntie. We're out here to get ours and get going!" What was instilled was to be a player, fuck everything moving. - **GIANNI, 31**

My dad died when I was 14 years old. My mom raised me and my two younger sisters. At 14 years old I took on being the man of the house. I got a job after school to help supplement the household income, and I made sure my sisters were ok when my mom was at work. I saw how stressed my mother was most of the time. I never talked to her about the things that I was feeling because I thought it would make her more upset, so I just kept my feelings inside. I was the only male in the house so I thought I had to assume the role of being a man. I never let anybody know when things were wrong with me. I just kept everything to myself. I wrestled with my emotions my whole life. Still to this day, sometimes it's hard for me to really express the way I feel. - **HUGH, 32**

I was taught to show my emotions growing up. I was raised around a lot of women and the men in my life weren't the kind of men who told me to 'man up'. I've had men in my life who used to rough me up, and make sure I did pushups on my knuckles on concrete. They weren't telling me to stop acting a certain way or stop acting like a girl. As I got older I got more in tune with my emotions. I remember watching television commercials of kids in impoverished countries who were living in devastating conditions, and this would actually make me tear up. I wasn't going to hold back my feelings when I was feeling bad about this. My emotions came out and I started to tear up. Any man that holds his emotions back is an asshole. I can also acknowledge children who do things that are adorable, I'm not going to hold back my emotions. What does this say about me? Relax guys, I'm human. - **JAMAR, 32**

I grew up with my mom's family. I'm closer to them than I am with my father's side of the family. It was my mom's side of the family who instilled the traditions of love, and taking care of one another. The community and tribe that my grandparents created is a "super power". I call it "Super Power" because we pour into one another constantly. We hike each other up, we tell each other, "You ain't shit!" when you need to tell someone that. And we have this way of prayer unlike any other family I know. We really believe in that. This is a foundation with discernment, having a relationship with the creator, but ultimately it's just love. My mother took a pivotal role in teaching me about how to love somebody. So because of this, it has allowed me to be open in such a way where sometimes it has driven some women away. A lot of women are not in touch with the depth of their own emotions - being open and honest. It is within the particular individual to be open to me and also have self-knowledge when it comes to her, in order for her to receive me. - **ANDRE, 33**

I was told, "Boys don't cry!" You never show your emotions. If I needed to cry go somewhere else away from everybody else, go be by myself and suck it up and deal with it. I was told there will be a lot of things that I have to do that I don't want to do, but I just have to do it. When it came to talking about my feelings the only people that I could talk to were my momma, my girlfriend or my homeboy. As a man, you're not supposed to be crying a lot unless you're going through a death or something like that, you know what I'm saying? I have a huge problem using my words when it comes to my emotions and my feelings. This is something I'm learning about and dealing with in therapy. - **KING, 34**

I was scared shitless of my mom so if I acted out, she told me where to draw the line, and there were lines that I never crossed. I was able to talk to my mom about certain things. I realized as I got older and started to date that most of the girls weren't great at communicating. This made me want to enhance the skill sets that I already had. My family was very social so I grew

up mimicking this and cultivating it. And I cultivated it because I noticed there was a lot of people that didn't know how to communicate properly.
- **ISAIAH, 35**


My grandmother raised me from the age of one or two, I was with her my entire life. I knew my mother but she did not raise me. I colloquially picked things up from how I was raised and socialized with different people. They would tell me to "Stop crying, don't be crying", and all of that stuff. Or they'd say, "I'll give you something to cry about". I had an aunt who slapped me in my mouth once because I said something out of turn. From that day forward, I stopped talking. I was about four years old and I became a very withdrawn child from that moment on up until I went to college. I became functionally shy. I didn't talk to a lot of people and I stayed to myself. I was raised as an only child so I just spent a lot of time on my own as it was. So for me, expressing my emotions just wasn't on my how to do list. Most of my emotions were anger, especially growing up as a kid in the ghetto. I had a long list of things that upset me. Growing up in poverty, not having what other kids had and just feeling that sense of emptiness or that longing for things that I wished I had. Going on field trips and seeing other kids with their parents and not having any parents with me. My mother and father were not there, so I had to get tougher, and I got angrier to meet whatever forces I came up against. Then there were also times when I did express myself and it would just fall on deaf ears. When I tried to explain how I was feeling or why I was feeling a certain way, I got brushed off or written off, then this would have its own impact on me too. I didn't want to suppress things. I had things to say. I wanted to be understood. As I got older, I learned how to communicate because I was tired of fucking things up. I am trying to get better communicating with friendships and in relationships, and I'm trying to be better and more patient. I had gotten to a space where I felt comfortable with myself. I am who I am and I do my best within this matrix. People either accept me or they don't. - **BRYCE, 35**


I was raised not to cry and don't show our emotions. I get what my father and uncles were saying but it's like when I don't show my emotions, a woman starts feeling like I don't love her. Just because I don't show my emotions doesn't mean that I don't love her. I feel like I should show my emotions. I'm not talking about boo-hooing in her face and things of that nature, but I'm going to show my emotions more. My mom and dad taught me how to listen to people. I grew up paying attention to people and listening so that I can understand what people are saying. That's why I take the art of communication to heart. A lot of time communication gets lost and we don't know what happened. - **RL, 36**

My dad was a tough dude. He dropped out of high school in the ninth grade and has been in the construction industry his entire life. So when it came to emotions, he had nothing to do with us dealing with emotions. His 'birds and the bees' speech to me and my brothers was, "Boys are supposed to be managed and girls are supposed to be fast, so y'all go play". My older brother on the other hand, took the time to tell me about women. He broke it down about emotions, showed me how to use a condom, and told me don't be out here breaking women's hearts. How I really learned about emotions is by watching my older brother. I had never seen him cry until at a certain part in a movie he became emotional over a woman being shot. After that I saw him cry at both my grandparent's funerals. - **MALIK, 38**

If there is one thing that I am in tune with, that would be, I know who I am. I know what I like and what I don't like. I am expressive. My dad is a man's man, meaning that boys/men shouldn't cry. This all went out the window when I saw him cry. How is he going to tell me from the age of 6 through 12, not to cry? My mom graduated with her degree and he cried because he was proud. This basically threw everything out about showing my emotions from that day forward, this gave me permission to feel! So at this point in my life I am okay with telling my significant other, "I am happy for you, I am proud of you", and shed a couple of tears because again, intimacy is transparency. Now on the flip side of that, if I get to a space where I am upset and I cry, then you have to be careful. My indifference is subject to my anger. - **WES, 42**

I don't express my pain, why should I? It doesn't matter. I don't want people to think I'm weak nor do I want people to think I'm vulnerable. So it's better for me just to keep these emotions to myself. I was raised to be strong, I was raised to be tough. Stoicism was a form of survival for me, it was my defense mechanism against society. I've never been taught how to deal with my emotions and it's something I've had to wrestle with throughout life. I did not have control over my emotions and any little thing would set me off! I was emotionally and physically violent towards my ex-wife. She had a very strong personality and was constantly in my face over certain things to the point where I just exploded. I'm not proud of what I did and to this day I still regret it. As Black men, we don't have outlets to share our feelings or emotions. I think more men need support groups to help with our healing process. We need to understand that it's okay to ask for help. - **PHILLIP, 43**

Showing my emotions growing up was taboo, especially in the African-American community. Boys would have been labeled as being soft and been told to 'man up'. If nothing else, we've been taught to have pride. Pride keeps you from sharing your feelings. - **CHRISTOPHER, 42**

I was raised in a home where you had to talk and express what I was feeling. When my mom would ask me "Why are you crying?" she wanted me to explain to her why and what was going on with me. So I was raised to express what I was feeling. - **DOMINIC, 45**

Growing up, I kept my tears back because I didn't want people to think I was soft. I remember reading this book that my ex gave me about being self-aware, and I got emotional; it touched me and I cried in front of my ex. This may have brought us closer together because it was such a vulnerable moment, I felt that she understood. This made me open up to her even more. This ended up actually being the worst relationship of my life because to this day I don't know what happened. We dated long distance and then we moved in together, everything that we had developed when we were apart just disappeared when we moved in together. I felt like she lied about the person that she was because there was a lot of deceit and manipulation on her end. - **GYNUINE, 47**

My mom was a minister and my dad ran the streets, he was a party guy. The differences between my mom and dad caused an imbalance between them to the point where they argued every day. I don't ever remember a day when they didn't argue, and when they did argue I would withdraw and go and hide behind the couch in the living room. I found comfort amongst turmoil alone, by myself. Even now, I never go back home to visit my parents. Growing up, I used to dissect my emotions, put them in a box and put the box away until I needed them. So as far as emotions go, now at this point in my life I am really expressive. - **DEL, 47**

Growing up I had an anger problem that stemmed from some of the situations in my life as a kid. So every time that I got angry, I understood that there was a level of regret that followed. I used to fight when I got angry because I wasn't that good with words. I felt so misunderstood. Nobody in my life understood emotions enough to guide me effectively. I grew up very poor, I'm talking about real poverty. We were homeless, living in condemned housing with plywood on the windows. We lived in the projects in an area that was high in crime where I literally saw people, often, get killed right in front of me, stabbed, shot, beat up. There was a lot of drugs and alcohol around me, and on top of all this, I never knew my father. My mother had five kids with five different fathers. I knew the names of each of my sibling's fathers but nobody knew my father's name. His was the only face that we never saw come around and my mom never talked about him. I don't know why. When I looked at all my friends at school, everybody talked about their dads on certain days at school and I felt this was so unfair. This developed a lot of resentment in me towards other people. So a lot of the anger came from us being so poor, I felt like the world was so unfair. - **DI-AMEN, 47**

I don't really remember being taught anything about showing my emotions, it was more so through socialization, like when men would say, "Be a man and suck it up!" I think there was shame about showing emotion that could be considered as a weak emotion. It wasn't until the break-up of an 11½ year relationship, where the first time in my life I had experienced something where for long stretches of time I did not feel in control of my emotions. I would have these moments of emotion that were a little startling because I had never allowed myself to express my emotions in that way. They were so powerful and I couldn't stop them. Although on some level, they were also kind of cathartic in some way and I realized that I didn't have to trip over something like crying. - **XAVIER, 50**

As a man, I'm supposed to be the protector. If I show weakness when it comes to certain things, certain women will look at me like I'm weak. But at the same time, I know I'm not weak, I'm really looking out for her best interest. Sometimes I have to fall back, and sometimes I have to step to it. Women are quick to say that men are weak. Watching my parents, I was shown that if I do show my emotions, that's how to become a real couple. I saw how my father handled things so this put me on track. So as far as living my life, I follow that same track. - **WILLIAM, 50**

I was taught that as a man, I have to keep my emotions hidden, however, I know this isn't really true. Because when I keep my emotions hidden, this doesn't allow me to be a man. Real men are emotional. It's part of our human psyche to show our emotions. If we don't do this then it's going to be externalized and a lot of times this becomes stress and stress becomes disease after a while. I've learned that it's okay to show my emotions.
- **ISAAC, 51**

I'm probably a product of my environment. My parents were not very loving. My dad was a hell of a provider for his wife and his children, and so was my mom. I think they show far more emotions and love in their 70's then they did as I was growing up. I rarely heard them say "I love you". I rarely saw them walk in the door and kiss each other. They were high school sweethearts and I think they got married because my mom got pregnant, and they settled into a life together. Now they've discovered that they're the best of friends after they got me and my brother out of the house. I'm a product of this. So from an emotional standpoint, I'm probably not empty, but I'm not the best at showing my emotions. If I were in an argument with a woman and she started to cry I would probably say, "I'm going to give you a moment to pull it together, and then we'll talk about it". This could be very frustrating if I had a partner who has a love language that I'm not tapping into from an affirmation standpoint. And it's frustrating for me because I show love by doing acts of service. So rather than challenging myself to be better, I just fall back into old habits. - **DEION, 51**

Dealing with my emotions growing up was interesting because when I was young, I had a really bad temper. Although I was a happy-go-lucky kid, if you got me riled up I would go off. I never hung in gangs or in groups, I've always been kind of a loner. I was taught to embrace my emotions and try to figure out where the emotion was coming from. My dad would always be like, "Okay, what are you feeling right now?" He would then ask me the question "Why?" With all of his questions, he caused me to self-analyze, so then by the time I got to the reason I was so upset, I felt silly. My dad was Buddhist his whole life. He raised me to where I'm not supposed to have expectations, because in the Buddhist philosophy, your ego produces expectations. When those expectations aren't met we get depressed and hurt, and this now leads to a bunch of other things. So I can't be disappointed in someone's behavior if I don't have expectations. So I just deal with things as they are. This may sound asinine, but I honestly don't walk with fear. I don't have any fears about nothing, I never have. My dad would teach me breathing exercises, at a young age. He was into the mind and mental health stuff. It got to the point where my dad would just walk up to me, put his hand on my shoulder, and instantly change my mood. This is how I was raised, as his test subject... LOL! We have a very interesting relationship together. - **MAVERICK, 51**

Growing up I was taught to show no emotions and show no fear. I was told that "I'm a rock. I have to be strong. Real men don't cry"... well this is all bullshit! I was adopted at nine months old and the youngest in the family; my dad died when I was three. My mom remarried to a man who was an alcoholic and because of this I really wasn't around the house much. I was pretty much raised by a bunch of hustlers, players, go-getters and drug dealers who were in my neighborhood. I was 11 years old being taught how to run a dice table. - **GARY, 52**

I was not reared with patriarchal ideas about being a man because I was raised by women and these women were very feeling and very emotional and emotive. So I didn't have to hide my feelings. I was raised to show my emotions and to allow myself to feel what's going on around me, and I've carried this with me through adulthood. My stepdad was very patriarchal. He was very traditional. He didn't understand the idea of showing emotion. What I discovered about myself is that there is probably a correlation between my relationship with my parents, or the lack thereof, and the necessity to seek the arms of a woman. Both parents should provide a level of love and intimacy for a child. They are the ones who should help to reinforce that I am cared for and that I am loved. My father was supposed to instill this pattern in my mind that he is proud of me, that I am loved, that I am seen as worthy. In my mind I was constantly saying, "Hey dad tell me you love me. Hey dad do you see me? Hey dad I'm over here, aren't you proud of this accomplishment that I just made? Hey dad tell me what you think about this." So with my mom I was seeking more nurturing to make me feel warm, loved and fuzzy. And to this day, this is what I felt I was missing and I am still going through self-analysis and seeking positive reinforcement. But, what I am learning is to forgive my parents and to forgive myself. - **MICHAEL, 53**

I was taught that emotions were important and that I should always express my emotions and say what I need to say and get it out of my mind. There was a point where I was expressing my emotions too much and I was told to drill it back in because I was too outspoken and too carried away with my emotions. - **TRUSTIN, 54**

Indirectly I was taught to be tough, be a man. As a Black man, if I was going to survive I had to keep my emotions in check. - **GREG, 54**

I was a little punk! I was raised to be a little punk. If I felt hurt I was going to cry, dammit! I never had a problem showing my emotions. I was raised by my mom and didn't really have a father figure in my life. So being around my mom and my six sisters, there were emotions everywhere. I'm not afraid to show my emotions. - **STEPHAN, 55**

My dad allowed me to be open with my emotions. If I wanted to cry, I cried. He never instilled in me that real men don't cry. I was always of the mindset that I didn't need the affirmation of another guy to tell me how to act, so I was never intimidated if I did cry. I'm an emotional guy. I don't like to squash my emotions. - **TARZAN, 56**

My parents came from hardcore situations growing up and I rarely saw them affectionate. However, they had mad love for each other and were connected at the hip. They were in sync when it came to raising us kids. So there wasn't a lot of love in my household, but I was taught responsibility as a man. I was a virgin all the way through college, because my father, being a street dude would tell me to go on out there and have sex if I needed to. "But let me explain something to you, if you pop up with a kid, all those plans you have for college and the things you want to do with your life will go all out the window. But go ahead and fuck your shit up", and I knew he meant it. So for me, I was taught more about being a man by how I handled my business, and being responsible for my family, more so than how I needed to love a woman. The church didn't instill that in me either, I had to figure out my own formula when it came to my emotions. - **MM, 56**

I was taught by the men in my life that men don't show emotions. My father would say, "You come from strong stock and you need to toughen up!" I never saw my father or my grand-father cry or show any emotion. So I thought being a man, you just don't show emotions. My mom was more nurturing, caring and loving. Whereas my dad's job was to get me through school, keep me out of trouble and out of jail, keep me respectable, and this is what he did. - **ORLANDO, 56**

I was raised by a single mother. There were no stipulations about showing my emotions. There were no conversations about "Suck it up or stop being a baby", none of that stuff. She was sort of tough and she didn't have those stipulations. If I cried, she would console me. I think it's totally wrong to tell a young boy to suck it up and don't cry because you're molding that kid in a way that he wasn't already. You are changing his mold and not letting his mold form. I think the people who are molding boys this way is because the same thing was done to them. - **DN, 58**

My mother taught me growing up, that if I argue with a fool, then I become the bigger fool. So when it comes down to emotions, I am very careful about my emotions. I am not highly emotional. Not to say that I can't be angered, because I can be. But I do have a degree of reasoning that the beast of the field do not. I am able to reason my way out of most situations and I agree to disagree. Sometimes I find it necessary to suppress my emotions, especially when certain hormones are being released in my body and I feel that I'm being driven towards anger or a heated discussion. I see the value in my ability to be able to do this. - **PILOT, 61**

From the age of 23 to 48, I didn't cry at all. To cry was some weak, pussy stuff! My mom would say, "Suck it up, you're not a baby." My mom was a single mother, she was a survivor who did for herself what a man couldn't do for her. She had a hard way to go and she had to make sure that her son knew how tough life was, so she built in me a device to create strength. One of those devices was to stop crying. At 23, after putting out my first album, I remember being on the couch, holding my girlfriend at the time, and I broke down crying because what I was trying to do, wasn't looking like what was actually happening, and I realized that in order for me to do everything that I needed to do I had to get the hell out of Boston. So in some way, that cry was me releasing my hometown and entering into a whole new existence. - **ANTHONY, 62**

# Chapter 7

## THE IMPORTANCE OF COMMUNICATION

The level of happiness in a relationship will often be determined by the number of honest, difficult conversations people are willing to have with each other. Without a doubt, communication is the foundation of a healthy, long-lasting relationship and constructive communication is essential for couples to thrive. Men agree, in order to build lasting intimacy with their partners, communicating on a deep level and listening with discernment are extremely important. Understanding each other isn't only about how much they say, it's also about comprehending the other person's perspective.

All men are not alike when it comes to their communication styles. Some men are completely comfortable expressing themselves while other men are not, because they think that what they are saying will be misinterpreted, or that their partners will not really care about hearing their points of view. Although all the men agree with the importance of communicating, some still struggle with expressing themselves.

To me, communication is the bread and butter of a relationship. In terms of understanding one another, each individual has their level of how good they are expressing themselves and communicating. Despite seeing how much I value communication, I can admit that I'm not the best at it, but I am aware that it's very important and I do my best to do it. When I'm in a relationship and we're communicating, I think it's best for both of us to keep an open mind, be willing to listen, and keep kindness in our hearts and with this then we can pretty much solve most of our issues. - **SHAUN, 25**

Communication is really big. I think it is important to let my woman know what's going on and what I'm up to. As an erotic dancer my hours can be really crazy and if I don't communicate with her she'll be pissed off. I don't like to keep her guessing. I also don't want to have that feeling of wondering where she's at, who she is with. If I feel like our relationship is dwindling down, I want to talk about it. This works both ways. Let's keep the communication open. I don't want to give up and quit so easily, let's work through it and try to build for a better future for ourselves and our children's children. I want to set the standard. I want my child to see us kissing in the morning and to see us saying, "I love you!" - **JOSHUA, 25**

Yes, I do find it challenging to communicate with women today because I don't feel like we're communicating to understand one another, it is more so a tit for tat type of conversation with us going back and forth trying to figure out who was right and who was wrong. I just got out of a relationship recently and tried to resolve our issues without conflict so that I could understand her better. However, in my marriage, it took me two to three years to try to understand her. We both had a challenging time trying to resolve our conflict. I feel like she had more issues within herself then with me. - **LAWRENCE, 26**

Communication is important, however I don't like to talk just to talk. It seems like my ex used to get uncomfortable in silence, and she thought that I didn't care about her. It's just I prefer to listen then to talk just for the sake of talking. I'm not an emotional person and I really don't care about too many things that are unimportant to me and the way I live my life. - **DONNIE, 27**

Communication is very important. In my last two relationships we had communication barriers. I should have been a lot more unapologetic. I spent a lot of time holding my tongue and not saying things that I should have, out of fear of hurting them or from the fear of how they would react to the things that I may have said. They were very reactive women, either being angry or sad or running away when we talked about certain things. I think it is really important for me to learn how to communicate with whomever I'm with because we all have different styles of communicating, and different expectations when it comes to communicating. I know I'm going to have to be flexible and adapt, unless I run into someone that is on the same wavelength as I am, and we are on one accord This would be a blessing to find. - **DAMIAN, 30**

Very important! 100% important. I feel as though I am a good communicator. As a young man, I was not taught to be a communicator. But with every woman that I've encountered throughout my life, they've all shown me what I lacked. They helped me refine my communication. A lot of these women that I dealt with were not the average woman who wanted to party, smoke and shit. They were women with substance, and communication is a part of substance. They taught me to open up and let them know what it is that I want because they are not mind-readers. - **GIANNI, 31**

I was not always great with communicating with the women that I dated. I was uncomfortable expressing myself and saying what I really felt about things. A few years ago I met a woman who was 10 years older than me and she challenged me a lot on speaking to be understood and not just heard. She taught me that there is a way to communicate with someone so that we really understand each other. This was very interesting to me because I never knew that there was a formula to clear concise communication. Now I cannot date any woman who does not know how to communicate or a least isn't willing to learn. So many people think they are communicating with each other but they really are not. - **HUGH, 32**

In life, in general, communication is important. It is something that I have to constantly work on. It's also one of the hardest things in a relationship.

When I'm that close or intimate with my woman, there are things I want to say to her and have her automatically understand. Sometimes I try to communicate with my girl and she may not get what I'm saying, things are not always so black and white. It is not always easy because sometimes I don't even have a complete understanding of what I'm trying to say, let alone trying to get somebody else to understand what I'm saying from my messed up mind. - **JAMAR, 32**

Conversations are always going to be tough when it comes to something that is worth anything. We can't be afraid to have conversations with each other. Even when we understand the ability to get past things that are misunderstood, it's not about right or wrong, it's about whether or not you understand. Because if something is good, it's only based on how well it is understood. - **ANDRE, 33**

It is very important because it allows us to be able to build and have a stronger relationship. Just being able to talk to each other is key, because if I don't know what's wrong, then I don't know how to help her. We need to be able to talk to each other about whatever problems we may have. We need to fix those problems and move past them, or we just need to move away from each other. We have to talk and figure things out. I've been married for nine years and I'm learning to not talk just to argue, but to talk to really understand my wife, rather than me getting defensive. And then we start talking over each other screaming our points. When all of this is happening we don't understand each other and nothing gets solved. - **ALONZO, 34**

No I don't have an issue with this however, my communication is not always received well because of people's own preconceived notions about how things should go. Or they feel as though they can't express themselves. A lot of people aren't used to my level of feedback. I have a lot to say about everything. So, it may feel as though what I'm saying is a criticism of someone and it's not. I give talking points so that she can understand where I am coming from. I want to be thorough to make sure what I'm saying is not misconstrued. - **BRYCE, 35**

Communication is a lost art, and most people are just not taking the time to sit down and have a conversation. This is bad because I meet women who don't even want to talk anymore, nor do they know how. I'm not perfect, women are not perfect. We just have to find that one person that perfectly fits each of us. There will be disagreements. The question is can we communicate and work through those disagreements? - **RL, 36**

I enjoy talking. I enjoy debating. And I enjoy seeing the logic in a lot of things and situations, so communication is important to me. To be with a woman who is well versed like I am is a turn-on! A woman that does not have an opinion or cannot logically think about things is dull and boring. They say women are more talkative than men, this isn't true. I've met several women who can't form a sentence or express her thoughts. She doesn't have to be like Michelle Obama, she just has to have an opinion and be able to express herself. - **RON, 39**

Yes I find it challenging to talk about what I want with my wife because she doesn't want to hear it. I think it could be due to the fact that she is anticipating what I am saying before I say it. I think that women think that they are smarter than guys, so when I say something, my wife doesn't think I know what I'm talking about. It's very frustrating for me. - **CHUCK, 40**

It's the #1 thing I need. But learning how to communicate is what's important, that's a must. The way I communicate may not be the way that she communicates and together we need to figure that out. My mom used to yell at me when she communicated and I didn't think anything was wrong with that. My mom loved me, even though she was yelling at me and I never thought it was a bad thing. So naturally, my way of communicating is yelling. My lady's mom communicated with her by talking softly and not as stern. So we had to find a better way to communicate with each other. I had to figure out how to take my levels down and she had to learn that I wasn't yelling, I was just loud because my whole family is loud. It was hard to find that happy place and I learned to compromise very well with whomever I am dating. - **TYLER, 42**

I came from a household where domestic abuse was active, and my father abusing my mother was more a matter of his frustration, of cultural differences and him not able to advocate for himself. My dad is Haitian. He lost his father at the age of six. I did not feel that he had the knowledge to teach me how to be a man because of the lack of a fatherly influence in his life so I sought another mentor. - **WES, 42**

I actually took a course on communicating and how to communicate. Prior to this I used to raise my voice to get my point across and this wasn't very effective in my past relationships. I come from a family of seven children so I had to practically yell to be heard. I realized when I got older it was unhealthy and it really didn't feel very good. What I learned from this course was to identify my communication style and triggers, but most importantly, how to hear what the other person is saying. Allowing them to speak and mirroring them by repeating back to them what they said. I use these techniques in all areas of my life now and it has made a huge difference in understanding people in general. - **PHILLIP, 43**

On a scale of 1 to 10, communication would be the 10. It's the same way as when you're working together as one. Communication is so important because you cannot harmonize, bring things in order or move collectively, unless there is communication in the relationship. I'm talking about communicating on all levels. Emotionally, this causes me to move around the other person in a certain way if I know she's challenging me in this way. We need to be able to talk about how we're going to raise the kids, pay the bills and supplement our income, if need be. But what's even more important than just communicating, is the quality of communication. There has to be an allowance for expression when it comes to communication. - **DI-AMEN, 47**

I will say this, I think what this question means is often different for men and women. I think there is a lot of socialization that went into the creation of men and women in our society, and this has, obviously, a myriad of manifestations. What I see as appropriate depths of communication is not always satisfactory for women. I think we often process things in different ways. So that when we're in a team dynamic, it's hard often to bridge those gaps, because I may look at it like we talked about it and we resolved it. A woman wants to make sure she's heard. If we are not communicating well, then this can go down a slippery slope of emotions, and this can be unsettling. Although I'm decently evolved, there is still a certain point of emotionality where I just shut down. I don't believe every disagreement or dispute needs to evolve into chaos, but I don't seem to be able to control her need for chaos in the moment where everything I say comes flying back at me. So despite the risk of being accused of shutting down, I'm going to shut down. It's a protective thing. We should agree to disagree. It is in these differences that we process situations. - **XAVIER, 50**

Communication is very important. I'm even okay with arguing. We can call and cuss each other out, I'm cool with this as long as we get the shit out! I have a problem when a woman sits back and says there is nothing wrong. Now I can clearly see something is wrong, so let's talk about it. What did I do? Now I do know that my mouth gets me in trouble, because I say exactly what I'm thinking or what other people are thinking, and they don't want to say it. Sometimes my words come out wrong and what I'm saying gets misinterpreted. I've been told that I lack a level of sensitivity. - **DEION, 51**

Communication is the basis of a relationship. If we don't communicate how are we going to get to know each other? Especially if we don't have 'true' communication. True communication is being real and authentic. If we feel a certain way about something, just say what it is your feeling. Let me know when I activate a certain emotion in you. When we are able to communicate in this way, it creates emotional intimacy, and this is what relationships need to grow. I learned the importance of communication, after going through my last marriage and not really communicating openly and honestly. Neither of us were really honest in our communication. Perhaps if we were both more honest with our communication, the relationship would have lasted much longer. - **ISAAC, 51**

To me, the sexiest thing in the world ever, is to find someone who is a fantastic communicator and we both are on the same page. The power of agreement is amazing! Whether it pertains to business or just having an intimate evening. It's powerful... just thinking about this gets my dick hard.

Intimacy is also about a person's ability to have sustainable, good communication. The lack of real communication is what is missing today and it is the reason why it's hard as hell to date. A lot of guys say they ain't trying to really communicate, they're just trying to "smash" as many women as they can and get their numbers up. But what is really happening is they're disappointed because they may be a poor communicator and they don't want to risk being exposed as being an inept communicator and they stay in this cycle. - **GREG, 54**

Communication is very important because without communication, how are we able to know what's going on with each other. We don't know what the hell each other wants. If we are not doing things that the other person wants or expects, then we need to say something. Sometimes to me, just texting a woman while she's at work and sending her a little rose emoji and letting her know that I'm thinking about her and her doing the same to me just lets us know that we're thinking about each other. - **STEPHAN, 55**

I was communicating the wrong way for many years. I was basing my communication on what other men were saying. I had to be careful about listening to my homeboys because they are not always right. I had to find a way to express myself to my wife. I'm still learning. I don't always get it right. - **TARZAN, 56**

Communication is important because I don't read signs from women. If a woman really understood this about me then she would have less headaches on her hand. I was raised in the projects, so the people around me were a little bit 'hard'. I grew up without the affection of love. I grew up with the strength and survival mindset. I grew up with two parents in the household, and it was instilled in me to be responsible and to take care of my family. It wasn't until I was older that I discovered my variation of being affectionate, or being able to display a lot more with expressing myself. I went through the cycle in my life of learning when and how to communicate and express myself. Women have an idea or a fantasy of how men should be. But as a man, I'm still learning and developing my self-expression that is unique and customized to me. - **MM, 56**

Being able to communicate in my relationship is the cornerstone. If I can't talk to my woman, and tell her certain things then we are going to have problems. I can't read her mind, and I think all women assume that men automatically know things about them, and we don't. I am a simple creature, all she has to do is tell me. Just let me know what I need to do and I will do it. Couples should always communicate and be honest with each other. If there is something lacking in your relationship, talk to your mate and let them know because they may not know. If women are not telling us men what's on their mind, then we are not going to know. As men we are going to assume that everything is good. If it's something I'm not doing or if it is something that I'm missing, tell me. This way I have a better grasp of what's going on and I can make adjustments. I can't read her mind and I can't read her moods. If I ask her if there is something wrong and she says "No", then okay I'm going to believe her. Women should just be honest. - **ORLANDO, 56**

Communication and honest communication is extremely important, first and foremost. What I find a lot out here today is women who are not necessarily lying, but they give partial truths. They need to be free to be honest and truthful. I am a man who speaks my truth. I'm unfiltered at times. I find with this new generation, communication is totally different. They hide behind texting and when people hide behind texting, the full truth is never presented. It's unfortunate that this is how the new generation communicates, old or young, it doesn't matter. That basic truthfulness is almost a lost art right now. I think this is due to the evolution of how the country has changed and how the roles have changed. - **KEITH, 60**

I think communication is important. The problem that I have is the interpretation of what communication really is. If my thoughts and how I size up communication is different from my partner's thoughts and how she sizes up communication, then we may think we are communicating, when in fact there is only noise between the two of us. Both of us need to be able to express our differences and our outlooks on a particular matter, or at least make the attempt to do so. Let's discuss how we both see the situation at hand and agree or disagree on our interpretations. If it comes to the point where we disagree, she needs to understand that I'm not disagreeing with her as an individual, I'm disagreeing with perhaps the outlook at that time. I try to make this clear as a differentiation. - **PILOT, 61**

Communication is critical because bullshit happens every day between me and my wife. Every day there is a navigation of communication. Our talk is, "Let's be honest, let's allow each other to speak" and the difficult one is "Let's not blame each other. Let's not start our conversations with, "You always do this..." - **ANTHONY, 62**

# Chapter 8

# SEX AND SEXUAL PLEASURE

S ex and sexual pleasure have always been sensitive and embarrassing topics of conversation for most people. It's the one thing that people have questions about, but only a few talk about. As an adult toy educator, I've had many conversations with hundreds of women and men about great sex and more pleasure in the bedroom. What I discovered is that people don't talk about sex because they feel embarrassed or ashamed, or they don't want to be judged, or they don't want to offend their partner. Some people even admitted, frankly, that they don't always know enough about it.

I wanted to find out from the men what their first sexual experiences were like, how they approached sex, different sexual proclivities, and if their manhood was attached to their sexual prowess. There are a wide range of fascinating answers based on each man's enjoyment, his abilities and skills. What gives one man his gratification, is different from another. Talking about sex can be quite awkward, and I found through this interview process that some men were more open than others in sharing sexual secrets that they have never shared before.

# FIRST SEXUAL EXPERIENCE

I lost my virginity to a woman who was 22 years old and I was 16. She was a friend of the family, so I had known her for many years. I always had a sexual appeal to myself. I'm not sure where I get it from, but I was always told at a young age that I was going to be a handsome young man or a sexy young man, and I think this older woman just took took advantage of the opportunity to have sex with me. I think she wanted to be the first one to experience me as a virgin and as an innocent young man. She was always playful with me and always nice to me growing up. Then one night she invited me over and I thought she was going to cook me dinner, but instead she started kissing on me and rubbing on me, and then she went down on me giving me oral sex. I didn't know what the hell was going on and one thing lead to another.  She took her bra off, then she took her pants off and and then her panties. Once she was naked, she guided me through having sex. - **JOSHUA, 25**

I was 21 years old when I first had sex with a woman and she was around the same age. In all honesty, I think there are delusions of grandeur around having sex. Society puts a lot of pressure on young people suggesting that sex is the greatest thing ever.  It's hyped up in movies, TV shows and video games. Sex was great, it was cool, but I thought I would feel different afterwards. I was a horny kid in high school and had sex on my mind and what not, and I finally get to it and it was like, "Well ok, what's next". I have been a porn connoisseur since I knew what a keyboard was. I started watching porn at the age of six. I was six year old on the computer typing in sex.com to see what would come up. My generation was raised on the computer and using software. We had a computer in the house and I was taught at a really young age how to use it. I was a pretty sheltered kid and I knew how to use webcams to talk to friends. Sex has not been an active thing in my life. I mean, you know, I get by when I can. - **SHAUN, 25**

I was 10 years old when I first had sex. It was with a girl whose mother was a friend of our family. She was 12 years old and my mother used to send us to my room to play. One day the girl asked me if I wanted to play house. She told me to take off my pants and she started playing with my penis.  Once my little penis got hard she told me to get on top of her. I didn't know what I was doing, I'm not sure if I even penetrated her but it felt good. - **DONNIE, 27**

I was molested as a child by a male family member when I was between the ages of five to seven. I told my mom what he was doing but she didn't believe me until she saw it for herself when she walked in on us. That's when she finally believed me and this was a few years after it had been going on. I'm in counseling around this now and am in the healing process. As Black men, I feel as though we don't take the time to necessarily heal from our post trauma. Whether we've been molested, or seeing our moms being abused, ya know, whatever it is. There are things as Black men that we really need to heal from correctly, and I feel as though getting help and therapy is one way that we all can heal. So I started going to therapy to heal from those traumas. - **KING, 34**

I was 10 years old and I hung out with my cousin who was 14 or 15. I was always kind of tall for my age. The girl was in the eighth grade. My cousin told me to pretend like I was in the eighth grade and act like I knew something. I was like, alright cool! He had this light-skinned girl, I had this dark-skinned girl. My voice was in between screeching and trying to sound deep. I was like, "Hey, how are you doing?" We went to the room and got in the bed. I was trying to take her bra off and could not get it off. She's on top of me and I'm trying to lick her breast. Thinking about this now, I must have looked so stupid, LOL! Next thing I know my cousin comes in the room with his girl and they get in the bed with us. So now all four of us are in the bed. I look over and my cousin's dick is out. So I reach over and put on a condom. I don't really know how to use a condom but I put it on. I went to penetrate her and she was making a face like it hurt. I asked her if she was ok and she said yes. So as I'm putting my dick inside of her it started to feel warm. I'm watching my cousin and started copying what he was doing to the other girl, because I'm trying to learn. I'm just pumping up and down looking real stupid. - **RL, 36**

I was 18 years old, believe it or not! Everybody is shocked when I say that because they expect for a man to have sex much sooner than that, and I didn't. And then after that, I didn't have sex until I was 21 because I was afraid of getting a disease... this was the biggest thing. Who can you trust? I was attracted to a lot of women. I even taught and talked about sex education with people who wanted to know about sex. They were coming to me as if I was a guru on the subject because of my knowledge. But little did they know, I was not having sex. I spoke so well when it came to educating guys on how to please a woman. All the guys, when I was in college, were coming to me to get advice because their girls would send them to me to get advice. My older brother would educate me on all the diseases you can get from having sex. He would say don't just do it until you are ready and if you do have sex wear a condom. I just made up my mind not to have sex. It wasn't like I didn't have opportunities to have sex, I just choose not to. A lot of the young ladies I was attracted to went to my college and that college was known to have a high HIV rate. I was so afraid of catching something that I just didn't have sex with these young ladies. When I came home from college I met a young lady that I would hang out with every weekend and she was so upset with me that I didn't have sex with her. We would do everything but it. We would kiss, hug, get all hot and steamy but I just wouldn't have sex, no way, I just pumped the breaks. - **MALIK, 38**

I was 12 years old when I lost my virginity and she was 15, she was my homeboy's sister. We were playing in an abandoned apartment and she took me into the closet and she said, "We should act like we're doing it to make everybody question what's going on". Of course I was excited about fucking her, she had a big booty too, LOL! Over the years I was more attracted to older women because they had more experience. And to tell you the truth, over the years I never dated anyone that was my age. The oldest woman I dated was 13 years older than me and we were together for two years. - **GIANNI, 31**

I was six years old when I lost my virginity. She was an older woman and she took advantage of me, she was a woman... I was six years old! I can't talk about this anymore. After that (molestation) it was that feeling of ejaculation that I wanted. Around the age of 12, I started reading a book called *The Female Anatomy* to understand a woman's body and then I started to experiment with girls. I would ask them if what I was doing did anything to them or make them feel a certain way. - **CHRISTOPHER, 42**

I think I was 15 years old. It was crazy because I got picked up by a girl in my neighborhood. I was outside sitting on my porch and this girl walked by and I said, "Hey, how you doing!" She walked over to me and said, "How are you doing?" We talked for a little while and she asked if she could come by tomorrow. So she came back the next day and we went inside to my bedroom. She was directing me on what to do to her. I had a hard-on just by the thought of having sex! She asked if I had a condom. She told me how to put my penis in her vagina. She spread her legs open, grabbed my penis and put me inside of her. We had a few minutes of pleasure. I ejaculated and then it was over. She was definitely well versed in sexual behavior, and it was my first time. She went home and I never saw her again. - **KADEEM, 44**

I was four years old and she was four years old. Yes, my penis got hard and I put it in her vagina. At four years old, I wasn't a regular four year old boy. I was more conscious, I knew what was happening, I knew what was going on. I knew what a vagina was and I knew I had a penis. I already knew this, easy, hands down. I grew up in the 70's. In my environment, not everybody was paying attention to their children and where they were at. It was a sad thing because even that little girl had come from a really bad situation of molestation so it wasn't as though it was very hard for us because she understood what was going on as well. I was molested by females. They would say that I was their little baby and they put me in the bed with them. They would have me use my hands on them or in them. I remember when I was really little, I was tiny, and one of the girls would put me on top of her and pump my butt between her legs. Growing up around the age of 13 or 14 this would always happen, even at church older women would approach me. I remember feeling aroused as a child before I even ejaculated. I had hat feeling of pleasure and excitement at the age of 7, 8 and 9. I developed a large appetite for sexual pleasure during this time and I had to get control of it so it won't be as though I was advertising myself. But if I was alone with a girl, I'd want to go again and again, like and all-nighter type of deal. - **DOMINIC, 45**

I think I was 17 years old when I first had sex. The first situation was embarrassing but because of my immaturity and my strict upbringing. This young lady snuck out of her house one morning and came to my house. She got into bed with me. I remember trying to put on a condom and it desensitized me and I couldn't do it, so sex never happened. Later that summer I had met a young lady who was much more experienced than me. She was a couple of years older than me and she initiated sex. I learned about sex through trial and error being with her. It was exciting to me because we did a lot of different things. I read a lot of books back then and we tried some of the positions like doggy-style or her being on top. - **GYNUINE, 47**

The first time I had sex, I was 15 years old. My brother made an arrangement to have a floozy come and 'freak me out'. It was my birthday and she was my birthday gift. She scared me to death. She unzipped my pants and I said, "Wait a minute, what is she doing". My brother said, "Boy just lay back!" and he shut the door. Of course I wanted it because I had never experienced a woman before. She was like 22 years old and she was very skilled in the things that she did. - **WILLIAM, 50**

I believe I was 16. She was a girl back in the neighborhood in Detroit. We were around the same age. The insane thing about this I just wanted to knock this out so that I can say I had sex. It wasn't like I really wanted to have sex with this particular girl, I just wanted to have sex for the first time. I thought, what if I pass up this opportunity and then don't have another opportunity and then I have to go into another school year with my friends teasing me because I'm still a virgin and all that shit! So I figure, let me just bang this shit out real quick, instead of going back home kind of embarrassed. No one knew the girl so I didn't have to hear any judgement from my friends. Then I didn't have sex again until I was 18. - **XAVIER, 50**

I was around 11 years old when I became sexually aware of myself. I would wake up in the morning and my dick was hard or it would get hard when I was sitting in the tub bathing myself. When I would clean my penis it felt good so I started masturbating. The first time I ejaculated I popped my cherry, so cum came out and there was a little bit of blood. I was like, "Oh shit! what was that?" It was such a sensational feeling that I wanted it to happen the next night, so I tried it again. The first time I penetrated a woman was when I was in the ninth grade. I grew up in a middle class family. We lived in a four-bedroom house, and had an in-ground swimming pool, and a mobile home in the driveway. So in my neighborhood I was the top dog! I met this girl while I was riding around with my cousin in a stolen Nissan 300ZX. We were riding down "The Shaw" - Crenshaw Boulevard. I saw her and got her number. I invited her over to my house and we had sex in the mobile home. We did a lot of foreplay, kissing and touching. I knew about fingering a girl and playing with her clitoris, from listening to older dudes. She took her panties off and I laid on top of her. Honestly, I don't even know if I penetrated her because I wasn't circumcised so I couldn't really tell. - **GARY, 52**

I think I was 13 years old. We had a sleepover and we played house in a tent with a bunch of kids. There was a mommy, daddy, kids, uncles, aunts, etc. Since she and I were the mommy and daddy, she said, "Let's try having sex!" So we got naked with each other and I tried to put my little pee-pee in her hole. It was very awkward. I did end up penetrating her and popping her cherry, but I didn't ejaculate. I remember thinking, "I just had sex. I don't have to think about this anymore. I can check this off my list of things to do." It was like that pressure to have sex was off of me. All my peers were talking about having sex ever since I was about 11 years old and I hadn't done it yet. - **TRUSTIN, 54**

I was practically 18 years old. I can't say it was horrible, I mean, I didn't know what I was doing and I didn't get the impression that she knew what she was doing either. She was my girlfriend and we had talked about having sex, like a lot of young kids do. I lied and said I had had sex before, 100 times! but it had never really done "it" before. It was awkward. She laid on the couch, lifted up her skirt, I pulled out my penis, still with my clothes on and tried to put my penis inside of her. I really don't think it went all the way in. - **JORDON, 54**

I was 16 years old when I lost my virginity. I snuck out the house to go to her house and we were just hanging out in her room watching TV. We were kissing and grinding and all the sudden we started slipping our clothes off, we were both nervous as hell. We were so nervous we didn't know what we were about to do. She's taking my clothes off, I'm taking her clothes off. I'm trying to figure out what the hell I'm supposed to do with this "thang". It was kind of scary because it was painful to her, it was her first time too. Because it was painful to her I was scared. I didn't know if I should stop or keep on going. It probably lasted less than 10 minutes. - **STEPHAN, 55**

I was 18 years old when I first had sex. I was riding my bike in the neighborhood and I saw this girl and she was riding her bike and her chain popped off. It's my nature to help people out so I went over there and helped her put her chain back on. I came to find out later that she did it on purpose. So once I did that, that allowed her to give me a reward, basically. And that reward was an invitation to go over her house and hang out with her. I didn't know her that well, I've seen her in the neighborhood before. So I went over and played the board game Life with her and a few other people. As it got later, the other people went to bed and the girl touched my penis and said she wanted to play with this. So this gave me the okay to move forward. I'm not the type of man to make the first move, to me it's not an honorable thing. We started kissing and what-not and then we went to her room. She undressed me and talked me through the whole situation, and then we had sex. Once I got inside of her I knew what I was doing. - **DN, 58**

# GREAT SEX AND MORE PLEASURE

I feel like sex shouldn't be going on for 45 minutes. I feel like sex should last for only 10 to 15 minutes. For me it's about the climax and the passion. When you have sex that lasts for 45 minutes to an hour, to me it's just fucking. If it's something we both want, the climax should happen soon. Kissing, rubbing, heavy breathing, her body shaking, bodies sweating, laughing together and then climaxing together, now that's great sex!

To please me in the bedroom, she has to stop thinking so much about herself. If she's going to suck my dick, then suck it. Don't suck it until it gets hard and then climb on top of me. In this case I feel like I'm just a piece of meat. - **JOSHUA, 25**


The first time I had sex, it was overly hyped more than I thought it should be. Great sex to me is when it is closest to the idea that I have about sex. I enjoy having sex for a long time so I enjoy it when a woman can keep up with me for the duration. I'm a simple person and not particularly demanding or needy. As long as she communicates what she wants, and I get the impression that she is enjoying herself, this would be enough for me to play into my ego and for me to get off. If I please her then this makes me feel good. But sometimes, I have to admit, it is easier to whip out my phone or turn on my computer and take care of myself. Then I'm back to my business to do whatever it is I have to do. Sex takes a lot of effort and I'm a lazy dude. So if the opportunity presents itself then I will have sex, I'm just not actively chasing it at this point. - **SHAUN, 25**


I think "great sex" is when there is a soul connection between two people. I'm a pleaser and I'm unselfish so I wouldn't want to get off first. My ex-wife and I, most of the time, would orgasm at the same time, so when this happens it just makes sex even better because to me this creates an even deeper connection. When you have sex with someone you leave something with them forever. - **LAWRENCE, 26**

When we are both able to 'bust-a-nut'... that's great sex! When it's wild and fun, like rolling around in the bed, smacking her ass, light choking, or pulling her hair. When I tell her to do something, she does it and she's into it as much as I am. When she's not pushing away from me while I'm inside of her and she just takes me all in. Hearing her scream and moan is a big turn-on. And I like having sex in different parts of the house.

To please me more in the bedroom, a woman can give me more head. Not all women are skilled at giving head and if she's not skilled then I will teach her. This is another thing about women being submissive, she has to be willing to learn new things. If I teach a woman the way I like to get head, and if she learns what I like, then this will please me. - **LOGAN, 28**

Great sex is when it is both liberating and giving. It is when we feel somewhat of an exhaustion. And what I mean by this is when we feel exhausted and empty after having some type of sexual act. But in the same breathe, great sex is also be an experience that we both share together. It's when we're both giving equally and freely and we're both giving an infinite amount of energy, leaving each other feeling empty and completely satisfied. This is what makes it great because at the end of our experience we both feel appreciated. I am a minimalist when it comes to sex. My expectations are a lot lower when it comes to what I want or what I need.

To please me more in the bedroom would be to have more attention from my significant other. There is so much expectation on the man to have all of the sexual prowess and to put forth all of the energy and the effort into pleasing a woman. A lot of times this gets lost when it is time for the woman to reciprocate or when it's time for me to be pleased. I think that there is an imbalance there. Especially when it comes to the expectation of how a man should be pleased versus how a woman should be pleased. It's not a particular act for me that's going to give me that satisfaction. It's more so the attention she gives me and her ability to lay back, relax and enjoy the experience with me. - **DAMIAN, 30**

Great sex, to me, starts off with intimacy. Knowing I can be myself and be vulnerable around her, first off, this is a turn-on for me. So if I know I can be comfortable with her, I'm going to do anything and everything she wants me to do! And from there, great sex is non-stop and heart pounding where I'm looking into her eyes, holding her head and just strcking the fuck out of her, oh my God!!! It's almost spiritual like, "Girl I feel ycur soul!" I don't have great sex often. The only person I ever had that type of connection with was my daughters' mom. We were together for four years, but again, my ego got in the way. I did not have this type of connection with my fiancé either. However, after we broke up, I finally pinpointed what it was that was causing a lot of my damaging relationships. It was my ego! - **GIANNI, 31**

The best sex I ever had was when the woman was open to receive me. And what I mean by that is she wanted me just as much as I wanted her. There is a big difference having sex with someone when you know we are both coming together to make sure the other person is completely satisfied. She didn't have any hang ups. She didn't have any conditions. She wanted to explore and try new things. To this day I have never met another woman who was sexually self-expressed as she was. Don't get me wrong. I've had a lot of great sex, but with her it was just different. I like when a woman wants to role play and try new things. I'm an artist, and very creative. I like when a woman is adventurous and playful in the bedroom. Sex can become so dull and boring, especially if you just have it in the bedroom. So if she is willing to explore and try new things, then I am very pleased. - **HUGH, 32**

Great sex to me is when it is spontaneous and passionate. It's when I am anticipating or longing for her throughout the day. It's when sex is long, hot, and wet to the point where we lose track of time. I've grown to understand that for women, it starts long before the bedroom. Sc if I want the passion to be there then I have to pay attention to her, connect with her and be playful with her. Doing things like smacking her on the ass, cooking dinner and feeding it to her, bringing her flowers, massaging her, and stuff like that. I don't do well with timid women, so if we've gotten to the point of having sex, I want her to just let loose. I think if I've gotten her to the point of being comfortable, before having sex then she will open up and really enjoy it and go all out. She will be just as nasty as I am and a lot of times women are nastier than men. So she just needs to be comfortable, let loose and bring out her inner hoe! - **JAMAR, 32**

I don't value great sex as much as I used to because real intimacy does not involve sex, it's the opposite. There is a big difference between fucking and sex. When having sex, I have to incorporate my heart, I know this sounds really corny. As far as I'm concerned, my penis is a tool. I can give life and I can take life. I can pleasure a woman and also degrade a woman based off of this "tool". Most men do not value their tools and they don't realize that they have giver and taker of life between their legs. So as far as good sex is concerned, it's done with the heart. Sex is not about what you can get, it's about what you can give. When two people are giving themselves to the other individual, that is good sex. It is good energy exchange. Good sacred energy exchange. - **ANDRE, 33**

Great sex to me is at least two hours long. Multiple orgasms. Sweaty and hot and real passionate. It's variations between fast and slow (penetration), and having the stamina to go on and on. I've been with women who were not as skilled in giving oral sex, so sucking my dick with less teeth would have been more pleasing to me. A woman's vagina is some of the best feeling stuff ever. It's amazing! It's great, especially if it's nice and tight and wet. - **KING, 34**

It's been some time since my wife and I had sex, but great sex to me is when there's a build-up. It's when our anticipation is high and we're building up the foreplay. This automatically makes everything more intense where our souls are tied to each other. We're mentally stimulating each other, emotionally stimulating each other, and talking dirty throughout the day. This builds up our emotional connection. I can even have great sex when we are hating each other. During a fight, there is a whole lot of passion between us. It's like I don't want to have sex with her but my body starts craving it. It's like, "Damn!" I want to be mad at her but I want to have sex with her too!

I like when she initiates the sex because I don't always want to be the one to start it off. I get really excited by this. My endorphins are heightened when a woman takes the initiative with me, this is a big turn-on. It's surprising how much this turns me on because I'm not used to a woman taking the initiative. Other than this I really don't care about me being pleased, I'm more focused on pleasing her. If she's satisfied, then I'm satisfied. - **ALONZO, 34**

Great sex to me is when we can both be fearless and we can both be open. It's not about us just getting off or whatever. If I can make her cum until she's shaking and she cums eight times, I like that because I like to please her. Pleasing her is my #1 thing. I want to make sure that she is taking care of.

It's that energy of us being fearless. It's being willing to do anything and being open to having sex more if we both need it or want it. I had sex with a friend that really felt like love. We hung out the night before and she ended up staying over my place and hanging out that weekend. We had sex in the morning. We would stop, eat, talk and have sex again... and again... We were in bed until about 6pm that evening. It was wonderful. This girl was really earthy, she reminds me of Lisa Bonet. She was really into her surroundings and herself and she was self-aware. It was like actual love-making. We weren't just doing it to pound each other out, we really cared about each other. I'll never forget it. I find this type of connection with a woman extremely rare. I've had sex with about 250 women and I have only had this type of connection with women three times. She, however, is the only one that I remember. I think this is because we were both on the same level, we are both self-aware.

For a woman to please me more in the bedroom, she just has to be open. I'm not talking about her eating my ass or anything like that but just being open and being free with herself. Telling me what she wants and telling me what she needs. If I can just read a girl's mind, I'd be the best. If I could just be in a girl's body for one day, I'd figure the rest out. The closer I can get to that, the better off sex will be. If she allows me to get in her head to understand what she's thinking and what she's going through, what's making her get closer to orgasm, then I can please her better and this is how I'm going to get off. - **ISAIAH, 35**

Great sex comes in those relationships and scenarios where that comfort and that intimacy is building. There is a certain level of vulnerability when our skill matches our emotional energy. It's like I can feel, prior to having sex, that she cares about me. There is a certain chemistry there, a certain energy, like we just got this vibe. Now I've also had those sexual vibes from women that didn't mean me any good, so this feeling is tricky. Sometimes she just looks good or she's connecting with some type of sexual fantasy or physical preference that I have. I may have a certain emotional connection to where I start feeling like this could be a thing. Now-a-days I have to like the woman before I have sex with her. She can't just be pretty with a great body, this isn't good enough anymore, been there done that. This adds very little to my sexual experience with her unless that emotional connection is there. Great sex comes when there is an emotional connection.

When a woman is being intentional in the bedroom, this pleases me more because she has my pleasure in her mind with everything that she does. She wants to please me, she cares about me as a person and wants to see me happy! I'm very intentional with how I approach sex. I'm the type of lover where I want to make sure she orgasms multiple times before I even think about orgasming myself. This is my "MO" (modus operandi). - **BRYCE, 35**


Great sex is the build-up first, I have to have the build-up. If I fuck her mind first, now here comes the sex. Great sex is when I can do every type of sex from rough sex, to love making sex, to dominant sex, to talkative sex. When I have all of that in one session and we're changing positions, and sweating, and we're wiping each other's face off, and we're looking at each other like, 'I'm gonna tear your ass up!... that's great sex! We're snatching each other's clothes off and going at it. We're in the bed, on the counter, in the bathroom, at the window with the curtains opened. To me, I'm just this type of person. I also love kissing during sex. And I like it because it's another sensation between the actual fucking part. I'm a great kisser. I know I have nice soft lips and my breath is good. I know what my lips can do when they're between her legs. So if our bodies are moving right together and I start kissing her... Ummm, I love that shit!

What pleases me in the bedroom is when a woman is really into me and she wants to please me. She's kissing all over my body and she knows what I like. But, what's really crazy is that I please myself more when I'm pleasing a woman. When I'm going down on her and she's losing it, going crazy and squirming, this is a turn-on for me. When I can make a woman cum multiple times in a row by just giving her head, this is it for me. - **RL, 36**

Great sex to me is when we are both into it! If one person is into it and the other person is not, this is crazy! When my wife is into it, I don't care if I'm swinging from a chandelier, hanging out a window or she's on her back in missionary position, and she is into it... that's great sex to me. Back in the day I used to be wild. If my wife is into getting wild, then it's on! One of the issues we had when we first got married, I couldn't communicate this to her, but after seven years of marriage we communicate very well. I tell my wife, "Listen, if you're not into it I'm going to stop". I know every marriage gets to the point where she'll just roll over and say go ahead and get some, I don't like that. It's like humping a log. I want to hear her moan. I want her to tell me where to kiss and where to lick it. If you need me to lick up under your arm let me know. I want her to be into it! As of right now, I'm totally pleased! I know most men are not pleased in the bedroom and that leads to cheating. - **MALIK, 38**

Great sex to me is when there is still an anticipation and we are communicating and connecting throughout the day. It is verbal foreplay. When I'm letting my wife know that I'm thinking about her and she's doing the same. It's a playfulness to the point where we are getting aroused. What makes this great is being able to break away from work and just focus on each other. My wife and I have very demanding jobs, so when we are able to do this, our sex is very powerful! We are totally into each other to the point where we are not worried about or focused on work anymore. We let the world go to a certain degree and we are only focused on each other.

I like it when my wife surprises me! For example, she tells me that she has a trip booked, so just grab some clothes and let's go. She has it all planned out and everything is a surprise for me. I don't need to know about the destination, nor do I care to know about the destination. It's accepting her being in control of the situation. This type of surprise is a big turn-on for me! - **CHUCK, 40**

Great sex is getting head and any position goes in the bed! Great sex is licking, kissing, and every position in the bed. I want the sheets to be torn up when we're done! Great sex includes everything. Like when I can grab her and pull her hair, she can grab me. I can lift her up and carry her to the bedroom after having sex in the living room and the kitchen. The older I get the nastier I get! I start out giving her oral sex. Then I put my dick inside of her, going fast and then slow. Then I pull out and go back to eating her pussy, tasting her juices again. I do this over and over again. That's good sex! Of course kissing and holding her if she wants it, I'll throw that in there too, LOL!

What would please me more in the bedroom is if a woman is more aggressive and completely open sexually because I don't need any restrictions. I want her to just come in and take it, take it all. That would be perfect! She can call me a hoe, I would be just fine with that. - **TYLER, 42**

What is "great sex"? I guess it would be having a really good connection with somebody. So there is the physical connection, where I see a woman and I get turned on. There is a mutual attraction that is hot and heavy and we just go at it and ravish each other, like a one night stand. And then there is the type of connection where I have really good energy with someone and we can talk and laugh together over stupid shit. Great sex is like a good high, where the best part of the "high" is after you're high. Some women think that after they climax once, it's over and they are done. They don't want to explore what's next.

What would please me more in the bedroom is a woman who likes to give head. If a woman doesn't like giving head then it doesn't matter. She can suck my dick more, move her hand faster, or whatever, but if the excitement of liking it is not there then this won't turn me on. So a woman who enjoys giving head is always a turn on for me. - **CHRISTOPHER, 42**

Lucky enough I have a great sexual partner and what makes her a great sexual partner is because we know each other. I'm at the point in my life where I am able to distinguish what please me personally and getting to this point in my life, it is easy to distinguish what is good and what is bad sex, if there is such a thing. I can either have sex to bust a nut or I can have sex to

make my partner happy or make myself happy. It's best when we can have an equal opportunity situation where we are both happy, this would be great sex to me. My partner is a great kisser. She is in tune with her body, she knows what she likes, she tells me what she likes, she asks me what I like and what do I want. There are levels in sex, and I could only get to those levels by advocating for myself by saying what I like and what I don't like sexually. I'm very hands on and I like being touched. I like being kissed and caressed. So just more caressing and more physical touch in the bedroom would please me more. I'm not complicated when it comes to stuff like this.
- **WES, 42**

Great sex is when I see her eyes roll to the back of her head and she's gasping for air. She's fully involved and cooperating by pulling her legs back behind her head or if she's on top, she grabs my chest while she's riding me. When she's grabbing my hips and butt, when I'm entering her from behind, to make me go in harder, this is the type of sex I love! I have been with women where the sex was like this all the time. Giving me more head before I penetrate her is what she can do more to please me. And then if I come and she wants more sex, well then give me more head so I can get hard again. - **KADEEM, 44**

Great sex is when the two of us are balanced with ourselves individually and then we are able to tune into each other mentally and spiritually before the physical happens. So if the woman is open and our two energies together are in like minds, then we can open up even more during sex. If we do this before we start into the physical aspects of sex, then this allows us to open up spiritually and it allows us to connect energetically together. We are both connecting in a quiet, meditative space together. If we practice this type of connection in this manner, then by the time we connect physically, it will be more than basic sex, it will be foreplay. Great sex for me starts before we get to the bedroom. That's where I'm turned on, before we get into the room, because if she feels right and everything is right, that's when the sex is going to be right. I don't want to waste my time having sex with a woman if it's not right. - **DOMINIC, 45**

I'm either having sex to enjoy my partner or I'm having sex just to cum. When there is intimacy involved, it's what takes place before and after sex. Great sex has nothing to do with the orgasm. If the intimacy is there and I know the woman and we've talked about what we like and what we don't like, then the orgasm is going to come. Good sex is when it's over and we're done with our business, and I don't get up to go grab that towel. I want to be in that moment and not disturb this quiet intimacy that we are sharing. It's like the calm after the storm, you know? If we don't have this then we're just fucking! The best sex I've ever had is when I wasn't fucking. I wasn't lusting after her and trying to hurry up and bust a nut because she looked good or had a big booty. I wasn't treating her like a porn star in the moment. There is a difference between porn sex and intimacy. I don't want to have sex with a woman like I'm masturbating to porn, like she's just a vessel for my semen. I can fuck her hard and cum but if my head is not with her then I am totally disconnected from her.

I would say a woman can please me more if she just rides the wave of emotion. A lot of times I can tell from the way she moves and the position that she takes, that she's just used to having sex the way she did with the last person she was with. When a woman rides the wave of emotion during sex, it's not predictable. Some women may want to kiss me or rub me on my chest, doing the things that I like. It becomes predictable if she is not really into it. If a woman is into sex, she's going to go where her emotion takes her. She may want to push me down and take control because that's what she's feeling. It's the things that she does that are natural and it's not an act. Because to me, when people have sex they are just doing what they always do, it's not tied into the person that they're with. It's not tied into the emotional intimacy. If a woman is not 100% into it, into everything, then I don't have sex at all. - **DEL, 47**

To me, great sex is when a woman is flexible and can work her body. She can squeeze her vaginal walls and she knows how to ride me being on top. I like when a woman can arch her back because it feels a certain way when my penis is inside of her. If she has a camel back then it's frustrating because I'm trying to get all the way in (her vagina) and she doesn't want me to get all the way in. I want a woman to be more spontaneous in the bedroom. I don't always want to initiate sex, I want to know that a woman wants me a much as I want her. So I like a woman who is more assertive, that would please me more. - **GYNUINE, 47**

Great sex is when sex is an experience. It should compare or even trump going to Disney World or Disneyland for a day! Here's the thing, some men approach sex with the goal of having an ejaculation, and I'm not talking about orgasm because an orgasm is a whole other thing. To me, great sex actually starts before we even get into the bed. When I talk about intimacy, I'm talking about love-making, when we're moving in this acknowledgment of love all day long. I'm sending her little texts saying, "I can't wait to see you later", or "I can't wait to get my hands on that body!", and she's doing me the same way. We are sending texts back and forth that are building up each other's self-esteem. We are keeping each other mentally stimulated and salivating for one another. So then when we finally get to the bedroom, we're going to take our time with each other.

I would say a woman needs to express her own sexuality in the bedroom. Express her own desire to be sexually fulfilled. I have had women like this....very few, and they are rare. However, they provide the best sexual experiences. The women who get in the bedroom and they literally start touching themselves, by doing this they are providing me with a cheat sheet. When a woman is touching herself, she is pointing out her most erotic zones, she's giving me a crash course on how to please her. That's what she's doing. I learn how to mimic her. I learn how to touch her in the same way so that she could feel my hand and just throw her head back and just enjoy herself. Watching her do this is also turning me on as well. She has already pleased me by giving me the course. Not many women will do this, but if I get one who does then I need to take notes.

I love being seduced! This is a woman using her greatest super power, ability to seduce. If she understands what seduction is, she can seduce her way into becoming a millionaire, even a billionaire. And what I'm talking about is being who and what she needs to be for this moment to get to the goal that she has in mind.... whatever that is. This is what seduction is. This means a woman has got to get into character. This means coming with the right tones in her voice. She's got to come with the right attitude. She's got to come with the right clothes on, or no clothes at all, whatever the situation calls for. Make me have no choice but to do what you tell me to do. I love this! - **DI-AMEN, 47**

To me, the best sex has always had an intellectual component to it. It's not someone that I'm just fucking. There is a certain level of mental turn-on. It would please me more if she just had a certain degree of engagement and commitment to the sexual component of our relationship. I need to know we're both making sure we don't lose this connection. As a guy, I don't always want to initiate sex and come up with something interesting to try. - **XAVIER, 50**

I'm visual so I'm having sex through my eyes first. I need to have the lights on. I need to see it, I need to smell it, I need to taste it. I need for us to be vibrating on whatever vibration level that we're on. Great sex is when we start having sex before we even take our clothes off. We're out having dinner and she comes back to the table and says, "I got you a present", and hands me her panties. My nasty ass will probably pull them out and smell them before I put them in my pocket. Then we go and sit at the bar and we're talking nasty, and we're rubbing each other, and she doesn't have any panties on. Then we get to the car and she's giving me fellatio in the car on the way to the crib. Then we get to the crib and all her juices are flowing, and she's on and popping! Yeah man! We've already had sex for like two hours! Then we get in the bed and we're so connected on all these levels and I'm just busting nuts, one right after the other! Boom! Boom! Boom!

I don't know if it is just one thing she can do to please me more in the bedroom. My eyes are my first point of arousal. I like when a woman loves herself. When she's touching herself and she spreads her legs and lets me look at it. I'm nasty, I want to see all up inside of her. I want to see her juices glistening in the light. If she's turned on, her nipples are hard and she's loving herself and breathing hard, rhythmically. She doesn't say it vocally but her pussy is saying, "Come get it!" This is a big turn-on for me when a woman wants to give herself to me. I don't have to ask for it. I like when she is aggressive with me. I love to be seduced because I am the lucky ass dude that she is choosing and she wants to be with me. It gives me a 'chubby' when a woman is all on me and she wants to be with me and she's self-assured and aggressive. - **DEION, 51**

Great sex to me is when both of us are satisfied. When a woman says, "Thank you!" after we're done and I'm like, "No thank YOU!" That's when you know the sex was good. Once a woman has decided that she wants to share her body with me, I'm pleased because she has given herself to me. This is the blessing there. What we do after this is just breathing and technique. I take the opportunity that she's granted me to totally enjoy myself with her. - **MAVERICK, 51**

Great sex to me is being able to connect with that woman and really move with a certain rhythm together as we're making love. And of course, cumming is always great as well! LOL! More head is always a good thing! It feels great! I'm a basic kind of guy. So more head and good rhythm while having sex works for me. - **ISAAC, 51**

Great sex to me is being married and being in love. It's being so connected where we know each other's touches. I only have great sex when I'm married. Now don't get me wrong, I've had some BOMB ass sex with other women, but great sex only happened when I got married because we have such an intimate connection, and we got each other. There is a lot more emotional and physical intimacy involved. Aside from the orgasm, I get the emotional bond that comes with marriage. It's the feeling of vulnerability that brings us closer together. I trust my wife with my life. It's hard for me to be this vulnerable with other women because I have to present myself as being strong. My wife and I are very sexually active, but I would really like it if she gave me more oral sex. I get pleasure out of pleasing a woman and I can literally be turned on to the fullest, to damn near ejaculation, just by giving a woman oral sex. It would be great to have a woman equally as turned on by giving me oral sex as well. - **GARY, 52**

There was this lady, she was a therapist, a relationship coach, and I think I had the best sex with her in my life! She sang after she came. What made it so good for me was the fact that she enjoyed it so much. She was so vocal, she was so emotive. Everything I did just seemed to derive this new energy every time I would thrust. She just seemed so excited. And the more and more I did, the more and more excited she became. She would tell me how much pleasure she was having and I would just go crazy. Before I even knew it she was already there, she was climaxing. This was just thrilling. As I grow, the things that I desire evolve or lessen. I feel the things that I wanted or thought that I wanted in the past, I don't need anymore because something else has satisfied that need. - **MICHAEL, 53**

Great sex to me is when I'm with a woman who is not afraid to let herself go. We are willing to please each other and let each other know that we are receiving pleasure. There was a woman I dated on and off for a couple of years, she was a little older, and sex with her was always good. She was very expressive and very unselfish and she was skilled in the art of sex and knew what she was doing. She liked everything we were doing together and she was willing to try new things. One thing that I really liked was that she made sure I was pleased. In my whole sexual career, she was the only woman who was able to deep throat. I had never experienced this with another woman before or after her. Also, with this woman there was a level of emotional intimacy, we were friends and could talk about anything together.

A woman who is uninhibited and not afraid to let herself go will please me in the bedroom. Some women don't want to be loud or make any noise. It's like they don't want me to know how good I make them feel because they're afraid of getting emotionally attached. A lot of women I know won't let themselves have orgasms because once they do, they get emotionally attached. So until they are ready for that they just won't have an orgasm, or they will fake it. - **JORDON, 54**

Great sex to me is combing both the mental and physical aspects. It's when I feel safe and at my best. It's when I feel desired or super aroused. But, it's also when things are being said that make my brain fire sensual receptors that open up my third eye, whether we're talking dirty during penetration, or confessing our love for each other. I become aroused and my endorphins are heightened because of the sexual triggers and the words being said.

If I'm in the bedroom, I'm pleased already! I enjoy just being in the game. Sex for me is not performance based, it's participation and agreement based. At this point in my life, it's about mutual experiences. There are times in my life where I may have other things going on and I didn't have room to turn sexual encounters into relationships. So, if we enjoy the evening, if we enjoy the weekend, and if everything was fantastic, let's mutually agree to do it again! - **GREG, 54**

Sex in my marriage was wonderful! We tried different techniques, different atmospheres, different areas of sensuality, different toys, different music, different dancing, different bathrooms, on the beach, in cars, different spas, etc. We were really in tuned to setting the theme and being in the moment instead of just taking off our clothes and going at it. We were very in sync, I know my ex-wife's body very, very well and she knew mine.

If the next woman that I am with could learn the art of Tantra massage, that would be great. I've only met one woman that I've been with thus far who understands tremendously the Tantra sex and Tantra practice. This is not a woman that I dated. I just had a Tantric session with her and it was powerful. - **TRUSTIN, 54**

Great sex to me is implementing EVERYTHING that we both want to do! We are both just letting go completely; Orally, sexually, touching, mentally, erotic noises and everything! It's a feeling that's hard to explain. It's like where everything in your body just lets go! For me, to making a woman feel great really turns me on more than anything else. If I can make a woman just explode juices all over the place, and her body feels good, and I make her feel this way, this is a HUGE turn-on for me.

It would please me more if she can take over... shit! A woman taking over is a huge turn-on. When she is assertive like that I know sex is about to be great! In my experience there is a low percentage of women who will actually do this. Women are scared to try new things. People are scared to talk to their significant other and to say, "Hey, can we try this sexually?" They are afraid that if they ask their significant other to try something new or different that they will get angry and upset and will just shut them down because they don't want to do it. - **STEPHAN, 55**

Great sex for me is based on two things. The first would be straight up attraction for that woman. If I'm attracted to her body size, she takes care of herself and she's in shape, in my own fantasy this is a turn-on for me. The

135

other thing that makes sex great for me is if she listens to me, even if I'm talking about nothing in particular. I may talk for an hour about shit that makes me feel strong. So if I feel like my woman understands me, and she's listening to me, I'm getting turned on. Just by her paying attention to me makes me feel like I'm connecting with her and for me I can't wait to have sex with her. I'm not into the rose petals, the showers or baths, silk sheets and all that other silly stuff. I don't give a damn if we were in a barn, it's the conversation leading up to sex that makes it great for me.

We have sex, and it could be amazing sex, but if I get up out of that bed and we don't have a connection, then I still have wondering eyes because I'm waiting for my next kill to see if I can find a woman better than what I just had. This is the hunter in me. This woman didn't make me feel anything. I busted a nut and the passion was good but I can get sex and passion from a woman ages 20 to 55. So what's going to be the difference? A woman who can engage me in deep conversation, I like her because we can communicate, we can talk, she listens to me and she makes me feel a certain way, period!

I've had women who've gone overboard to try more to please me in the bedroom. I don't need her to do all of that. When she does this, now I'm disconnected from her and feeling like on the outside looking at her performing and I'm like "Shit! I didn't pay for this ticket!" I don't need all of those theatrics, sex is all I need. I didn't ask her to do all that shit. So now, I'm looking at her and thinking, "Well damn, if she's letting me do all this stuff to her, then how many other niggas has she done this to?" This now becomes a problem. So at this point in my life, at the age that I am, if we're hanging out and having a good time and then we come home and she's hugging me,and we're laughing together and we lay down and we're cuddling, to me this is sexier than anything she can put on coming into the bedroom, I seen that movie a thousand times.- **MM, 56**

I'm a simple man. Great sex to me is if she has an orgasm. This is what I'm there for. I want her to feel good because this is a big turn-on for me to see her have a good time and I'm pleasing her. I want to make her happy. I want to be so good that she invites me back. It's all about pleasing her and this goes right back around to communication. I don't want to put on chaps, have a whip and bring in a midget, if she's not into that, and vice versa. We won't know what each other likes unless we talk about it.

I'm a simple creature, so it doesn't take much for me to be pleased in the bedroom. The worst sex I ever had was good to me. If a woman's vagina is little or big, it's still good to me. Busting a 'nut' is the best feeling in the world! So long as I'm getting a nut, then I'm good. - **ORLANDO, 56**

I would consider great sex to be when I can get the response from my wife that I satisfied her. I don't always perform at my highest level. I may be tired, stressed or whatever. I have a very high sex drive, and I thank God for it. So there were times in my life where my testosterone levels were low and my wife would tell me that I wasn't performing at my highest level. We've had a good, robust, intimate, passionate, sexual relationship, so when it starts to downslide or I was underperforming, my wife would tell me she wasn't satisfied. I have to be honest, I was offended at first and my manhood was challenged when she would say this. She is very frank in telling me that I have to do something. And what she meant was for me to go talk to my doctor about it and take some things that would help me perform better, and I did. So we would use natural performance enhancers when necessary. - **TARZAN, 56**

Great sex to me is when the pussy feels exactly right. It's snug, juicy, has friction and is smooth... it just fits like a glove. It's when when her emotions show me that she is completely involved. She's all in and she's completely uninhibited. When I am pleasing her so well that she can just let go! This in turn makes me all in. When I can just let myself go to that place that's sort of an out of space experience, like we're in another world. - **DARRELL, 57**

Good sex for me would be when the day went 100% well because this is all included for me in that same experience. No fighting, no arguing, just a great day, and then the day ends with sex where we both have an orgasm and we fall asleep behind it. When we both completed each other's needs, this would be really good sex for me. During the act of sex I'm with a woman physically but I'm not really with her mentally. I'm in my own head thinking, 'you better get yours because I'm going to get mine'. So I really don't care what she's doing or what she's saying, if anything I want her to shut the hell up because I'm trying to concentrate. I got to get as much sex in as I can before I decide to cum. On the other hand, women make all this noise so I have to remove my mind from what she's saying in order to satisfy her because when it's time for me to cum I don't give a damn what she's saying.

I am pleased when she can make moves first because I would rather have a woman that's a little forward, it's sexy. It's almost like you brought the stripper home. To have a woman come on to me is very sexy. When she tries to reach in my pants to get my 'stuff', it makes me feel like I'm being serviced per se and it makes me feel wanted. I get hard instantly. I've even had times when I was working at the computer and a woman would crawl under the table, pull my pants down and give me head. She'd get me off, swallow it all and go on about her business. I never even looked down! I miss that lady! I love that kind of stuff! - **DN, 58**

Great sex is all about intimacy. It doesn't even have to be about penetration. It's embracing and caressing, some call it Tantric. This type of connection and pleasure can get me off sometimes more than penetration. It's an enjoyable act because now we are pleasing each other without the crescendo of busting a nut. It's the leading up to penetration that makes it so satisfying and prolonging the ejaculation. Also, I have to really like the woman because if I don't care for her, then I'm not going to sleep with her.

When a woman is more of the aggressor, this is a big turn-on for me. I'm a workaholic, so to come home and have her seduce me, this is like a bonus at the end of the day. I like when a woman says, "I know you've been working hard all day, let me take care of you". - **KEITH, 60**

Great sex is sex that I have to work for. I think there is a certain thrill to the chase. Anything that comes too easy for me I may not appreciate as much. If I have to work for it and think through it and it's at the tip of my fingers but I can't get a grasp on it, and finally through some ingenuity or some circumstance that I have created, I'm able to reach that fruition, then it's more pleasurable for me. There are several factors involved in sex. The chase does spur my curiosity and since sex, in my mind is mental, this satisfies the mental aspect. When there is a chase aspect leading up to sex and there is an uncertainty whether or not I'm going to get some, and then I'm able to pull it together because of my ingenuity, this is powerful and exciting to me. How a woman responds when we are engaged in the physical aspect of sex is also powerful and exciting to me. This could be the sounds she makes, her body motions, how she's feeling, how we are engaging together, how she's enjoying sex with me, and how we are enjoying each other... all this leads up to great sex.

A woman showing her emotions and showing her willingness to please me is what I would like more of. I like it if she has the ability to take a cue sexually because in some experiences that I've had, it's almost as if she's feeling like, okay, you got me, do what you please and I'm just going to receive. Rather than just being a receiver, I would prefer that she is a giver also. and tries to make it a 50/50 encounter, rather than a 0/100% encounter.
- **PILOT, 61**


I have explored and have been curious about sex since I was young. It wasn't just let me do it, I wanted to understand what works for women and what works for me. Great sex for me is a choreography of expression where the hands, the feet, the toes, the nose, the eyes and everything can be at play. Honestly, I got to tell ya, the parts also need to fit well. I've been with women whose vagina was too big for me, and I'm sure there may have been some women where my penis was too small for them. I'm not sure it was great even though all the mental stuff was there. Mentally and physically all the movement and choreography was there. The willingness to please was there and if the parts fit well, then oh my God then sex was incredible!

Also, I'm very visual, so for me, I get turned on if she drapes her body in beautiful lingerie that is interesting and attractive, instead of wearing granny draws. I get that women want to wear granny draws but when you come to bed, can you make it look hotter than that? When a woman is free and giving sexually and she has a willingness to initiate acts that I've already shared with her, this is what I like. I don't want her to weaponize sex by saying, "If you want me to do that, then you've got to do this". I want a woman to do the act because she cares about me and she loves me and she wants me to be pleased. If I have to ask for something that I like, this kind of pisses me off. - **ANTHONY, 62**

Great sex to me is when we are mutually satisfied. It's when she is able to reach an orgasm and I have done all the things that set up the possibility of that happening. With the kissing, the caressing, being close, the visuals, the aromas that take place, the lighting in the room, the time taken to please each other and our energy towards each other… all of these things. When I'm with a woman who wants to please me and I want to please her, it's pretty hard to deny that there won't be an amazing outcome. One thing that is most erotic for me is being with a woman who can't wait to do the things for me that I like. I don't have to ask, she just does them. This is a turn-on because I had self-esteem issues as a kid. I had raggedy teeth, I was really skinny and I felt that no woman would want to be with me or like me for me. Because of this I would go out of my way to please people. So for me, I enjoy when a woman looks at me and says, "I would love to have a drink of that tall glass of water right there!" - **PAUL, 66**

# MEN AND FOREPLAY

I've been into porn since I knew how to hold a mouse and a keyboard so for me, foreplay is using that foreplay tab. Basically anything that is not sexual penetration in my eyes is essentially foreplay. There are different levels of foreplay. This could be sexting, sending nude photos where we're getting each other riled up and what not, to the point of now being ready to have sex. I enjoy kissing and have been complimented on my kissing abilities to get things going pretty well. - **SHAUN, 25**

Foreplay to me is rubbing on her, kissing on her, blowing in her ear, sucking on her nipples, kissing between her thighs. Getting her wet before I even penetrate her and just showing her how much I really want her in that moment. I'm going let her get hers before I get mine. I like to eat pussy! I learned how to eat pussy by reading the Kama Sutra and watching videos, I take that shit personally. I feel like if a woman can't cum while eating her pussy then I don't deserve that woman. After she's loose and wet I can penetrate her and enjoy the ride for 15 minutes and then go and make a sandwich after that, and do it all over again. - **JOSHUA, 25**

Foreplay to me is touching the woman all over her body. It's caressing and kissing on her from head to toe. Really making her feel wanted and loved. There is no time limit with foreplay, it could be three minutes, it could be 30 minutes. I pay attention to the woman to know when she's ready for me to penetrate her. I can tell by her eyes, the way she's feeling. If she starts to squirm or get a little jumpy and she gets moist, then I know she's ready. - **LOGAN, 28**

Foreplay would be a little mental stimulation, like for instance role-playing with a game like *Strangers at a Bar*. I've done this before. Even if I know the woman already, I like to play a game where I go into a bar and I want her to meet me there. She has to look for me and spot me out. And when she finally spots me out, she comes over like she doesn't know me and let's try to get to know each other all over again. - **GIANNI, 31**

Foreplay to me is creating a certain ambiance, it's the whole vibe. Once the vibe is right, it's licking and touching, and using feathers, and caressing, and making out, pulling hair, slapping and biting. - **KING, 34**

I think foreplay starts all over again right after we're done having sex, until we have sex again. It's not about me coming home from work, trying to get some and then starting foreplay. Literally, as soon as we're done having sex, I start to do things that will allow me to have sex with her again tomorrow. I'll do shit like leave her just sprawled out on the bed and I'll do some pull ups and push ups right in front of her and walk out the room like I wasn't even tired and I could have kept going, that type of thing. It goes from one side of the spectrum of being cocky, where I just tore her apart, to me being really romantic the next day while we're out to eat and making sure everything is taken care of. I'll always be a gentleman, holding doors for her, pulling out chairs, asking her what she'd like to order, and things of that nature. I'll be really sweet, you know what I mean? It's about power and mystery for the girl. It's about her not knowing everything I do. If I can provide any kind of mystery or if I can do something unexpected, then I'm going to do it. - **ISAIAH, 35**

Foreplay is intimate conversation, I want to fuck her mind before I fuck her body. When I take my time with foreplay and now I fucked her mind, what comes next is her physical body. Don't get me wrong, sometimes I just want to get into it and have that rough sex. But when I take my time and we both have that mindset of being turned on, we're both already losing it! I may have pre-cum or I may make her cum before I even touch her. I'm going to use whip cream, honey and ice. I'm going to kiss her in places that she's normally not kissed and that will make her jump. I like to surprise her by doing things and touching her places that she normally doesn't experience. I'm going to kiss her feet and her ankles, then move all the way up her body and be real soft with it. Those sensations are going to shoot up her legs, her thighs and up to her chest. I'm going to make sure that everywhere I put my lips, my tongue, and my hands, is going to make her hair stand up and give her goose pimples. I want to see her body start to shake. I love foreplay, I believe foreplay is important. - **RL, 36**

Foreplay could be anything leading up to sex. A scavenger hunt could be foreplay. A lot of people don't understand this. I've done this with my wife before where she's come home and I made an origami scavenger hunt. This scavenger hunt may end up in the pillows where I made the room all nice with candlelight. I call myself a hopeless romantic, because I am. The crazy thing is, my wife is not into romantic acts like the roses, rose petals, and milk baths, it's just not her thing. But if I buy her a really good book or take her to get her nails and feet done, this is what she likes. So the foreplay leading up to the act of sex is totally different for me. It doesn't necessarily have to be oral sex or tickling her with a feather, it could be a whole array of things. Now don't get me wrong, the tickling of the feather and getting the ice and playing with the nipples and all of that, that's cool if that's your thing. I know a lot of guys will say they are not the average dude, but for me, I'm truly not like everyone else - **MALIK, 38**

Foreplay is a lot of kissing, a lot of touching and definitely oral sex. However, I really consider foreplay to be all day long. I like to get her wet all day long! Starting with a phone call saying, "Hey boo whatcha doing? Go ahead and touch it for me right quick!" I like to play with her all day long. And guess what, if you do that all day long it's easier by the time you get her to the bed, she's already wet! - **TYLER, 42**

Shit! Mental stimulation is foreplay to me, the meeting of the minds. We could be talking about anything. Just the explanation of a thought or an expressed thought that has some intellectually stimulating nuance can create sexual tension that starts in the mind and then it evolves into a soft touch caressing her hands, her arms and her face. It's having that skin on skin contact. - **CHRISTOPHER, 42**

Simple, if she talks I listen. It doesn't even have to be verbal. It could be a touch. It could be a glance. It could be a kiss on the forehead. Foreplay can last all day if we let it. With touch, it depends on how we are being touched and where we are being touched. It depends on the moment, our moods, and the words being said. It could even be a perfume that she is wearing that elicits a certain emotion in me. - **WES, 42**

Foreplay can be many things. I find when there is physical play involved like wrestling and chasing each other, I get an erection quicker this way. I think this is because this is fun and playful and it gets my adrenaline going. There was one female that I was dealing with before I got married, and we were being playful and she bit me on my damn nipple! I was like, "What the fuck!" Honestly, I actually liked it! She liked pain herself, so when she bit me on my nipple I was like, "Oh, that's new!" - **KADEEM, 44**

Foreplay can be anything. I can involve Impact Play with floggers and paddles, whips and wrist restraints like a collar and leash. Shit... I'm kinky! I really use foreplay to lead to hot sex. I can get into orgasm denial because I want to build that crescendo so high, to the point when I allow her to have that orgasm it is super intense. - **XAVIER, 50**

For me foreplay is all about Tantra massage. The way my flow is, I set the setting and create the atmosphere with candles, with incense, with music, and with lighting. We have a light diner and some wine and then I put on some nice music, this is stage one for me. The second stage is getting in the comfort of being touched lightly with oils. Most women, I find have not experienced being touched or caressed lightly without having sex. They can't relax with just being touched because they are thinking all this man wants to do is have sex with them. But when they are able to just tune into the touch, with no sex going on, then they are really, really able to relax. This is something different for them. Most men, when they want to have sex with a woman, they start touching them all over their breast and they're all over the place. So I usually take my time. Forty-five minutes of Tantric massage is the way for me. By the end of the massage, a woman will let me know what she wants to do next. - **TRUSTIN, 54**

Foreplay can be sexting; exchanging text messages about what we like sexually. Sharing what I want to do to her, what I like to have done to me, what turns her on, and what turns me on. If we are together, it could be kissing and fondling each other, It could be a foot massage or stimulating conversation. Oral sex is foreplay, I like giving a woman oral sex. - **JORDON, 54**

Foreplay for me is all mental. It's talking about what I want to do and how I want to do it. Foreplay is not about penetration, it's about communication. It's getting into her head. It's customized to each individual woman. Some women want you to talk dirty to them. Some women want you to ask about their day and rub their shoulders or their feet, this could be foreplay to them. It could be helping the child with homework while she takes a bath and doesn't have to worry about it. It's understanding my woman's triggers, mentally or physically. - **GREG, 54**

Foreplay for me begins with a little bit of mental stimulation... like talking sexy and talking about sexual things. I love foreplay and will do things like kiss her on her neck and her ears. I'll get close up on her and move around her body without actually touching her, and then start touching her, rubbing her breast and her buttocks. And then it's on! - **STEPHAN, 55**

Foreplay can be talking about an upcoming date that we're having later in the week. Or when we're just flirting and talking. It's lots of kissing and touching, just getting ready. I love foreplay sometimes better than actually having sex because I like to know she's involved and wants to play. Fucking is great, but I know once I start fucking it's not going to be forever, it will eventually come to an end. But the foreplay is where the long lastingness of it all is. - **DARRELL, 57**

# SEXUAL FANTASIES & FETISHES

I had a threesome and it was amazing! It was everything that I thought it would be. I was sitting on the couch with one girl on my right and the other on my left. Both girls are kissing my neck and then one climbs on top and starts fucking on me and starts kissing me and then the other one sat on my face. That shit was hot! There was no jealousy and everybody was into it. It was the girl who initiated it. She texted me and asked if I wanted to have a threesome tonight and it just happened. I would definitely do this again with different women. - **JOSHUA, 25**

I don't know if this is a fetish but had a girl eat my butt before. I never asked for it but that shit was crazy! I really enjoyed it! - **JOSHUA, 25**

I wanted to see what the thrill was with having a threesome and I've had them so many times so now the thrill is gone. I'm like I'm over it... I'm cool. Now if she wants to go there then okay, but I'm cool with the one-on-one because I have a lot of tricks and moves for that ass! - **GIANNI, 31**

I had a fantasy of being handcuffed and chained down to where I didn't have any control. I love being dominant in the bedroom, so taking all control away from me is a big thing. This was different for me because I was giving up my control and I couldn't do anything about it. I couldn't move, I couldn't scream, I couldn't run, I couldn't change the situation, I had to trust my partner. This took a lot of trust to give up control. Normally I just had to trust myself in situations. - **KING, 34**

I had an ex who liked to role play. She would wear different wigs and she would put on accents and become someone different, and this was really cool. This wasn't by request, it was just something that she wanted to do. I still find myself fantasizing for a woman that is that creative in the bedroom and who has that much fun. - **ISAIAH, 35**

I had sex on the beach at night with the moon reflecting off the water. What made it more interesting was we had to sneak on the beach because it was closed. It was an experience that I will never forget. I'm a voyeur, I like having sex out in the open. If we're coming from the club and we both want to do it, I'm going to throw her leg on my shoulder and get to it. It's like being sneaky and having that feeling that we might get caught. - **RL, 36**

I've shared sexual fantasies with my wife. She knows that I love all that stuff, I'm a freak. This may sound crazy but I've had sex with my wife on the hood of my car in the rain. People just don't understand what rain does for me. Have you ever stood outside when it's raining? So imagine that feeling with the rain coming down on your body and having some good sex at the same time. Now a good fantasy for me is me trying to fulfill one of her fantasies. I also want her to tell me what her fantasy is so that we can make it our fantasy. - **MALIK, 38**

I've had a foot fetish since I was 5 years old. It's something that I wish I could change... it's like a drug! Growing up I thought I was weird because I didn't know anyone else who had this fetish. Feet really turn me on! My girlfriend took me to a foot party for my birthday and she indulge me with another girl. I pleasured all four feet and it was really hot! I have about five foot girlfriends where we just do the fetish thing and that's it, we don't have sex. It's cool, it's respectful and it's innocent. - **RON, 39**

It's been a while since I had any fantasies. It's funny that you ask this question. The last fantasy that I had was my wife wanting to give me a ménage a trois for my birthday. I think ménage a trois is overrated because there is competition in terms of how I'm going to satisfy my partner which I think is a waste of time. The underlining impression is who is going to please and satisfy her (or him) better. Somebody's going to want more. If I've been kissing my wife the same way for 25 years and you bring in Joe-Schmo from down the block who kisses you differently, then you want that reward. It's a rush, a competition. I never played out this fantasy because the man that my wife wanted to bring in was a man that she was having an affair with. - **WES, 42**

I don't really have sexual fantasies or fetishes. I've taken sabbaticals so I have control in my mind when it comes to sex. I look at things that may stimulate most people, however, I really get turned on by confident women. - **DOMINIC, 45**

In college I had a foursome with two men and two women. It was me, one of my best friends and two girls. We were in two separate rooms but we ended up swapping girls. But he ended up coming too fast so I ended up with both girls. It never happened again after that but I may want to try it again. - **TYLER, 42**

My sexual fantasy is to be with two women. I remember when I was little watching pornography I always wanted to try it. I won't say I have any fetishes, however, I do like big boobs! I've dated a few women with very big boobs and they would place my penis between their boobs. I would be titty fucking them and they would still be sucking the head of my penis. It was great! - **KADEEM, 44**

I was in this situation where this guy wanted to watch me have sex with his wife. The guy said to me, "My wife is FINE isn't she?" I said, "Hell yeah!" He asked me if I wanted to fuck his wife and I said "Hell yeah!" So me and his wife went into the bathroom at this club and he came in there. The bathroom was small and he was just standing too close to me. My penis wouldn't stay hard, it just didn't work. I just wasn't comfortable and I couldn't perform. This guy and his wife were swingers, they've been together for 16 years so this works for them.- **GYNUINE, 47**

Toes and armpits are my fetish. Toes are like grapes in my mouth and I don't understand my attraction to armpits other than them being a very feminine area on a woman's body. For me it's just very stimulating. I don't try to understand this because when I do, now I'm labeling myself and I'm having to put my ideas into a box. I'm not trying to go around analyzing what I feel. What I feel is God given. - **MICHAEL, 53**

SEX AND SEXUAL PLEASURE

I really don't have any fetishes but I've had a ménage a trois. The first time I had a ménage a trois, was funny because I didn't last two seconds! My second wife was the most aggressive out of all three wives and she initiated it. I talked a lot of shit about what I would do to two women so she invited a girlfriend into our bed. My ex-wife is full on bi-sexual and enjoys being with women. - **GREG, 54**

Yes, I'm a very oral person, and I'm very attentive. My fetish is that I like to make a woman have an orgasm from oral sex, and if she squirts that's even better. I have ejaculated giving women oral sex, this is a real turn on for me! - **JORDON, 54**

I have a fetish with bathrooms, I love bathrooms. Just slipping away and having sex in a really nice bathroom is a turn-on for me! - **TRUSTIN, 54**

Yes! The fantasy was making love outside on my balcony in the rain. It was great! We were both butt-naked, out in the open, but there were trees all around us so no one could see. I was standing up behind her and she was bending over the railing, the rain was coming down on both of us. Because this was not a natural way I usually have sex, it made the experience even more exciting! It was everything I thought it would be. - **STEPHAN, 55**

I have a booty riding fetish where I enter her from behind. I love the way this feels! Whether I'm penetrating her having sex or if she is fully clothed, I just love riding booties! Even when I was a kid, around the age of 12, I used to grind the pillows, just trying to figure out what was going on with my "little thing". - **STEPHAN, 55**

I've done some crazy shit! Like having sex on the fire escape in an electrical storm... that shit was hot! There was an element of danger but it was also fucking hot because all this water was pouring down and the fire escape was ice cold and super hard. It was kind of painful but at the same time she was so soft. Usually for me I find myself having unexpected sex out doors and this is really great because it's different. We're in nature which makes it unusual just being outside and there is this element of voyeurism where someone can see us. It's kind of being stealthy in a way. - **DARRELL, 57**

I don't really have any fantasies but I do have a fetish. I get off having sex with dolls. This is no different than a woman with her dildo, it's just the other direction.  I grew up as a Jehovah's Witness so I never masturbated. I was taught if I masturbated that would send me to hell. When my dick would get hard I just ignored it because God would strike me upside my head. The reason I tried it is because I'm single at the moment. When I go out with a woman that I don't really see dating long term, to have sex with her is like taking a little piece of her soul, and I don't want to do that. So I figured, let me just get a doll and I can unload 'my weapon' before I go out. By doing this, I am able to have a quality relationship with a woman with no pre or post thought of having sex with her. This way I really get to know her, for her, and not her body parts.

I use this doll because hand masturbation just doesn't do anything for me. I don't have any thought process. I need a different type of stimulant. I don't get hard by looking at naked women or porn, my mind doesn't work like that. Having sex with a doll feels amazing because her boobs, butt and vagina are perfectly formed and they feel exactly like human skin. Her insides are made exactly like a real woman with the ripples and everything. If I close my eyes I would not know it wasn't a human. It's nice and tight. I actually have the best orgasms in my life! Because there's no inhibitions, there's not thought that the person may not like what I'm doing, and there's no noise to cause distractions. I'm 100% in my own mind and I'm 100% selfish. I don't have to use any part of my mind for another person. It's totally different being with a woman versus being with a doll, they are two different kinds of pleasure. It's like women who love to use their dildos while having sex with a man or after they have sex they want to use a dildo to complete the process. - **DN, 58**

My fetish is the Black female form. A woman's body that is thick, with thick, well formed, thighs is a turn-on for me. This is both a fantasy and a fetish to have sex with this type of woman and being able to enjoy her physically. I find it interesting having sex with these types of women, because although it is my fantasy, sex with them has not always been great. I had to reassess what it is that drives me when I see a woman built like Serena Williams. I've been greatly disappointed with women who are built like this and their ability in love-making leaves much to be desired. I don't know if it's because they think the way they are built is enough and they don't have to do anything but be. - **PAUL, 66**

# MANHOOD AND SEXUAL PROWESS

Yes, I think my manhood is attached to my sexual prowess. There are some days that I want to have sex and I just can't because my mind races so much so it will be hard for me to get my penis hard. There are days when I get off of work and there's a female that wants to see me that I've been talking to and I get to her place and I'm ready to go, but during intercourse my shit doesn't stay hard. This happens because I've been dancing on women all night and my mind is on other things. I'm thinking about how much money did I make. Or I'm thinking about another female I saw that night. I always want to have sex but I can't do it every day. - **JOSHUA, 25**

I think part of my sexual prowess is being able to please a woman. This is part of my manhood. To me my manhood is everything that I bring to the table. - **LAWRENCE, 26**

Definitely my manhood is attached to my sexual prowess. I went to Clark Atlanta where I think it was like seventeen women to one man. Some guys are go-getters and they make a lot of money. Some guys are really good looking. For me I'm very social and I was known to get the baddest girls. It became an identity for me. I think as I got older, I had the reputation and ability to get a certain woman. I wasn't into cars or whatever, I was into getting a lot of girls. I really took pride in this when I was younger and then when I turned 27 I was like, "Oh shit! I got to make money!" It wasn't about being cool or having good looks or anything, it was about making bread. I had to get my shit together. - **ISAIAH, 35**

This is a good question, let me think about it for a minute. My manhood is based on my sexual prowess and my personality. And I say this because of how I am and what I have experienced, especially being an erotic male dancer. I've always thought of sexual ways to please a woman with things that I've learned along the way. I even like watching porn because by watching porn I can learn certain things. I like experimenting with different ways of pleasuring a woman. I like to explore a woman's body to see what turns her on. For example, I may kiss and lick the back of a woman's knee, this shit will make a woman jump.- **RL, 36**

Yes, my sexual prowess is attached to my manhood. Women will talk trash about a man if they're not good in the bedroom. I try to do my best and this is why I'm very observant during sex and I pay attention to her. I don't want that woman looking up at me thinking, oh my God, he thinks he's tearing it up! If I found out the truth, that she was not sexually satisfied, it would probably set me back a little bit sexually. I think women need to express what pleases them more to men and let us know if we're not doing it right and if we're not pleasing her sexually. I think it is important for me to know if I'm not satisfying a woman because then I can fix it. I'd rather know this then being on top of her humping away and she's not satisfied. - **TYLER, 42**

Absolutely my manhood is attached to my sexual prowess! It had, at times, deleterious impacts on my relationships, specifically with two women that I was in love with. How this has manifested negatively in both of those relationships is by having full disclosure about our sex lives. This just made sense to us at the time to talk about it. However in retrospect, I'm not so sure that was a great idea because I couldn't handle what she told me, I didn't need to know. As a man I can get in my head wondering if sex is the same for her as it is for me. I had hang ups about what my girlfriend has done with other guys. And yes, this had an effect on how I felt sexually as a man. - **XAVIER, 50**

Yes my manhood is attached to my sexual prowess because I like to perform (in the bedroom). I'm a high achiever, whether it's in my relationship or in my business. I want my wife to see me as her king! when Tarzan calls, Jane (cums) running! - **TARZAN, 56**

This is a hard question to answer. I wouldn't want my manhood to be attached to my sexual prowess but I know that my goal is to please her, whether that be my stamina or my technique. I don't think I attach my manhood to sex because I think I'm more of a man then just my penis. - **STEPHAN, 55**

My manhood is defined by being a father and being a grandfather and seeing my seed develop into two beautiful young ladies who are going to change the world. I can step back and see this foundation, this is what being a man all is about for me. - **TRUSTIN, 54**

Not 100%. My manhood isn't attached to my sexual prowess. However my sexual prowess has a lot to do with my ego. Poor sexual performance can mess with a man's belief in himself. Men who have erectile dysfunction issues, man, their self-esteem is shot! - **GARY, 52**

This answer regarding my prowess would be different per each sexual partner. How I please my girlfriend now and how I pleased my ex-wife are completely different. Every woman has a different blueprint. There may be some consistencies. For example, I love kissing. My ex-wife hated kissing me because she thought my lips were too big. My girlfriend now loves kissing me and she loves the size of my lips. So my sexual prowess is not connected to who I am as a man. It is a form of expression of who I am as a man. I don't use my prowess as a tool to subjugate how or when I get sex, I use it to express myself with who I am with. - **WES, 42**

There is an element of my manhood attached to my sexual prowess because as men, we define ourselves typically by how well we perform in the bedroom. This goes back to the teaching and the programming of the man, he is supposed to be sexually virile. Growing up it was about how many notches I had on my belt or how many women did I get. There are men on high blood pressure medication, diabetes medication and they're under a lot of stress, and they can't perform in the bedroom. Their ego, their swagger and their confidence is based on their ability to perform in the bedroom. When this is taken away from them they will feel really down. If you look at history, men were defined by their ability to impregnate a woman and the only way to do this is through intercourse. If a man can't get his 'Johnson' up, then he can't get his 'Johnson' in. - **KEITH, 60**

Well, yes. My manhood is attached to my sexual prowess. The pride of being a man is to be able to please his partner sexually and that has to do with his ability to get and maintain an erection. If a man is not able to get an erection without the aid of drugs or other things, then the first thing he thinks is that he's not a "man" anymore because he can't get it up. But for me, I tie my manhood in my ability to be a leader, especially in the realm of the work that I do. Also if I'm on a date or in the company of a woman, I think she would want me to be decisive. - **PAUL, 66**

# REASONS WHY MEN CHEAT

Yes I have cheated because I felt like I wasn't getting what I needed out of the relationship that I was in. As far as sexual pleasure, I want my dick sucked! Can I get my dick sucked? Why should I have to go look somewhere else to get what I should be getting at home? I don't mean to do it but I don't get everything I need out of one woman and I'm just starting to learn this. Every woman brings something different to the table. - **JOSHUA, 25**

Yes, I've cheated on plenty of women. Man, I feel bad even talking about this right now, but my daughter's mother, the one I was with for four years, I regret it so much because she was a great woman, but I cheated on her because of my ego. When I cheated it wasn't even because she did something wrong, she was perfect! She was my definition of a woman. She took care of business. She was faithful. Anything I needed from her, she was willing to give. I felt like there was something better for me out there, because I was looking for the next 'thrill' and hanging around with the wrong crowd. This led me to look elsewhere when the whole time the complete package was right there. The ego is a killer! - **GIANNI, 31**

The one common thread that all men have is the want to be wanted, the want to be respected and the want to be supported. Without the support of his woman, this may easily be the reason why a man will cheat. I'm not advocating for men cheating, I'm not saying that. However, the lack of support at home may make a man seek attention elsewhere. - **HUGH, 32**

I cheated on my wife during our marriage. The reason why I cheated was because I didn't advocate for myself. I did not voice my displeasure with my wife. Sexually I wasn't satisfied. So instead of teaching my ex-wife how to please me or letting her know what I like, I sought sex elsewhere. I did not deal with the teaching process, the transition or the growth process that could come from it. I was not open to building the intimacy that could come from learning, I was like fuck it! You're not giving it to me and you don't want to give it to me, so I'm going to find sex elsewhere and get it

when I can. In not advocating for myself, and removing that transparency, this also removes the intimacy because transparency breeds intimacy. So that took away an element that could have potentially brought me and my ex-wife closer. When she was no longer interested in sex, her lack of interest made me disinterested, and this is when the marriage began to fall apart.
- **WES, 42**

I met a woman who hid things from me and wanted to change the core of who I was. For example, I like watching sports and this girl that I was dating didn't like me to watch sports. Well, she wasn't going to change me and this became an issue. I overheard her saying, "When we get married, he ain't going to be doing all that once I move in!" So no matter how good the sex was, that relationship was not going to work, and this is why I cheated.
- **TYLER, 42**

Yeah, because the opportunity presented itself. I was married during this time and It was with a woman that lived in the same complex as we did. I was driving and I saw her coming from the store and I asked her if she needed a ride. She came onto me. I asked her, "What's good?" and she said, "Whatever you want it to be". So I dropped her off, then came back to her place, we drove to the park and had sex. - **GINUYNE, 47**

Oh yes, I cheated because I had excessive compulsive behavior. I wanted another woman to fulfill something that was missing with my wife. Now, for whatever reason I felt that my wife didn't provide that for me. It was not her fault, it was my fault because I did not allow that void to be filled before I was married. Therefore, I saw this other woman as being the fulfillment however, I discovered that she really wasn't, because the things that I was missing weren't there to begin with and I couldn't use another woman to fulfill that. - **MICHAEL, 53**

During my first marriage, I would go and get massages and after the massage, I would get a Happy Ending. Is that considered cheating? I knew going into my first marriage that my wife had some issues that drastically affected our sex life. I naively figured that once we got married, it would be different. I can count on one hand, how many times we had "good" sex in 10 years. When she wanted to get pregnant she was open to having sex all the time, but by then I didn't really want to stay in the marriage, so I wasn't going to get her pregnant. - **JORDON, 54**

Yes, I cheated. Even at my most satisfied periods in my relationships I would still see other women that have certain qualities that I found attractive and my dick would get hard. I would fuck them so good and then go home and still love my wife. I've cheated on my wives on ten or more occasions in 25 years. These indiscretions mostly happened towards the end of my marriages when we were separated or broken up and just not in a good place. - **GREG, 54**

Yes, there were two women that I cheated on. The first was a woman that I dated for a while and she let herself go. She gained weight and this was very unattractive to me. I hate to say it but a lot of men cheat because they met this physically beautiful woman in the beginning of their relationship and then she begins to let herself go. It doesn't always have to do with the woman having children because this is not the case for all the women who let themselves go. So men want that woman to look the way she did when they first met and when that changes they move on. And the other woman I cheated on was because of a lack of sexual satisfaction. She started out doing certain things to please me, then after a while sex became unimportant to her. A lot of people want to say that sex is not a major part of a relationship, I'm sorry but I think it is. I'm a very sexual person. I'm the type of person who wants it in the morning, throughout the day, and when I go to bed. I'm not an every couple of days or once a month kind of person, and this is the way this woman have become. - **STEPHAN, 55**

Yes, I cheated because the opportunity was there. I was horny and she was hot, and she wanted me. I probably cheated like this maybe three or four times in my life. This not what I do, but I've done it. Each time I felt horrible about it, like really horrible because I knew that she would not approve. She was investing her whole heart into me and here I am fucking some other chick. So yeah, I've done it and this is when I was younger. The person I am now, I don't think would cheat on a woman that I'm dating because I know what it's about. I know it's just sex and I know I would feel shitty afterwards. So I just wouldn't do it again. And I certainly wouldn't tell her because I don't know if she could handle it. - **DARRELL, 57**

# MORE THOUGHTS ABOUT SEX

When a woman sleeps with me the first night, the fact that she gives it up so easily makes me think, damn! she probably does this a lot! - **JOSHUA, 25**

Yeah, I do get bored with sex. It's the thought process of getting bored with sex, it's never inside the moment. I've had women who were not good sexually, but it didn't matter because I can cum regardless. I think the thought of having sex with certain people is pretty boring. Like, for instance, I dated a woman who only wanted to have sex in a certain position. She denied me sex and I never know if I was going to get it or not. This is no security for me sexually. So because of this I turn myself off so that she can't turn me off to protect myself. This is an emotional thing. - **HUGH, 32**

I jerk-off every day or have sex every day. It just feels good. Maybe it's a stress reliever, but once I cum I can kind of operate my day after that. Even if I have an early day, I try to bust-a-nut real quick. - **ISAIAH, 35**

I learned about sex from looking at my cousin's porn tapes. I ended up getting addicted to porn around the age of 12. I'm not going to lie, I still watch porn every now and then. People act like porn is a disease. We're grown now, everybody has probably seen porn at one time or another. I prefer watching home-made type of porn. I like when it looks real between the two people at their house.- **RL, 36**

I got introduced to porn through magazines and bootleg cable around 12 or 13 years old. This is when I became curious about understanding women's bodies and understanding myself. It was during this time in my life that I began to shape myself sexually because it allowed me to learn how to please myself first. It allowed me to understand how to please a woman and it also allowed me to know how to let someone else know how I want to be pleased. - **WES, 42**

When I met my wife initially, it wasn't a sexual thing. We did not have sex until six months after we met. We spent our time building our relationship first. We had multiple diners and conversations getting to know each other, and eventually the sex part came. - **PHILLIP, 43**

I have been taking sabbaticals away from having physical sex. These sabbaticals are for me having control over myself. I know why it's happening, so why should I feed into it? I control my sexual urges, they don't control me. - **DOMINIC, 45**

I remember being attracted to the singer Freda Payne. I was so turned on by her album cover at the age of three. Internally I knew something was going on, I couldn't necessarily articulate it but I know now what it was. I didn't start masturbating until sixth or seventh grade after getting my hands on some Playboy magazines and pornography. The interesting thing about it is it's like I think there was more shame associated with masturbating when I was coming up then there is now. Back then it was a hidden type of thing, you never talked about it. It's funny, I had this philosophy for a long time that if I had a girlfriend, then I should never masturbate because all my needs should be taken care of. It's not my philosophy so much at this point in my life however, I still kind of believe in it. Now I implement masturbation into a two person scenario and it becomes more kinky.
- **XAVIER, 50**

I find it challenging being a single man in Atlanta because sometimes I just want to fuck. I don't necessarily want a relationship. I have to be honest as a man and let women know this up front. We can be agree to be fuck-buddies but the after a while, she wants to know where the relationship is going now that we're having sex. So now in my mind, I'm thinking, we signed up for sex, I thought we both agreed to this. Now she wants to flip the script. It was just a transaction, a barter system. - **DEION, 51**

I was 13 years old the first time I had sex and the girl was 17, it was with my sister's friend. My sister had a sleepover. I got up around 2:00 am and I made me a bowl of Captain Crunch cereal. One of her friends came into the kitchen to get some water and I ate her pussy. Prior to this I was just being a boy bothering my sister's friends. I would walk past them and rub their butts or their titties and they'd punch me and kick me out the room. I was eating pussy for years before I even penetrated a woman. - **MAVERICK, 51**

I can't just walk away from a woman after having sex with her, even if the sex was bad. I would rather try to figure out why it wasn't good and maybe we can make it better next time. The point of utilizing sex, for me, is for greater companionship. It is actually painful for me when a woman pushes me aside after sex and say' "get away, get on your side of the bed!" - **MICHAEL, 53**

We had sex education in school, however, the actual physical act of sex I learned from looking at Playboy magazines. I masturbated many times as a kid, I was around 13 years old when I started. I played with my penis for so long and then at one point something started to happen! I ejaculated and it was like, 'wow! This is fantastic!' The feeling was so powerful and overwhelming that I thought, ok, I'm on to something now! - **MICHAEL, 53**

I've only ghosted a woman once and this is because the girl instantaneously started saying, "OK now you're mine! this is my dick! Now this means that we're together!" It was very scary seeing a woman, just because I had sex with her, to think that now she owned me. - **TRUSTIN, 54**

I rarely ever cum from oral sex. I enjoy it. I enjoy the 69 position, I enjoy all of that, but I rarely cum. I enjoy penetration. I've only cum a couple of times orally and I just think it has to do with body position and how my body works. It's not anything personal or any sort of physiological block, it is just ergonomics. It's just like some women can cum face-down, some can cum vaginally, some can cum clitorally. It's just knowing your body. For me the joy of sex is the journey. For a lot of guys, after they cum, that's it. But the journey for me is enjoying the ride. Trying to assess the performance based on the end result is not good for me. Just like some women, they may not orgasm but they enjoy the making a man cum. - **GREG, 54**

I think it is very important to have sex before you get married. Why wait until after the fact to find out you're not compatible that way. I know sex isn't everything, but it's important. So I will never do that again. I waited six months to have sex with a woman only to find out we weren't compatible. **JORDON, 54**

I learned about sex watching old black movies, like Richard Pryor and Dolomite, and by listening to my peers talking about what they did and what they were doing. I also watched porn on VHS tapes back then. I started masturbating around the age of 13. I got a hold of my mom's Jet magazine and I saw the woman in the centerfold. My little pee-wee would get hard looking at this sexy girl and I didn't know why it was happening. I grabbed my penis and started touching it and it started feeling good. The more I touched it, the better it felt. It started tingling and the faster I played with it, the better it felt. Then all of the sudden semen started coming out and I got kind of scared, but it felt good as shit! I was like "Damn, I didn't know I could do this!" So instead of me jerking off, I started grinding pillows instead and I did this up until the age of 16. - **STEPHAN, 55**

Pussy is the confession booth, because a man will tell you anything when he is inside of you! He doesn't need to be tortured, just give it to him good and he'll tell you everything! - **GREG, 54**

When it comes to oral sex, it's rare that I find a woman who enjoys doing it, especially in the way that I enjoy doing it. My first wife didn't like to do it at all and my second wife used to do it until she got pregnant and then she won't do it because she say it would cause her to have a miscarriage. And then after my daughter was born she stopped altogether. - **JORDON, 54**

A woman asked me, "Is that all you men think about is sex!" I replied, "If you don't think about sex then there is something wrong with you". She asked me, "How could you be with one woman one day and another woman the next day?" I said, it's called biology. - **GREG, 54**

Knowing that only 25% of women can orgasm through penetration, this statistic doesn't surprise me at all. I've experienced it where only a few women that I've dated have actually climaxed. This is confusing and I'm still trying to figure out what makes a woman climax, what can I do to make that experience happen. I've had some women tell me, "I don't know, it just has to happen". I had a woman tell me the only way she could climax is by spooning, which I thought was kind of weird. I want to try to satisfy a woman as much as possible. To feel a woman have an orgasm is the most amazing feeling I've ever felt. So I want to know how to make it happen. If it's not happening, let's talk and figure it out how to make it happen. If I'm with a woman and she can't achieve an orgasm, I'm still going to love her. - **STEPHAN, 55**

I thought oral sex was a fetish, I did not know it was a necessity. I was mostly focused on the penetration. I thought that both parties had to consent before I went down on her. My wife likes this from time to time. As a matter of fact, if I hadn't done it in a while she would say, "Hey, you have not eaten me. You haven't gone done there and played with lil' girl". She would tell me what she wants, and as her husband, I had better damn sure listen. So, yes I have to make sure I pay some attention to her and I better make sure I know how to perform oral sex. - **TARZAN, 56**

Sex is not satisfying for me without intimacy. I can be physical with my wife but after that's done, what kind of communication or interaction are we having in our home? I learned that intimacy goes beyond the bedroom, it is sharing other things in the home that make my wife feel loved, appreciated and special. - **TARZAN, 56**

I don't judge a woman on her sexual prowess because she had a life before me. I can't get mad over something she did sexually with some other guy. I can't expect a woman to be virgin up until the moment she meets me. I just don't want to hear about it. I don't want her to sit there and describe her encounters with me in great details. I don't want that image of her stuck in my head. - **ORLANDO, 56**

I had a female friend who stripped down in front of me asking me to have sex with her one more time before I got married and I said, "No". Every mistake that I had made in all of my past relationships were because of a freedom of self. I felt that I was going to go into this marriage without there being any shame or mark or open door to a little bit of proclivity on the side. And this was the best decision that I ever made. - **ANTHONY, 62**

# *Chapter 9*

# DO MEN REALLY WANT FEEDBACK IN THE BEDROOM?

Let's face it, talking about sex can be an embarrassing conversation. We are led to believe that sex is something that comes naturally, and we should instinctively be good at it, which just isn't true. Even though sexual issues are very common, most couples don't discuss them. Not all men are confident when it comes to sex. Pleasuring a woman is not something that he is taught. From a young age, men are taught how to perform most basic human tasks, and when they get older, they learn how to study and get a job. But are they just supposed to know how to have sex? Men may have grown up in an environment where sex and pleasing a woman was rarely discussed. Or the two are completely different entities and objectives. And if it was discussed, it was more about how many notches they have on their belt as opposed to how to really pleasure a woman. Feeling inadequate in the bedroom is something no man wants to experience. As one man stated, "The pride of being a man is to be able to please his partner sexually". But what does pleasuring a woman have to do with sex?

Oh no, please tell me what you want! I highly value communication and I am definitely not a mind reader. There is a lot more focus today around consent and permission and making sure everyone is on the up-and-up. Every woman that I've been with, we literally had a very basic conversation that has been casually woven in after flirting and talking about what we like in the bedroom. Then we'll start 'sexting' – having sex through text messages, describing what we like and how we like things done. This is a pretty successful way to communicate, especially since I can go back and read what she says and reference it right before we have sex. I work smarter, not harder, LOL!!! So we just go off of this action, and it's always worked for me leading up to sex. I don't know what previous generations were like, but this is what my generation does. - **SHAUN, 25**

I just broke up with this woman that I've been seeing for four years. Right now I'm not looking for a relationship, I'm just looking for sex, casual sex. I tell a woman this straight out the gate and if she just wants to have sex then we can do this. If she starts to get too clingy, I will stop communicating with her altogether. I'm not really interested in hearing feedback from a woman, my only purpose right now is to fuck and move on. The moment she starts asking for things then I'm done! - **DONNIE, 27**

I'm very open to hear her feedback when it comes to the bedroom because I aim to please. I'm dominant, but I can also be submissive to her if she asks for something. I'm willing to try new things if she's also willing to learn new things, this is how we keep each other happy. And if we keep each other happy, teach each other what we want and explore each other's body, then there is no reason to step out on each other. - **LOGAN, 28**

To be honest, I want feedback because I don't want my significant other to ever feel like she's missing something when it comes to sex. So if there is something that I'm not doing or if there is something that I can do better, I want to know that as opposed to her feeling unfulfilled sexually. - **DAMIAN, 30**

The first go round, I want to do my own thing and see how she likes that, but as we progress and we keep going, I would ask, "Baby, how do you like that? Do you want to kiss like this? Do you want me to touch you like that? What do you like? Tell me what's on your mind." - **GIANNI, 31**

It all depends on how she tells me what she likes. If she is demanding and is a drill sergeant, then this is not going to work for me. But if I do something and she sweetly offers suggestions on what is going to feel better to her, then yes, I want to know. One of the biggest turn-offs for me is a woman who seeks to emasculate me in the bedroom, this won't work for me. - **HUGH, 32**

This is hard for me to answer, because I really don't want to answer this question truthfully because it comes from a lot of trauma in my life, to be completely honest. It's hard to answer because as a person who has been taken advantage of, I have a hard time with control and giving up that control. So for me, it all depends on how much control I am giving up. But this is something that I can honestly say is difficult for me. Now, there are things that I'm willing to do but it takes time. - **ANDRE, 33**

I'm open for feedback because I know every woman is different. So I'm open if she lets me know what she likes and what she doesn't like. I don't want to end up doing something, and I think I did a great job and then she tells me that she really doesn't care for that. I guess this is my ego, in a way, but I do appreciate her being honest and just telling me what she wants and doesn't want. - **ALONZO, 34**

No, I definitely want feedback. I'm super cocky but I'm not retarded. I was with a girl who would lay down on her stomach and play with herself between her legs. Most women won't do this. I know that she probably likes that position for having sex because I'm reading her, so I really think it's about paying attention to the woman that I'm with. I know that everybody's different, so it's just about learning each individual woman. - **ISAIAH, 35**

I love feedback. I actually ask for feedback during sex at times, depending on if I can't read her breath, or her moans, her body movements or what's she's saying. I spend a lot of time checking for this and her reactions as I'm going. I like to get into a rhythm and then listen to what she is saying. Sometimes I have post coitus conversations, asking her, "Hey, how was that? What did you think about that?" Especially if I know I was putting in extra effort, working for a while. I like to talk about it and see what worked for her. - **BRYCE, 35**

I'm open for feedback. I don't mind feedback if it's going to make certain things that we're doing better. I think everybody should be open for feedback. I think a guy should be able to tell a woman what he likes too. I'm not saying that either one of us is bad at what we're doing, it's just knowing what's going to get us both excited and turned on. I love to learn about a woman and I want to learn everything about her body so that I can please her fully and get her to the point of orgasm. I want to be the ultimate lover. I want to know her body. I pay attention to a woman's body and how she reacts to certain things. I want to remember those things that I do to turn her on and after sex we can talk about it and discuss what she liked. I know I'm a very dominant person in the bedroom. I'm literally like Fifty Shades of Grey... or fifty shades of black. I know how dominant I am and how strong my personality is in the bedroom, even if I'm being silly and playful, or not. - **RL, 36**

I'm open for feedback because if I do my own thing and she doesn't like it I'm gonna feel like a fool! I don't like to look like a fool. Tell me what you like, let me do it, so you can get yours, because I'm going to get mine regardless. I've been like this since I was younger. There were other young ladies who sent their boyfriends to talk to me because I would tell them, "Listen, you gonna get yours regardless. You have to understand and figure out how to please your woman". There is nothing about ego when you ask your woman, "Hey what do you like?" If I'm not eating her right, then tell me how you want to be eaten. If I'm not kissing her right, tell me how you want to be kissed. If you want me to kiss your neck, let me know this and I won't grab your hair and pull it, I will kiss your neck. - **MALIK, 38**

Of course I want feedback, any man who doesn't is a selfish lover. I've been with several woman and with those women that I've talked about sex with, none of them like certain things done to them sexually the way the others ones have. It would be pretty messed up to be sucking on a woman's clit when she prefers a softer licking. I've been with women who love me to play with their breast and suck on their nipples. And then there were other women who were not aroused by that at all. You've got to learn your woman and the only way to learn is to get feedback. - **RON, 39**

Oh yes, I want feedback. It's like going to school, how am I going to get the "A"? If the teacher is telling me how to get the "A", I'm going to pay attention. Getting feedback also says what she doesn't want. Sometimes it's not necessarily what she says but it's what she doesn't say. I want to know how to increase and/or have better sexual situations, so if I give her what she wants then she'll give me what I want. Unfortunately, not all females know what they want. If I strengthen this communication with her then she is happier and more interested in having sex and she's more excitable. And honestly, just being excitable is key to having sex. - **CHUCK, 40**

I never asked a woman what she wants, I always watched to see her reaction. I feel like it's a turn on for a lot of girls when I search around. But honestly, I really would prefer that she tells me. The women I've been with, after a while tell me what they like and I rather they tell me instead of saying nothing at all. - **TYLER, 42**

Absolutely! I don't want to be in a situation where I'm not pleasing my partner, I don't have time for that. I don't find it challenging, and I'm not here to waste time. The objective as to why we are here is I have an erection, she is aroused, and there clearly is an attraction. If she wants to get this thing going, then she has to let me know what she likes. I also do know that there are women out here who do not want to teach their mates. I prefer to know what she likes so I can build on that, let me know before we get this party started. There are also times in a relationship where discovery is necessary. Do what you like, I am your canvas. - **WES, 42**

If I'm attracted to somebody then I will do what I feel, because I just love her body and want to touch every part of her. However I am also open for feedback because I want to make sure that she is pleasured. Also, I don't have a one size fits all approach when it comes to women, I would prefer to talk and figure out what works best for us. - **CHRISTOPHER, 42**

I would love for a woman to give me feedback. I remember dating a woman in my 20s and she would tell me what to do to please her. But with my wife, she lets me know what she doesn't like and then tells me how she likes it. Sometimes it's emasculating in the way that she says things**. - KADEEM, 44**

I would prefer for her to say exactly what she enjoys because it's easy. If you're an adult and you know yourself, I think it's even better. Because when it's time for that, those are notes for me to have. I will now know what she enjoys and vice versa, versus guessing. If the woman is not verbal then I'm kind of just shooting in the dark and it is what it is, versus just saying how she enjoys it. When you're shooting in the dark that connection takes longer. - **DOMINIC, 45**

I'm open for feedback because my goal is to please her and the only way I'm going to know how to please her is if she knows how to be pleased. If she doesn't know what she likes, then she can't get mad at me. So I encourage a woman to tell me what she likes and how she likes it because that's the only way I can help her get to where she needs to be. If we're in the act I may say, "Tell me how you want it." Some women are receptive to this and some women would prefer that I just do my own thing. - **GYNUINE, 47**

Oh no, I definitely want feedback because every woman wants something slightly different. Women even want something slightly different from one day to the next. This is something that I pay attention to. If I get caught up based on what the last woman wanted, then it ain't going to please the next woman. So a lot of time in my first experience with a woman, I'm giving her what I had mastered giving the previous woman. I can't expect her to like it because it may end up being something bad or uncomfortable for her. - **DI-AMEN, 47**

I am the youngest in a family of all sisters, so growing up they would always talk about their marriages and their relationships. Being this close to women, they would always put me up on the game telling me what women like, what they don't like, and how to treat women. Women would think that I was a sucker because I was a nice guy around them. I would rather a woman tell me what she enjoys. I wouldn't want to be that guy who disappointed a woman in the bedroom, thinking that I was doing something. So because of this, I listen to them and if we're not sexually compatible, then it is what it is. - **DEL, 47**

I'm open for feedback, of course. I wanna know if I'm satisfying her or not. I want to know what she likes because I'm there to satisfy her so that we can take it to the next level. I feel if a woman enjoys having sex with me then she'll come back for more. So I'm open, yeah sure, let's try it. - **WILLIAM, 50**

Absolutely! Because I don't want her ass leaving me feeling unsatisfied. I want her to say, "Wooo ok! I want some more of that!" She knows her body better than anybody. So tell me if I'm getting it wrong and that's not the way she wants it. Tell me what would make it better. I'm not offended by this. I want her to say, "Touch me right here, lick me right there, I already see you're a man, so when we get to your dick we're good!" I follow instructions. I want to come in as king dick and bust her back out! - **DEION, 51**

I learned over the years, my dad told me, if I have the right conversation with a woman, by the time I lay with her, unless it's a quickie and we're just doing our thing, I should already know what she likes, because we've talked about it. If she's got to give you instructions in the bed, it should just be tweaking what I've already known or learned about her. Sex should be all figured out before we even get there, because if it's not, then what the hell are we talking about? My dad would tell me the best way to please a woman is to ask her what pleases her. The mere fact that a man even asks a woman this question, is a step in the right direction. Other than that we're just shooting in the dark. - **MAVERICK, 51**

I love feedback because I want to please her. So feedback, to me, is essential. I welcome feedback. How do I become a good lover if I don't know what pleases her. - **ISAAC, 51**

It's very imperative for me, for men, to listen to what a woman is asking for in the bedroom, how am I going to satisfy her if I don't know? That's retarded for a man not to want to know what his woman likes. It's crazy for a man to think he's doing something and he's done and she didn't even get off! - **GARY, 52**

I like both. I am open for her to tell me because I want to know what she likes to make sure that she gets her pleasure. If she doesn't tell me what she wants and likes, that's ok too because I am certainly Mr. Macho, I do like to be assertive. I've been told I'm aggressive. So I do not have a problem with taking the lead and doing my own thing. Although I do like to get feedback because I want to do the thing that she requires me to do. - **MICHAEL, 53**

I actually would prefer her to tell me what she likes, on occasion. I don't like to do things if a woman doesn't like it because I'm a pleaser, I think, when it comes down to it. I do things not just because it pleases her, it pleases me to please her. Obviously I don't want to do anything that is not pleasurable. I will however draw the line at choking a woman if she asked me to, I wouldn't feel comfortable doing this. I know this is a turn on for some people, auto erotic asphyxiation, is what it's called... I personally wouldn't do that. I'm not into inflicting pain and I know some women like that. - **JORDON, 54**

I am absolutely open for feedback, tell me what you want! I'm a pleaser, I want her to have a good time, so tell me what you want. I'm not a selfish person, I think it's about acknowledging the other person in the relationship. I need feedback, I'm not trying to be licking her ass if she doesn't like it! Same with me, don't get so excited and start squeezing my balls... that shit hurts! I think that men and women have to test the waters before we get in the bedroom when it comes to how we communicate. Then we'll have a pretty good idea if the man is going to be dominating and they're not going to listen to the woman or if the woman thinks she knows it all. - **GREG, 54**

Yes, I'm open... tell me, please! Because when she tells me, it gives me a road map on how to please her. I don't want to be fumbling around and doing

something to her that she doesn't like. She may not like the way I go down on her, and I'm down there and she's thinking, "Oh, I wish he would stop!" So if she's telling me this upfront, then I have an idea of what she likes.
- **ORLANDO, 56**

No man, no fucking man on this earth, unless he's a punk-ass, wants to hear a woman give him instructions for fucking... they just don't! I don't want to hear shit! I want to feel like I figured it out. So when I am open to getting instructions it should be subtle, very subtle. There is a masterful skill that a woman has in letting a man take charge in the bedroom. With my second fiancé, after we had a rhythm of what we both were cool with, she would say, "You know, we been doing a lot of fucking. Let me show you how I like lovemaking, let's do it this way". But that came after really knowing that whatever we do have already works. Then I would want her to show me something a little different so we can take it up to the next level. - **MM, 56**

I want her to tell me. I want to know, but I think I can figure it out. If she's the type that communicates well and is expressive, like when I hit a certain spot and she lets me know with extra moans, or says "Yes, yes, that's it!" It's all good. But I don't want her to necessarily say this is what I want you to do. "Do this... stand over here... turn over here... etc." This could be a distraction and it could get me out of the mood because I'm so busy thinking about what she's saying and forgetting about the spontaneity of it all. - **DARRELL, 57**

It depends because some of the stuff they ask is either embarrassing or just stupid. Although it's really not, because that's what she wants, it's the same with what a man likes. But when it comes to the sex part, I don't really want to talk about that stuff. I just want to do it, but I don't want to talk about it, and I think it has something to do with my manhood. If I never do certain things and a woman asks me to do something different, the first thing that comes to my mind is, oh she must have done this before, and then I have a different thought about that woman. So in my mind the woman is not as pure as I thought she was. There is a jealousy component that comes up where I think she must have done this with other guys, so now I feel a little weird because I'm thinking, I may not be that great at it or I may feel a little inadequate doing it because she has all this experience doing that thing I've never done before. If I hear about things that she likes to do, then the next thing that comes to my mind is her doing this sex act with her exes. If a woman was smart, she would act like she's never done stuff like that before, but somehow hint that this might be fun. Just don't put it in my head that she's done it before. - **DN, 58**

I would hope a woman would say, "To the left or to the right, back up or move forward". If she expresses what she likes, then this makes it easier for me. We are not taught about sex. A lot of times as guys we go in there and we don't know what the hell we're doing, we're just poking around. Also, the mindset of women have changed and they have become more of the aggressors and more sexually open in terms of saying what they want and what they don't want. - **KEITH, 60**

I'm open for feedback to a certain degree. For example, if she said that she needed oral sex in order to get her going all the time, then I would probably establish some limits. I have my limits also and by saying this, she has just exceeded my limits in this instance. I'm not always open to the idea of doing whatever it is that pleases her and I don't expect her to also be open to whatever I want to do that pleases me. - **PILOT, 61**

I like feedback because I want to be good! Tell me what I need to do, at least once. If I'm not hitting the mark, let me know early on in the relationship and then I can run with it. A lot of women that I've been involved with have difficulty communicating their preferences, and it could be because they've been slut-shamed in their lives - by their culture, society, their parents, or boyfriend. I guess if she comes to me, liking sex, she may be looked at as less than, when this is not really true. This is a deep thought that has been planted in our girls from the time that they're young. I think women have to do a lot of work to overcome this thinking so that they can be sexually liberated. - **ANTHONY, 62**

I don't really want her to say anything to me. And what I mean by that is I just want the union to be so natural and so spontaneous that nothing has to be said. This is difficult to find, however, with the right woman this is possible. For her to say, "No, no slow down!", or "No, no, not so hard!"... this is not cool for me. And it isn't from the aspect of her not being able to tell me what to do, nor is it making me feel like I don't know what I'm doing. I think how things are said and how we both communicate is critical. If I hear care, concern and respect in her voice, and the eroticism ensued as a result, I can't help but to comply and do what she is asking of me, as opposed to a woman who sounds like a drill sergeant. These types of conversations don't come up when I'm with a woman. I begin the process and pay attention to her. When I'm physical with a woman that I've never been with before, as she reacts I take note and go forward from there. I only get feedback if we happen to talk about the experience afterwards and we're reliving the moment by talking about it. There is no one way to please a woman, that doesn't work for everybody. There could be an instruction manual on the mechanics of how to please a woman, but that doesn't work for everybody. The fact that every woman is unique and is an individual means that I would have to learn from the woman that I'm with. - **PAUL, 66**

# Chapter 10

## COMMUNICATING HIS WANTS AND DESIRES

Revealing sexual wants and desires to your partner can be scary, especially when you're unsure of how a partner may react. When it comes to sex and a man's sexual prowess, his ego, emotions, and insecurities oftentimes hinder him from freely expressing himself. Men don't want to feel ashamed or humiliated for having certain wants and needs in the bedroom. Our society puts so much emphasis on sex. It's difficult to ignore in our lives because it's everywhere in our culture. It's reflected throughout media advertising in fashion, music, TV shows, and movies. Because it's so prevalent in our society you'd think we would all be more open, relaxed and comfortable with talking about it, but often the opposite is true.

Talking about sex can be a sensitive and awkward topic that raises feelings of embarrassment, shame and inadequacy. There are men who would rather pretend that they are satisfied sexually rather than upsetting their partners, and risk that it might tear their relationship apart. Men also fear discussing their sexual needs in the bedroom. They'd rather say nothing than risk having an argument that may or may not improve the sex. They also don't want to feel vulnerable and open if their partner disapproves of their request. As a result of this, they are left feeling frustrated, unhappy and guilty. They would rather keep up the pretense to avoid an argument or say nothing in fear of having no sex at all.

When it comes to expressing my wants and desires, some days I beat around the bush and hope that she can sense that I want to be intimate, and other days I just come right out and say, "I want to tear that wig off and put it on my head!" I'm trying to have the Wild, Wild West in here! The way I express myself depends on the woman I'm with. Some women are open to talk about things, so I can be really open with them. Some women are more shy and reserved so I don't talk about things that will make them feel uncomfortable. And then there are women who may not be into the things that I am into sexually, so I don't want to appear to be a freak in their eyes. I don't want them to place that stigma on me, judging me and thinking that I'm nasty. - **JOSHUA, 25**

I try to communicate what I want in the bedroom, but I felt that the last woman that I was with saw this as a weakness and we were not able to really communicate well together. If I had issues, I felt she was the one person in the world that I should have been able to express these emotions with, she should have been the one I opened up to. She did not receive me trying to communicate with her very well. I hope she learns that communication is key in a relationship or else she will not have a successful relationship. - **LAWRENCE, 26**

I do find it challenging because I have a pretty wild side and I don't want a woman to judge my freakiness. If a woman is game when I take the lead and she is satisfied, then great! But if she is rigid then it's really not that important to me and it's actually annoying. If I'm really not into her then I can fuck her but I'm not trying to work so hard. My ex and I were perfect together sexually. I'm still getting over that relationship. - **DONNIE, 27**

Yes I do find it challenging. In my experiences I think that there is a certain level of insecurity women have talking about sex, and I hate to generalize it like this. But, I think that there are more women than not, that are not truly comfortable in their ability to please a man, so because of this I have a communication barrier. In my relationships, I don't want to be the person that causes hurt feelings or causes insecurities, especially when it comes to something like sex. I don't want her insecurities to get in the way of experiencing sex freely. - **DAMIAN, 30**

Aww hell naw! Being able to talk about what I want sexually creates a sense of adventure for me and allows me to express myself creatively. And then this also becomes a surprise to her and catches her off guard. - **GIANNI, 31**

Yes, I do find it challenging to communicate my wants and desires with a woman because I don't want to hurt her feelings. So most of the time it is challenging because I don't know if I'm going to step on a landmine, so I try to be careful. But even being careful I can come off as being timid and this is not a good quality for any man to have. And honestly, I don't want to deal with the stress. - **JAMAR, 32**

I used to find it very challenging because of my own insecurities, and not sure how I would be received. But the woman that I dated who was 10 years older than me, changed that for me. She encouraged me to speak up and share my fantasies and fetishes with her. I did not feel like a pervert with her. I felt like my needs were important. So now I don't divulge everything all at once, I feel out the woman to see what she is open to exploring with me. - **HUGH, 32**

Yes, I do struggle with telling a woman what I want in the bedroom because of my misunderstanding of control. Control is a falsehood of security. The real power lies in being free. Freedom is something for me that I'm not very familiar with. - **ANDRE, 33**

In the past it was challenging to talk about my needs, this was before I started getting counseling. Now that I'm in counseling I find it a lot easier. I'm able to verbalize my needs and my wants. Before I would not verbalize these things and I would let it fester up and I would explode into anger. Now I can verbalize and communicate what I want instead of getting to the point where I want to explode. - **KING, 34**

The challenge for me is feeling as though I can be open without it changing the dynamics of our relationship, or how I am viewed within the relationship. Yes I do find it challenging, because a lot of times women take it as a failure as if they haven't hit the mark, or if they're not perfect. A lot of

women will take it as an attack on their ego. And they'll say, "I never had a complaint before!" This is not a complaint, I'm just asking her to make an adjustment. There is a difference. I wasn't saying she was bad, I was just asking her to do something else or to do more of something, and she didn't do it... and I didn't like that. In my experience, women will take it personally, as if they failed and their feelings are hurt because they don't feel like they did it right. I think some men feel this way as well, which is why as people, we have all these issues and these conversations about sex and how it impacts things. People are not being pleased. No one wants to have conversations with someone telling them that they weren't good, because now there is this whole feeling of "I'm afraid of what comes next". A woman may start feeling like, "Since you weren't pleased, does that mean you don't want me anymore? Am I not good enough for you? Are you going to go and find somebody else?" We should be able to have these conversations to the point where we can all learn and grow from the feedback. I think as a culture, we don't have an open relationship with conversations around sex.
- **BRYCE, 35**

I find it somewhat challenging depending on the woman that I'm with. I'm not trying to offend her by saying something that may hurt her feelings, but at the same time, I have to get her used to who I am. We got to keep it real with each other. She tells me what she feels and I tell her what I feel without us getting emotional or in our feelings. We should be able to talk to each other without feeling some type of way and growing from there. I want to be able to talk to my significant other about anything. Some men feel like if they talk about their needs then it's going to make them seem like they don't know what they're doing, or that they're weak because they're telling women how they like sex and certain things that they want. It makes the man feel like he doesn't know what he's doing and he will jump into defense mode. It's all about how he presents what he's saying to a woman. Men have to open up their minds and pay attention and listen to what a woman is saying instead of jumping into defense mode so fast. Collect their thoughts and then have a talk with them. Don't talk at women, talk with women. A lot of times men just talk at women, they don't talk with women. This is where men go wrong, they don't actually listen. - **RL, 36**

When we first got together, yes I found it challenging because I didn't know how to communicate with a woman, and that's the honest truth. I thought I knew how to communicate from being in past relationships, but apparently I did not know how to communicate with a woman. My wife introduced me to The Five Love Languages, I had never heard of this book before. And after reading it, we both worked on enhancing our communication. In my mind I would say something and I would think in her mind that she would understand what I was saying. Apparently what I was saying made no sense to her at all. I know I was saying complete sentences, I know I'm not dumb, I know I'm speaking English... and she would say "That makes no sense to me, you're not communicating with me." So I really had to learn how to communicate in her love language. I had to learn how to speak better to her and to be clear about what I want and what I need. Communication opens up everything and a lot of men don't understand this. I even try to explain to some of these guys like, "Listen! Listen to somebody who's been there and going through this. All you have to do is find out your woman's love language and communicate through that, and you will get whatever you want!" - **MALIK, 38**

I only share my wants and desires with someone that I may want to have a future with. I won't waste my time having a conversation or waste my energy on someone with whom I know this ain't going to work out. It's only easy if me and the woman that I'm with have that open line of communication. The older I get I'm more direct because I don't want to waste any more time. When I was younger it was more challenging for me to open up and express myself. - **TYLER, 42**

I feel that communication has gotten misconstrued over the years. Communication to me is simply an expression of a thought or idea. People now-a-days use communication as commands or demands, and that's not what it is. It is the expression. The freedom to express ourselves. It's not the freedom to be abusive or demanding. True communication is where I see you and I'm not yelling at you, we are hearing each other. It is very important, fuck yea! Women have a way of listening but not hearing. They listen from their version or assumption of what is being said to them as opposed to what they are saying. Because most of the time men will tell women what they want but women are just not listening. So it doesn't matter what he says, they have this preconceived answer of what it should be. So men feel like the women aren't listening to them anyway so why should they say anything. - **CHRISTOPHER, 42**

Yes because I'm not growing with my wife sexually. We are not thinking outside the box or maturing in this area so that we can find out more things about each other. We are both to blame for this. If I can't relay my desires to my wife where she understands and is open to try it then the conversation becomes more challenging. - **KADEEM, 44**

Men were never taught to talk about sex, and because of this we're missing, as a society, the vehicle in which we need to have conversations around sex. The only thing we're taught is if you do it then wear a condom. Nobody is telling you anything else. There were older men in the neighborhood where I grew up who would sit us down and talk to me and my brother about how to talk to women. His advice was to be friends with them first, don't feel like you want to go right in their pants.

No I don't find it challenging to communicate what I want, I've gotten beyond all of this in my early 20's. Communication is the best, regardless of how I feel inside. If I'm able to verbalize what I want and share it the best way that I can then that's great. But if I don't discuss what I'm feeling and she makes things up in her head about it, then we're just playing guessing games. A lot of females stay in their head about things. Women will say they want to get to know me, but yet they don't ask me questions, and since they don't ask questions then I feel they are not really interested in me. In relationships, we have to talk. The only way to find out what's going on with each other is to talk to each other. - **DOMINIC, 45**

No, I don't find it challenging. Now whether or not she receives the information is another thing. I had two situations with bad sex that were very, very disappointing. And the crazy thing is, I'm willing to bet that she thought it was me, but it was really her. She couldn't take all of my penis, she couldn't be on top, she complained about all the things she couldn't do. We ended up stopping in the middle of sex. It was just sad, I didn't even cum. In her mind, she probably thought I was the bad 'lay' when in actuality it was her who was the bad 'lay'. We never spoke after that. If I were to see her again I may bring it up.

Everybody gets on the defensive and they're not listening to each other. So a woman may become defensive and feel like a man is telling her that her sex is bad or whatever, when in actuality he's just trying to tell her what he likes, which is the same thing that a woman would do. I think this varies from individual to individual, some men may be afraid that the woman may hold back on sex and not give him none if he tells her what he wants. But in actuality, a closed mouth won't get fed. Some men don't want to take the risk of not getting anything so they don't say anything. I know a girl who likes to get 'eaten out' but she doesn't suck dick. So to me, a woman can't expect more than what she's bringing. It has to be a fair exchange. - **GYNUINE, 47**

No I don't find it challenging to communicate what I want because at this point in my life I'm more confident and I'm able to communicate how I feel. As a man, I'm 97% ego and 3% emotion. Most women that can keep a man, cater to his ego. This is a delusion on the man's side. A man is thinking he has a partner, but in reality, he has a cheerleader. Black men don't know how to show their emotions like white men are, we're not taught this. We're taught to be protective and don't show our emotions, toughen up, don't be soft, don't be SIMP (a simpleton, a sucker, an idiot). - **DEL, 47**

There is a challenge communicating my wants and desires because of what I see in the general population, especially with this whole Me Too Movement. If I look at what's really acceptable in a relationship and all the messaging going on about, "Don't objectify me", along with the feminist movement, and things like that, then this kind of shuts down my ability to express my own desires. I don't want to make my woman feel objectified, or reduced to this sexual object to the point where she just doesn't even want to have sex. Women have to understand that they are sexual objects, as are men, but she is other things too. I hope she sees me as a sexual object as well. - **DI-AMEN, 47**

No because the goal for both of us is to cum, this is why we are here. I want to feel good too. So if she's using too many teeth giving me oral sex then I'm going to say, "Baby can you back up off the teeth? Make a better 'O' with your mouth." I'm trying to be in sync with her as much as possible to have a beautiful orgasm together. Hopefully we connect in mind and spirit first, and then in body. I've had incredible conversations where we were diving in on these multi-layers of eroticism, and I got a "chubby" growing in my pants and she's probably got a little moisture in hers. Our vibe is so freaking intense and we both have incredible energy like we're vibing on violet, our auras are violet. We've been engulfed in rhythmic conversation and completely turned on by each other.

Sometimes men have a hard time talking about their needs, especially if he's been with his partner for a long time and sex has become mundane and there is no more spice. He's afraid to ask her to suck his dick or to ask her for something out of the norm. He's worried that she may say, "Where did you get that from? You ain't never asked me for that!" This will make some brothers pause because his woman may start tripping. Now in the same breath, she's probably thinking about the same thing he wants to ask, but they're both afraid to ask. Just like he's kind of tired, she's probably tired of the same old dick she's been getting from him. - **DEION, 51**

I don't have an issue with telling my lady what I want. I used to have those issues growing up but I got over this because I realized that if I don't tell the woman what my needs are then how is she going to meet them? Men who can't talk to their women about their needs and desires don't truly value themselves. If a man values himself then he has to be able to express those values. So if he doesn't value himself, from an intimate level, and he has a need and cannot express that need, this has everything to do with what he feels about his own value. - **ISAAC, 51**

I learned through my years of trying to converse, that conversation is the key. If I can tell my wife what really does it for me, then she'll know how to get me off. It's the only way to learn from each other. When men are not able to talk to their partners about sex and their needs, this is a malfunction that happened to them early on. Men are not taught to converse. We're taught to be hard, we're not taught to share our feelings. When kids are little, girls are given dolls and taught to play house and boys are taught to go outside and play football. And if you put the girls and boys together to play house, the first thing the parents think is that they're trying to have sex. When in actuality, that boy is learning the development of being a man when he's playing with the girl. - **GARY, 52**

Yes communicating my needs can be challenging, but also, it depends on the woman. If I see this right away, this is a red flag and it starts to remind me of something that I don't want to do or something I don't want to deal with. If she is not inhibited and doesn't have a lot of hang ups then I don't find it challenging and I feel free as a bird. If she is inhibited then I would feel hindered in expressing myself and this becomes a struggle in itself and I don't want to live with that. - **MICHAEL, 53**

No, I don't find it challenging at this point in my life. I had to learn to be comfortable expressing myself... it's a learned behavior. I became comfortable after taking classes and going on Tantra, going to different retreats and doing different intimate exercises with women. I think many men find it challenging because they are embarrassed about their knowledge and embarrassed about what they know and don't know. Especially with Black men, they are so afraid of being put down. Black men, by nature, are more expressive in their love-making than white men.
- **TRUSTIN, 54**

I don't have a problem communicating. Does she understand what I'm saying or is she willing to accept what I'm saying when I do want to communicate? - **STEPHAN, 55**

I find it a lot easier now to communicate with my second wife, because I learned her language and as long as I am communicating back to her in her language, then we are able to talk, share our opinions and resolve issues.
- **TARZAN, 56**

If we are in a conversation about sex, then no I don't have a problem talking about my wants and desires. It would only be challenging if I sensed that she wasn't really interested in knowing this information, then I would not be comfortable initiating the conversation. If she was giving me some sense that she was open for this type of conversation, then yes, let's talk. I think some men may not want to be perceived as being a sexual deviant. Some women are not going to be open to hear what he wants or what he has to say. I think guys want to hear what the woman likes and what her desires are before they start sharing what they want. Guys caution themselves from saying too much because they don't want to be perceived as being a freak. The woman may just like being in the missionary position and he wants to do all this other stuff. She may one of those women who judges a man and ask him where he learned that. - **ORLANDO, 56**

No, it is not challenging for me because I cut through all the red tape. I'm a very direct person. I can be quiet but when I speak I say what's on my mind. Now how she takes what I said is what's going to be important. This is where the challenge comes in because in a relationship we both have two different fucked up points of views, we were raised two different ways. So if I tell her something and then she turns around and tries to impose her opinion on me, we may clash because maybe we don't believe in the same things. We have to be respectful of each other. When I come to her and I'm straight up and clear, it allows me to see her for who she really is. - **MM, 56**

I want to be able to talk openly about what I want in the bedroom, but I don't have a significant other right now so I don't know. If I were in a relationship then I would like to, sure. I wouldn't be in a relationship with a woman that I couldn't be honest with at this point in my life, I wouldn't even do it. The next relationship that I get into will be the woman that I marry and I'm not going to marry anybody that I'm not completely honest and open with. - **DARRELL, 57**

Yes I do, 1,000% and it's probably because I was shy as a kid. This ruined a lot of my relationships when I was younger because the girls I really liked, and those who liked me, I couldn't look at them straight in the face. I felt totally incapacitated physically and mentally if the subject of my wants and needs came up. If they asked me about another guy, I could talk to them about that. But when it came to me, it was over, I was done. - **DN, 58**

I don't find it challenging to talk about what I want in the bedroom because I'm pretty easy. I wouldn't want to date a woman that I had to teach about sex. In a lot of my relationships I didn't have to ask for anything because the women came with skills. Now if there was a woman that wasn't as skilled in the bedroom, yes I would feel a little awkward because I'm trying to feel her out to see what's going on. Like does she have an issue or a problem, or some traumatic history? When it gets to the point where I have to start educating a woman or trying to figure her out, or if I have to become a psychologist to find out if she has daddy issues or mommy issues, then this becomes too much for me at this stage of my life. - **KEITH, 60**

I have at times found it challenging to communicate my wants and desires with women. It all depends on the circumstances because each woman is different. How a woman is rigged makes the difference. I've been with a woman since my divorce and she told me what she was taught as a little girl growing up in the church about sex being nasty or whatever. Every time before she has sex, the messages that she was taught as a child come to mind. This put her in a certain disposition with her thoughts. Therefore, she was a bit ridged and not so eager to be able to do anything beyond traditional sex, and she even had some reluctance towards that. So this was challenging and sometimes discouraging because it also took on the form of her saying "not tonight, not tonight!" - **PILOT, 61**

Not in general, but I do find it difficult for my wants and desires to be received or understood. It's funny because the women that I have chosen to be the most intimate with are not as free with their sexual expression as the women that I have not been the most intimate with. There are things that I haven't done with my wife that I've done with strangers in the past because my wife has boundaries. For me it's a little bit weird because I can only be X rated however, XXX would be nice too sometimes, LOL! - **ANTHONY, 62**

# Chapter 11

# DO BLACK WOMEN APPRECIATE BLACK MEN?

I overheard two men talking one day and their conversation was about their lack of appreciation by women. One man was mentioning all the things he does for his woman - taking her out to dinner, concerts, sporting events, helping her with her bills, etc. He then said in anger, that she never says "Thank You". The other man chimed in and said, "Women today just don't value a good man. They think men are supposed to do these things for them". They were both obviously upset and concerned about the state of affairs in dating women today and their final statements were, "Man, fuck these women!" It shocked me that this was their recourse, when all they wanted was for women to show a little gratitude.

I wanted to get an overall consensus from these fifty men to see what their opinions were on this matter. I was very surprised to learn that a large percentage of these men do not feel appreciated by Black women. Men understand that Black women are more empowered and more successful as the times change, and because of this their perception of how to treat a man changes as well. They see that there is a culture around the lack of appreciation toward Black men. It is perpetuated through the media via reality television shows that are centered around failed or failing relationships and man-bashing. They feel as if Black women are being pitted against Black men as though they are the enemy. Men also acknowledge that the lack of appreciation goes both ways and is often brought upon themselves by their lack of appreciation towards women.

No, women don't appreciate men. I feel like women think they are doing me a favor when I have sex with them, like I'm lucky to be hitting their pussy. I had a woman actually say this to me. I'm like what?.....You the one doing all this screaming and hollering over there." I just put it on her, she's the dead body, not me! This whole Hot Girl Summer shit has given women a different perspective on their lives and their sex lives. Women feel more entitled to dick then men do getting pussy. Hot Girl Summer is about women living their best lives, not worried about being in a relationship, saying "Fuck relationships!", and acting like their pussy is golden. Girls acting like this make me want to protect my energy, protect my soul and protect my integrity as a man because these women nowadays just see me as a piece of meat. They think every man wants them and that they can have any man that they want and in reality, that's not the case. I want them because I want them right now. I don't want her tomorrow, I don't want her next week, I don't want her next year, and I'm not going to send her a text message on Valentine's Day. - **JOSHUA, 25**

Hell no, women do not appreciate men because their expectations are really high. It's hard enough to connect with women when dealing with everything else in life too. I hold myself to a high standard. Women today are impatient, they want everything too soon. I'm building right now, I can't give her the world. My wife had expectations of me, but she never held up her end of what was expected of her. A relationship can't be 100% one person, it has to be 50/50. We both have to put the same effort into the relationship. In my marriage, I was the one working and taking care of everything. I was the one trying to communicate the right way and she didn't even try. - **LAWRENCE, 26**

I think there is a lack of appreciation today by women in regards to men. I feel this comes with the times and the changes between the generations. As we get further away from the structure of a two-parent household, the knowledge and the relationship that we shared with our parents no longer exists. We are moving in some cases, into a one-parent household. I feel that women are getting to the point where they don't need a man for certain things in life. This changes the perception of what it's like to truly appreciate what a man is and what a man can bring to a home and to a relationship. - **DAMIAN, 30**

Yes, I do think women lack appreciation towards men, however, it's not all women. But from my social media and what I've observed, a lot of women don't appreciate the fact that there are a lot of men out here that actually want to get to know them or want to do better by them, but they keep chasing after the wrong kind of guys. They transfer their bad experiences of what happened with the wrong guy they chose, onto every other man out there. They are ungrateful to all the good men still out here. Come on now, we are all human, we all have the same emotions. Men don't just heal that easily, it takes time and sometimes we just need that extra help to heal.
- **GIANNI, 31**


I think the reason women don't appreciate men is because they don't feel appreciated themselves. By nature, I think women are warm and nurturing and if they are with a man who allows them to be this way and he is not running a game on her, then she really wants to support him and their relationship. There are so many Black men who are lost, and they don't know who they are. So if a man doesn't know who he is or if he doesn't know his worth then how is he going to appreciate a woman? - **HUGH, 32**


I feel like women have had it hard for long enough so why not let guys feel what it's like and let them feel underappreciated a little bit. There are a lot of guys who are dummies and assholes who disrespect women, so if a woman doesn't appreciate them then it is their fault. I don't think there is a lack of appreciation, I think there is a lack of good men. I have come across women who don't appreciate how good a guy is, and there are a lot of good men out here. - **JAMAR, 32**


Black women are being pitted against Black men as though we are the enemy, and it's working. The media, the individuals that control the narrative, are continually trying to make it seem this way. It's not just digitally (with film and television) but if you look back during slavery, Black men were raped in front of Black women in order to make them less dominant. Now-a-days Black women are continuing to allow this to happen by ways of the government. The government is forcing men out of the home by giving free assistance to women, as long as Black men are not present in the home. It's a constant game. Now we're in a place where Black women feel as though they can do everything Black men can do, and this is hard. This lack of appreciation is based on history, it's generational. If a woman comes from a home where she saw her mother taking care of everything and her dad wasn't around, she may grow to believe she doesn't need a man. She'll find ways to do things on her own. So if a man isn't acting right, then she can go get another man, or even another woman for that matter. I think the frustration also is that Black women don't feel supported when a Black man dates and marries outside of his community. We don't support Black women as much as we should. Also if the woman grew up in a home where she didn't have two Black parents or she had parents of two different races, she may not see the value of a Black man and what he offers and just who he is. - **ANDRE, 33**

Yes, there is a lack of appreciation, especially for bi-sexual people. I feel as though Black people view bi-sexualism as a mental disorder, more than a sexual preference. It's very hard being a bi-sexual Black man in this country. I feel as though the mass of people feel like it's a chemical imbalance or a mental disorder that I have because I can't 'make up my mind'. The end goal is to be happy and to be in love with somebody. - **KING, 34**

I think there is a culture around the lack of appreciation of Black men. It's easy, when you look at reality television shows like Basketball Wives, it seems the whole show is centered around failed and failing relationships. You get this circle of women coming together and bashing the men that they're with, or who they're not with, and then complaining about what he's not doing. There is a culture of women absconding from their responsibilities in the way their relationships play out. - **BRYCE, 35**

Everything has changed between men and women, especially with the lack of communication. I also think that men are not as appreciative to their women the way they used to be. Men and women are acting the same. Men are not being men anymore and women are now acting like men. Men are starting to take the back seat to women, it's like now she's wearing the pants. There's not a lot of 'real' men out here now. Where are the real men who protect their women, provide for their women, cover their women, and still communicate and love their women? There is a lack of appreciation because it's so easy for us to go and find somebody else. Now they have all these dating websites and dating apps. So if there is any conflict in the relationship, ok cool, I can just go find and fuck somebody else. Because what one man won't do, the next man will. Women are not appreciating men anymore, and if a woman has gotten hurt, then she's going to go do the same thing to the next guy. There is no love in a lot of relationships today. When that red flag comes up they're gone, they don't even talk about it, they'd rather leave and look for someone else. No explanation or no discussion. - **RL, 36**

I don't think all women lack appreciation towards men, but I do think Black women give up on men to quickly, and yes, some men give up on women too and usually for both it's over stupid shit. The only way I think to grow in a relationship is to understand that it's a process and there are going to be highs and lows. I remember a woman telling me she left her man because he didn't call her back right away. This man was out here hustling trying to get his life together and the woman was so insecure and controlling to the point where she would stalk him at work. Women have to own up to the fact that they bring their past into relationships. All the pain, heartbreak, cheating, insecurities, abuse or whatever that their past men did to them, they bring it to the next man they deal with. - **RON, 39**

There are young women out here in their 20's who are bouncing around from man to man trying to find the one who will give her more material things than the last man she was with. They are choosing men who provide money and convenience for them and in return the women will have sex in exchange for these things. I really feel bad for the younger people in our society today because relationships seem to be all about convenience. They won't even talk to a man unless things line up for them or if they can get something from him. Also, if a man is NOT the breadwinner, a woman will push him to the side as if he's blocking her success. If she is a career driven woman then she may say that she does not need a man   There are women who will pay a lot of money to look beautiful on the outside, but they don't always do the work to make them beautiful on the inside. They are looking for what can be gained from cosmetic enhancements. I really think this is just the way society is at this point in time. - **CHUCK, 40**

Yes, I do feel there is a lack of appreciation by women today, because I think women are more successful now and what I've noticed is that a lot of women who are older constantly state that they don't need no man. Just this week I was with a girl and she had a goddamn vibrator in the bed! I was like damn! The girls I'm with don't seem to understand how much I care for them. When I have sex with them the way that I do, I'm doing it because I like them. There are some men out here who just want to get a nut and go home. I think some women take advantage of men. This girl that I was dating was very open about telling me what she needs sexually. However, when I want to have sex, she's like "naw", but when she wants to have sex, she's like "okay come on!" When I pursue her she refuses me, but when she gets horny I'm always right there for her. She can take advantage of me anytime she wants, I'm always available. Now I don't feel that all women lack appreciation, it is subjective. - **TYLER, 42**

Yes, I feel that women lack appreciation because they are petty. However, I also feel there is a lack of appreciation on both sides, with men as well. Simply put, a relationship is about servitude between one another and if this is not happening then it is all fucked up. She thinks a man is supposed to do certain things like pay her rent. Servitude is when a man calls and asks, "Hey babe, I'm heading home, do you want me to bring you dinner?" and she says "No thank you, I'm already cooking for you". Instead some women will say, "That nigga knows I just got off work, he better bring me some dinner!"- **CHRISTOPHER, 42**

I feel this way with some women. But I also think some women just don't give men a chance. As Black men, we have certain ideals and things that we want to accomplish in our lives. We know that being with the right woman who has our back, respects and appreciates us, can allow us to soar together as a couple. Women nowadays are so independent that they got their own and they don't need a man, so they say. I think it's great to see a woman who is doing her thing, but when it is at the expense of emasculating a man, especially a Black man, this does not help us get to know each other. Women still have this ideal of a man being a protector and provider, but on the flip side, they toss around their independence like they don't need us. When do we get to the point of needing each other? - **PHILLIP, 43**

Yes, but I also understand why there is a lack of appreciation. The lack of appreciation stems from the lack of connection between women and men. Women don't know their role and men don't know their role. They are coming together with individual agendas, not a collective agenda So when we don't have that knowledge of understanding then lack of appreciation is the product that is produced out of that. - **DI-AMEN, 47**


I think women don't appreciate themselves like they used to. Black women are the original women. They are beautiful, curvy, thick lips, etc. Everyone right now wants to be Black, and Kim Kardashian started it. So now, women who are naturally beautiful are getting fake butt implants. Atlanta is the home of the injections. Women want to be this "perfect" physical version of themselves and they want to advertise their bodies. Now women have all this outside beauty and they don't take the effort to solidify who they want to be as a person inside. So what ends up happening is women base their value on how attractive they are to somebody else. The minute a man stops looking at them, then what? Now she will never be able to appreciate a guy who just wants to get to know her because she doesn't know herself. She doesn't take the time to invest in knowing herself. There are a lot of good guys out here looking for good women. They understand that Black women are the backbone of who they are. But if the women don't understand this now we have problems. - **DEL, 47**


Yes there is a lack of appreciation because I think women have an entitlement factor with them. They may have dated a guy like an entertainer, an athlete or celebrity, and because that one guy was able to buy them things and do certain things for them, they assume that every man is supposed to do the same thing, and this is just not how it is. Some women value a man's title or his wallet, and this does not necessarily make him a man. - **GYNUINE, 47**


I won't say all women lack appreciation. Maybe men aren't representing themselves well. If he is not a viable asset or if a man doesn't have a strong foundation and isn't grounded, then women can sense this. There are a lot of good women out there, it's just so hard to find them now-a-days. It's hard to find someone that I can trust and have my back. - **WILLIAM, 50**

I think there can be a lack of appreciation but I think this is not necessarily a woman thing, I think it's a human thing. I think the Black male has sort of been demonized to a certain extent and propaganda has been put out and women believe the narrative that 'men ain't no good', that 'he's a dog', 'he ain't this, he ain't that.' I don't even know those dudes personally. Most of the brothers that are in my circle are stand up, incredible men that are educated, career-oriented brothers that take care of their families. Or if they're single, they want to be in a monogamous relationship and they talk about these things. So I think the script could be on both sides of the fence in terms of whether or not women appreciate men or not, and vice versa. Nine times out of ten, I think it is the lack of what we put into a person. I think a woman is a receiver. So if a man puts all the things that she requires and the tangibles that she's looking for into her, then a man will get that back two-fold, or maybe even five-fold. I also think the same thing can be done for a man. If a woman puts in him all those things that he needs, whatever that may be, she'll get back the same. I think we just get lost in translation with that. If a woman isn't used to being treated a certain way and a brother is trying to come correct, then she doesn't know how to handle that, or vice versa. If a dude ain't used to a woman speaking life into his ass, and she's challenging him on a level that he ain't used to being challenged, in a way that makes him a better man, than he won't know how to handle that shit, and defense mechanisms come up. - **DEION, 51**

Yes I do think there is a lack of appreciation by women today in regards to men. I think this is due to the outgrowth of what society puts on Black men. Society has criminalized our natural inclination. Black men want to be strong, stand up family men who can make money and work for ourselves. Historically there have been roadblocks, but now the roadblocks have become more subtle. They have become more sinister really. In some cases we find that the women that we love are the weapons that are used against us the most. For instance, with my first wife, her aim was to utterly destroy my life. She was all about having power, she wanted to compete with me. This is wack! Why did she want to compete with me when there is this whole world out there to compete with? She was the only person that took me to court to literally try to break me, and she is a Black woman. - **MAVERICK, 51**

198

A lot of this to me is a matter of consciousness. If I'm conscious and I appreciate myself, then I'm going to attract women who appreciate me. I've heard men make this statement about women, but I also feel that if men appreciate themselves, and if they love themselves, then they're going to attract women that appreciate them and love them. There are a lot of women who don't love themselves so they're going to attract men who don't appreciate them. So it truly stems from a lack of self appreciation. It's just like when women say, "There are not a lot of good Black men out here". They don't realize that by making this statement, they're creating their reality because of their belief system. - **ISAAC, 51**

To a degree, and I would venture to say 60-70% of the time, we brought this lack of appreciation upon ourselves. If we don't know how to communicate our needs, our desires, and our goals to women then how will they know? Women are the most feeling creatures there are, they are emotional. In today's world, I don't find a lot of women, and men for that matter, that love unconditionally. I think this is because women outnumber men, 26 to 1, and of course this has to do with the process of drugs and incarceration. Women have built up a wall between themselves and men and they have placed many conditions on them. Men have to work harder to build their trust. And some women have been in raggedy relationships from the get go. How is a woman going to appreciate a man if she doesn't understand him? - **GARY, 52**

I don't know if a lot of women have been taught how to appreciate a man, I think this is something that is taught as a kid. If a woman doesn't know how to appreciate the guy, even if it's little things, there will be problems in that relationship. If you talk to any guy and he is in a bad relationship or is unhappy, chances are he'll tell you, "Oh she doesn't appreciate what I do for her". Women need to understand that a "Thank you" goes a long way. And as men, we don't need it constantly, but it would be nice once in a while if she said "Thank you". - **JORDON, 54**

Yes there is a lack of appreciation, because the women today have their own credit, they have their own lives, they have their own things going on, so for them they don't feel as though they need a man in their lives. It's not the same way my mom or my grandma used to feel that they needed a man to rely on. So, every once in a while when a woman is feeling a little horny, they can call up a (male) friend and get what they need and then move on, so they don't have to deal with a man in any other way besides sex. This is exactly what's happening. Some women don't appreciate men, they just want them for their penises. Women are talking freely and openly about it now. Women will say, "Just give me what I want and I can do what I want to do without having to deal with these men". - **TRUSTIN, 54**

The lack of appreciation I think is two-fold because to me, some women have become so independent that they feel that a man ain't worth nothing to them anymore. And not only that, women have become so independent that they have their head stuck up in the air so that when men try to talk to them they think they are too good to speak to them. Also, these days, women have a preconceived notion about what a man should be like, it's becoming commercialized. A man has to be six-feet tall, with a beard, or whatever the trend is now. So instead of women listening to their heart, and following their conscious, they are going after what they see is the trend. Women are doing this to their own detriment and they are having the worst relationships. I see it all the time on social media. They will meet two, three or four guys within one year claiming that each man is 'the one!' - **STEPHAN, 55**

I think women appreciate the men that they're with and they will support him. But I think men have to appreciate and support the women as well. If they understand each other's needs and they're able to talk about what they thrive on in the relationship, it's natural for women to be nurturers and to take care of their man. I think there are a lot of women who appreciate their men, of course, there are also a lot of women who don't as well. If she loves him then she'll take care of him and look out for him and appreciate him. I think if a woman is not doing all of this then she's not really in tune to him as much as he may be into her. Her focus is elsewhere. - **ORLANDO, 56**

I don't think I've ever felt a lack of appreciation, but I hear it when women are talking. She may bring up how much she hates the man that she was with before. So in my mind I make a mental note not to be like those other men. Also, I feel that this woman may be difficult or a problem because she's already complaining. If a woman talks about her ex, it's best just to say he was alright, and just leave it at that, don't go in depth about the relationship. - **DN, 58**

Hell yeah, there is a lack of appreciation! However, there is equal blame because men have figured out that the woman is going to take care of everything - the household, the kids, all that shit. She's going to be a superwoman. So men have gotten lazy and they figured out that if a woman is going to do all of that, and she doesn't have room for him or and she doesn't make him feel needed. If I'm not feeling like 'The Man', then fuck that, she can do this by herself. And men know that women can take care of these things by themselves. Men don't even really consider that she is not able to do this by herself, she has got to do it by herself because she has been put in this situation to do it by herself. So this whole communication thing between men and women is really kind of messed up. I think the appreciation part comes when men present their 'real' selves, which is hard to present because it only comes when he's talking to a real woman. - **MM, 56**

Absolutely there is a lack of appreciation today in regards to men. One of the things I have noticed is that there are Black men out here sacrificing themselves; and I'm talking about good guys sacrificing for the family unit. What I learned is that if that mother is bad-mouthing the father of her children, especially in front of her little girls, the little girl will grow up totally disrespecting that Black man and disrespect her daddy. So if momma doesn't show an appreciation in front of her children, and not just her daughters, then how can they respect that man? We see a cycle happening. So when we talk about lack of appreciation, women project onto men what they've seen and heard around them. Society wants to group all Black men together and say 'they ain't this' or 'they ain't that', or whatever. Some women are not choosing to see that there are a lot of good men out here. Every man is not a bad man. - **KEITH, 60**

I think women still appreciate men, but if we want to put it on a comparative scale then I would probably say, "Yes, there is a lack of appreciation". I think there has been a change in attitude and maybe even circumstance. The more that women depend on something the more that they appreciate it and I don't think women, in today's world, are as dependent on men as they were in the past. There are more women in the workplace and more women that have respectable positions. In the past it was more men who had these positions and they made more money than women. Times have changed. - **PILOT, 61**


Yes, I do think there is a lack of appreciation and it's due to a lot of stuff. Black women are more empowered with all the opportunities available out here. Also, the incarceration rate for Black men is so high and there are a lot of households dominated by Black women. So year after year with women in these positions, when a man comes along they don't know what to do with him. They don't know how to appreciate a man, and I'm not saying all women. It's just the place and time we are living in now. - **ANTHONY, 62**


I don't find that there is a lack of appreciation by women today because I'm not the same man I was thirty years ago. I have a lot more self-esteem, self-worth and confidence. I present myself in a way that puts me in a place where women want to be around a man like me, who is articulate enough to put a sentence together and cares about his physical appearance and hygiene. I tend to want to be around these types of women and have been fortunate enough to be with them. And these women appreciate who I am and what I am doing. - **PAUL, 66**

# Chapter 12

## THE STATE OF BLACK RELATIONSHIPS TODAY

While the men are divided on how they feel in regards to relationships today, one thing that is certain is they understand that in order to build a strong and lasting relationship, they need the support and strength that a black woman provides for them. Some men have shared that there are certain emotional pressures placed on relationships that cause a lack of communication, mistrust and a general lack of understanding between the sexes. There are past wounds that both men and women suffer that need to be healed in order for couples to develop true intimacy and make their relationships work. They need to infuse a brand new energy and thought processes in order to cultivate the landscape of relationships.

All the men agree that black relationships are constantly misrepresented in the media. There are not enough images of authentically strong black families who are loving, protecting and providing for each other. They believe the black love scene is starting to fade as it is being overshadowed by negative perceptions and dysfunctional behavioral attitudes among men and women. We have to change the narrative around our relationships and stop seeking validation from society and pop culture. We have to create our own reality if our relationships are going to be successful. There is a lot of good happening out here within the context of black-on-black love. Let's shift the blame we place on each other and take onus for the individual roles we all play in cultivating healthy relationships. Only we can change the narrative and recreate our own reality of black love.

"This is an interesting question with the current state of our social progression at the moment. I think there is a huge wave of feminism that is taking over, particularly with my generation, it is being brought to the forefront of our society with the Me Too Movement. While there is a huge look at women's roles, there is a lot of talk on this. Now on the flip side, there is a society of people who are also shining the light on men's roles and how we view things, what we want, what we do, and the things that affect us in certain ways. So with feminism, should there also be "Men-ism", a men's movement as well? Women are bringing up the roles they play in society, and while I do think it's nice that a lot of these things are being brought to the attention of society, I don't necessarily think there needs to be a course of action that needs to be taken on all their issues. What about the men's issues, like men's suicide rates and stuff like that. What about the roles men play? Sometimes I think men are not always appreciated as much as we would like to be. I think a big part of being a man is the sacrifices we make. - **SHAUN, 26**

I feel like it would be better if we can go back to the 1980s because there was less ability to focus on the outside world and just focus on our relationships. We've got to build within before we can expand out. - **LAWRENCE, 26**

I feel really good about black relationships today because I see my close friends around me falling in love and getting married. It really brings me joy to see my friends happy like this. I'd rather see us getting married rather than having babies out of wedlock. Marriage solidifies our union. It's a stamp that says "We're in it together!" I love seeing black couples happy and when couples are happy there is a lot less foolishness going on. - **LOGAN, 28**

Black relationships today are tough. I don't want to say that they suck because there are so many successful and loving black relationships. There's just this stigma of black relationships not lasting or black relationships not being created in a healthy manner, and this overshadows the good love that is happening out here. There is not enough good love being openly spread and seen right now. There is not enough of this to over shadow what the bad perception is. There are other cultures that look at our culture as black people and they think that none of us know our dads and that the mothers are the heads of every household. - **DAMIAN, 30**

I think there are certain segments of people who want to see black relationships thrive, and we see it every day on Social media. There is a lot of black love out there. But then there are also segments of people who want to be in relationships but are carrying too much baggage from their past, both men and women. They lose trust, they lose hope, and they lose faith. So these people never hook up and get together because they are too wounded from their past and they can't seem to make things work. And then there are those people who have no clue what a love relationship is like or how to create one. They are perfectly comfortable with calling women bitches and hoes and in turn, the women openly receive these insults.
- **HUGH, 32**

I personally think black relationships are fine. I am a believer in having companionship and love and this doesn't really have a color to it. Just because you may have an inter-racial couple doesn't mean there isn't black love within that relationship. I think it is a big media propaganda type of thing when they talk about how many black men are with white women and vice versa. I also think who people date also has to do with the access of people they have around them. I am in an interracial relationship, my girlfriend is Puerto Rican and Mexican, as far as I'm concerned, she's the same as me, she just got off the boat earlier. I would find it difficult to date a white woman, but then again, I say that now but I don't really know what my future holds, and what type of woman can come and blindside me.
- **JAMAR, 32**

Black relationships are constantly misrepresented. I really love the author Bell Hooks. She changed the way I looked at the digital age. Reading her work, The Isis Papers really made me even more critical of what I allow myself to be susceptible to because of representation. There are not a lot of black couples put out there digitally, through the media. From what I can tell with Hollywood is that they are trying to push this narrative of black women being with white men and vice versa. The media doesn't show how beautiful black couples are. What was so great about President Barack

Obama and his family, they were this family that talked about black things and lived a very black life, you know what I mean? They had black culture in the White House. We don't see this kind of black love a lot. As far as relationships go, a lot of black men are confused about what type of woman is good for us and our children. Men don't choose a woman necessarily without a purpose, we choose a woman based on the type of mother she's going to be to our children. Beauty and every other superficial thing is just for show. - **ANDRE, 33**

It's hard for black men. We deal with so much as far as, who we are supposed to be and what we're not supposed to be. I'm not expected to be in touch with my emotions... no, not at all. Society expects black men to "shut up and color!" These are things that have been stripped emotionally from a black man, look at what we've been through. Black men are still dealing with this. There needs to be, first and foremost, accountability, and there also has to be empathy. This can only come from our community. In order for things to get better socially and in the world, the first peoples of the world have to take back what is theirs. Now, this may sound very radical but, let's think about this. We as black people are dealing with PTSD, we don't have a knowledge of self. So as far as intimacy and relationships are concerned, we have to realize that on both sides, that we are dealing with some serious issues. And while men and women are together we have to individually give the other person enough time and enough space to deal with this. This should be a prerequisite when it comes to black love. Most men have not even dealt with the experiences that they grew up with in the home or any other experiences that come with being a black man. Are they even willing to deal with these issues? - **ANDRE, 33**

I feel as though, in a sense, there was a time where black love was really lacking, from what we were shown in the media. But now, in 2020, I think black love is strong, it's not an idea anymore, it's something that's tangible. You can go on Instagram and see Black Love. It's not something that doesn't exist. You don't have to watch the Cosby Show to see it, it's everywhere. You can see Black Love riding in the car next to you, or in the grocery store. Black love is alive and well! - **KING, 34**

Before social media, I didn't have any negative views on relationships. I grew up having real relationships. My friends were getting married and having kids. I've always seen black love, it's always been around me. Now with social media I see all these things happening in black relationships. And sure, maybe all this was happening when I was coming up, I just never saw it. On the other hand, I do think black relationships are thriving and they are getting better. There are so many happy relationships and so many happy and successful couples out here. I know of a lot of happy couples personally, and I just want to see them keep growing. - **ALONZO, 34**

I don't just look at a black woman as a potential mate. I can look at any woman and think I may be able to marry her if we are compatible, so this is a harder question for me. I'm not always thinking about this on a black on black perspective. I look at other cultures that are dating inside of their race and I see their relationships being strong, for example the Latin community, and I don't really see this within our culture. I think it's also due to our history. Here in America, the whole slavery thing and what it does to us mentally when we think about each other. I love Black Love, I like the idea, however I'm just not attached to it anymore. I feel like I can see myself loving any type of woman. Granted we have our challenges by dating other cultures because we are not always understanding of that person being from another culture. This is one of the toughest things being a black male because it's rare to find people who understand us. - **ISAIAH, 35**

Black relationships today are highly fractured and there is a lot of blame shifting. Women are the gatekeepers of our relationships. You have women having children out of wedlock and then they try to control the child's father in how he moves and how he spends his money. Women will lock their best qualities behind what I would call "Relationship Paywall". And what I mean by this is unless we are in this relationship with titles and all of these things, like a wife or girlfriend status, then she won't even actually care about what's going on with him. Women want that reassurance and I'm not big on titles. I treat all the women that I've dated or slept with, as friends. As we continue to grow within this friendship, then I will determine if exclusivity is right for us. I'm not just going to jump in and claim someone to be my girl just because we slept together and we like each other. We don't know each other well enough to have that level of commitment in my opinion. We need to kill the blanket statements that we apply to genders and not try to project them as universal truths. All men and women are not the same. We all have different stories from our life experiences. There are just as many men out here who are angry, pissed off and confused as there are women. - **BRYCE, 35**

Relationships are not what they used to be. For instance, television shows like the Cosby Show, with Cliff and Clair, or Martin and Gina or like the Jeffersons, that's black love regardless of what they went through, they always loved each other, fought for each other and had each other's back. We don't have this anymore because everything has changed. We see more homo-sexual, LGBT relationships or inter-racial relationships in the media as opposed to strong black relationships. The black love scene is starting to fade. What happened to that strong black love that we used to have, like when couples were married for 40 years and they're still in love. It always boils down to the communication, or lack thereof. Couples have to communicate to have that love again. Black love is what's missing. Nowadays the media tries to push all this other type of love on us. Our community needs to see strong black men and strong black women who are loving, protecting and providing for each other. Instead, we're seeing couples arguing and men hitting women, this is just too much. As I get older, I see people giving up on love. Like me, I always say, "What happened to that 'real love'. Where couples invested in each other and stayed together and fought for their love. This is the type of love that I always wanted and the type of love that I'd rather have. I don't want a situation where we've been together for five years, married for two years and then we get divorced. I want that love that sticks around. I want that love that no matter what we're going through we can stick it out, we got each other's back. We don't dog each other out if we're going through something. I want that type of love where we pray for each other together. - **RL, 36**

Well, this is kind of a loaded question, I will try to answer it to the best of my ability. I think a lot of black couples that I have seen and that I've known personally are a lot stronger today than some couples have been back in the day. Although some of us are quick to get a divorce and not quick to work through this whole marriage thing, because it is work. And a lot of people don't really realize that until they get into a marriage. I think it's stronger for us today because for those of us who grew up in a two parent household, we want to be like our parents were. We want our relationships to last 30, 40, 50 years until, like they say, "till death do us part". So the couples that I've seen trying to make it work, most of the guys I know, they're not cheaters, they stick to their women. They try to learn and understand their women. Like I said. If we work together, we'll be stronger. In the past 20 years the dynamics of the black relationships have changed. It went from back in the day when men were actually courting women, kissing, holding hands and things. And now today, people have sex first and then they get to know each other... and this doesn't work. We need to go back to dating, let's get to know each other. Then maybe we might do something and perhaps build something together. Don't get me wrong, I see many couples today trying to build something for a lifetime together. Not just for themselves, but for their children and their grandchildren. And I just love seeing this. - **MALIK, 38**

I still feel positive and good about black relationships today. There are different social classes in the black community, as there are in every community. People get into relationships based on the level of people they attract. When it comes to black love, we date who we are comfortable dating. We have to have a happy medium with who we date. People only know what they have been taught and what they've been shown so this is why people accept the relationships that they are in today. It's not that it is their last resort, it is truly what they know. - **CHUCK, 40**

It's bad, ya know. It's like men and women are together, but they're not together. We are connected, we have a bind as a people, but there's this buy in that doesn't occur whenever there is friction and that's the problem. We are not trusting each other. We don't know how to talk to each other. How do we surrender to each other if we don't see the problem? We are at a little secret war with each other. We have to learn how to play on the same team. - **CHRISTOPHER, 42**

I think we are in trouble because the transparency of men is being challenged right now. There is a shift in how black male masculinity is being perceived. And in this shift there is a transparency, a vulnerability and these are cracks in our foundation and not a lot of people know what to do with these cracks. Right now in 2020 we are seeing more men challenging each other vs how it was back then. Back then, when I was younger, if I did something fucked up my cousin may punch me in my chest. Whereas today we are more apt to say "yo bro why are you so mad all the time?" Back then we were reprimanded whereas today we're saying "Yo bro, are you alright? Let's talk about it". Not a lot of men can respond to this question because they are not used to being vulnerable and communicating their feelings. They may just respond "yeah I'm good", when clearly they are not. The issue is men have not been taught how to express themselves this way. Not a lot of men are actively doing this which leads to a high suicide rate amongst black men and black single women. Honestly, right now, black women are moving at such a rapid pace that they don't have time to coddle men. Black men don't necessarily need to be coddled, they need to be caressed. There is a difference between being coddled and being caressed. For example, if I have a fucked up day at work, and I come home, the first thing my girl says to me is, "How was your day?" I share my day with her whether it was fucked up or great, she's going to give me a hug. And now I am whole and the outside world exists no longer. Now, being coddled is different. It's when your woman says, "oh baby come here! Let me love up on you!" I haven't addressed that I had a fucked up day at work. So being coddled doesn't eliminate the issue that I had prior to coming home. So now I bring that anger home and my home is no longer my peace. I have a girlfriend who is mad, my kids say daddy is angry all the time and no one has asked me how my day was. So therefore, there is no caressing, there is no hide-a-way, and I'm just mad because I have not been able to express myself about my fucked up day at work, nobody cares. - **WES, 42**

Men have just as difficult of a time finding a good woman, as women have finding a good man. We each individually have to self-evaluate to see what works for us in relationships because what may work for you, may not work for me. Our life experiences are different. We need to come together and create goals for our relationships according to what works for us, rather than conforming to what society say we should be. Black relationships are unique, we don't always fit into a certain bubble or system that is in place. Our experiences are very different from other cultures. Women have this litmus test where they compete with men, saying if a man can't do this for her then she won't do this for them. As men we feel like there is so much competition just being in a relationship with a black woman and we have to wonder is she really worth all of this. I want a melanated sister. I want my legacy to look like me. I love black love. What I'm starting to observe is that the women who feel this way, it has more to do with her their insecurity and how she feels about herself. She's trying to project that onto me. Sometimes loving a sister is challenging. They need to look at themselves and take ownership of the roles they play in the relationship as well. - **PHILLIP, 43**

I feel that here in the United States, because we've been under such a colonial mind-state, society has done what it was programmed to do which is to keep us apart. Because, you know when we come together as a people, we grow as a people. So here in America I think it is part of the system of not really allowing us to come together. There are so many forces that are working against us in that sense and there is not a voice that is large enough to bring that consciousness to all of the brown-skinned folks like at one time. So right now it's a battle for us to unite and grow strong in partnership but it can be done. - **DOMINIC, 45**

I think the biggest problem is that both men and women, but I'd say mostly women, have unrealistic expectations. They expect more from a man then they expect from themselves. I think a woman looks at what her father did and expects the man to do the same thing. I try to explain to women that your father is obligated to do certain things and your man is not, it's a choice. Women will say that they need a man who is a provider, but what does that mean? If I meet a woman in her 40's, she already has a job, she already has bills, she already has a place to stay, so the only thing I believe my job is as a "provider" is if you trip, to catch you. But it is not my job if you are financially irresponsible, to pick up your slack for your responsibilities. - **GYNUINE 47**

Black relationships are doomed, they are doomed! It's sad to say it. Society plays a role in it too. Have you ever noticed how controversial it was to see a white man and a black woman in a commercial or vice versa? This is all part of a bigger plan to eliminate the black man. When you eliminate the black man and the black children, then the population density becomes smaller and smaller and smaller. So the state of relationships now, makes me cringe because now you hear black women say, "I'm tired of these men, I'm going to go and get me a white man". Or you'll hear a testimony from a black woman who is married to a white man, and this invites other black women who are lonely to try a different nationality as well. Meanwhile, the guy who got his cake and is eating it too is destroying the lives of the woman that he married and he's really not investing into the life of the woman he's cheating with. So now his wife is sick of him and divorces him. She gave him three kids and his body doesn't look the same as it used to. She's now out here realizing that it is really hard trying to date men. She starts doing crazy stuff, doing the same thing that the men do, dating younger guys and becoming a sugar-momma, or worse. She may stay in her marriage because she doesn't want the relationship to end, so they invite someone else into the bedroom and they start swinging. Everybody starts having sex with the same people. People start getting diseases, etc. There is a reason why the HIV rate in Atlanta is so high. This is what's happening.

Now, today, it's a little tougher for me to date because I have old school values. It is definitely tougher dating women here in Atlanta. I found myself settling a lot with the women here. Even though we were unequally yoked, I found myself settling and compromising a lot, trying to convince myself that maybe she doesn't need to be everything that I am. This wasn't being true to who I am and I realized that I'm just going to have some lonely nights. I made a decision not to take the 'blue pill' that everybody takes. I was pretending and trying to force relationships like everyone else. - **DEL, 47**

Overall, I think the state of black relationships is sub-par and it's evident in the fact of how many people are not just getting married but staying married. If you look at the last long lasting marriages in a big way, we look at our grandparent's generation, that was it. Our parents did not have long marriages, it was very few. Then I look at my generation down to our children, and they can't even sustain a relationship let alone a marriage. This is happening because there is an under appreciation for one another. The problem with black men and black women is that we have moved away from our original culture, and this is a problem. We are literally out of our minds. Because what's in our minds is the European concepts of how we should treat one another, and this is a problem. We have to get back into our

African-central mindsets. We've got to get back there because that culture always bred unity. There was always a cohesive movement between the people, especially between the households. Although we were married within our households, there was a village that looked out for one another. This is basically what it comes down to... it's a cultural thing. People think that it's ok to just choose something out there, obviously this is not true. Look at how things are working out for us. This has not worked out for us.

We have to start collectively seeking out a solution because there is no doubt that we have all identified that there is a problem. The sickening thing about it is that nobody has been interested in solving this problem. I really think this is because there is a lack of love. I'm talking about love that includes everything and everybody, it's self-less. When there is a lack of love, the true version of love, we are in this position to be victimized because we're looking to go out and get something to satisfy ourselves, not caring about nobody else. Some people give only so they can get, which is still a very selfish thing. One of the true acts of love is to give and expect nothing in return. So when they don't get what they expect, that's when people fly off the handle and they become a victim and start talking about how horrible the other person is. This is what is reigning in our mindset these days and we're not looking to solve the problem that we know is there. Which is this lack of connectedness between the black man and black woman intimately.
- **DI-AMEN, 47**


I'm in Texas and I see a lot of black men pushing up on white girls, and honestly, I think it's for the sex. White women are a little freakier, and the black women are more reserved. Black women ain't gotta hold back, if I mess their hair up I'll get it fixed. Black women are making their own money so they think they can act bougie and do what they want to do. Then you got the thug girl on the other side who doesn't know how to act out there in public. - **WILLIAM, 50**


I am completely ecstatic and excited about black relationships. People say that black folks don't get married. However, every time I turn around on Facebook, there is somebody's ass getting engaged. I'm not buying into this narrative that all the black men are running around trying to find somebody that doesn't look like black women. I think right now in the state of where we are, we are finding a brand new energy about who we are. So I think, the more we love our damn selves, the more we're going to find somebody who looks like us. There is some truth in that whole thing. While she might be fine and white, she won't get my ass. I can't talk about what my life experiences are, and she can't relate to them. It just ain't going to happen. Or for a sista who's tired of dealing with these brothers and she goes and gets herself a white boy, his ass at the end of the day still won't get her at her core. Now don't get me wrong, they can love each other, but there are going to be spaces and gaps to where they just won't get each other. Sometimes there are subtleties in the world to where we immediately get it because we've experienced it and a white guy or girl will never get it. It goes right over their head. - **DEION, 51**

I think the feminizing of black men in this country has wrecked the relationship balance between black men and black women. I think black women have given black faggots too much of a pass. I see black women talking to their sons in a store, yelling at them saying, "Get your ass over here before I fuck you up!" When I see this I say, okay, there must not be a man in their house. She is a stressed out, single mother, trying to raise this boy, I get that. But remember now, she is raising that boy. So when he grows up and he's toxic and his girlfriend talks to him the way his mother did, and he puts his hands on her, the woman can't say he did this because there is no man in the house. There is always an angst that I get when I brooch this subject. - **MAVERICK, 51**

From my viewpoint, black relationships are great! I think that we have to first love each other. We have to be the change that we want to see. So I know that in order for black relationships to work, my relationship has to work. Overall, I do see there are some challenges in terms of black relationships, especially the way we communicate with each other. I really think this all comes back to self-love and intimacy. Us not truly loving ourselves because we've been fed this conditioning that black is negative and white is good. We have internalized a lot of Christian concepts where Jesus Christ is white and God is white. God is an intimate part of who I am, so if this is disconnected, then how can I truly love and connect with my own self, from a spiritual perspective. It's all connected. What is your self-concept? What is your God concept? All of this comes back to you, you know what I'm saying? If it's not empowering you, then you're going to have all kinds of problems in your relationships. - **ISAAC, 51**

I think black relationships can be improved upon for sure. Politically there is a division between men and women. They are dividing us by taking the man out of the equation. The legal system, if you look at the incarceration rate, there are more blacks in jail than any other race. There is also the issue of entertainment and those images we see and how this plays upon the relationships with our youth. Now, society is no longer taking the men out, they're after the babies. They have black men locked up and if you kill the head the body will abide. Just look at our youth, and the music they're playing and the videos that are being played, and how they depict young black men. They're slapping a woman and beating women. And now the videos have switched up to where the women are more dominant. Women are taught to be more dominant then men and men are now playing the "bitch" role. I'm just not going to put on skinny jeans, I'm sorry it ain't happening! I don't want to have to point my toe to put on a pair of jeans. It's cool for the church to teach us how to love god and reverence God, but after that, what's the next step? They have to show the black man and the black family how to empower themselves. How am I going to build wealth to leave to my children's children if the church doesn't provide me with the keys? Where are our leaders? And the leaders that are put in place, what are you teaching? Without empowerment, we fail before we start. - **GARY, 52**

Black relationships are in trouble. I understand that black men and their ancestors had witnessed cultural trauma, which has transcended into generational curses. Black men saw their women raped in front of them over and over again, incessantly, night after night, by their masters. And now she's got to come back to her husband and deep inside he begins to feel hate and discontent for his wife. Now she comes back to her husband and has to be subservient to him also. This sets a pattern of psychosis in our DNA. There is all types of literature that supports this theory of divide and conquer that has been practiced to break apart the black family, and it has been pervasive since the middle passage. As a result of this conditioning, we now are incapacitated and we feel inadequate to manage a family. This reality maintains itself stuck in the back of our subconscious. - **MICHAEL, 53**

What I am observing locally is that relationships look good because healthy people tend to hang out with healthy people. So you'll tend to be surrounded by the same energy that you're about. Social media wise it looks bleak but then the only people that seem to be connecting with social media in mass are the millennials. I'm in education and I notice that the Inglewood school district has 85% women. Many of them are single, mad, horny and upset. So if I look at relationships from this standpoint then it's not good. - **GREG, 54**

I know black women have it hard out here. Obviously there is a shortage of good black men. And when you think about all the black men in jail or gay or married, the numbers just aren't there. But, I think what gets overlooked a lot is that it's hard for us (men) too because when you think about the number of women who are gay or married or not date-able, and what I mean by not date-able is that a lot of women are crazy, a lot of men think women are crazy. And a lot of this is our fault because of the way we treated black women and the way black women have been treated their whole lives. Many women have grown up being mistreated not just by the men they date but also by the men in their families. When we reach a certain stage in our lives, we have all had experiences that perhaps were traumatizing to us. It's hard because the older men get, our tolerance level towards certain things gets shorter and I know when I meet women, I don't wonder whether or not she is crazy. I wonder how crazy is she, what baggage is she bringing into the relationship and how affected is she by her past? Because my fuse is shorter, if I go out on a date with a woman and she shows any sign of being crazy, that's it, it's a wrap, I lose interest. The most important thing is finding someone who we are compatible with more so than being in love, if we're not compatible then it's going to be a very bad relationship. - **JORDON, 54**

I just think people need to slow down in order to cultivate the landscape of the relationship with each other. Instead of thinking about 'hitting it', we should think about cultivating it and making it grow. If we look at the couples who are successful, they've cultivated their relationship. They remove their egos. They are vulnerable with each other. They are open with their feelings with each other and they squash any negativity that may cause harm to their relationship. I think from a church perspective there is a 51% divorce rate. From a millennial's perspective, I think people are more into social dating and hookups versus long lasting relationships. I read that there is a 40% decline in sexual relationships between millennials because they are all about technology, social media and text messaging, and this is not intimate. They text their emotions and how they feel as opposed to having a conversation face-to-face. This is not the way to communicate. Millennials have a lot of fears when it comes to relationships. They are afraid of their lack of experience and they are afraid of getting hurt. They feel that they don't live up to another person's expectations, or they feel that they're not good enough or worthy because someone else may have more (social media) LIKES then them. - **TRUSTIN, 54**

I think today, we need to be trained on how to be in relationships and we need to have role models. We have allowed Hollywood, movie stars, entertainers, and athletes, to define what our relationships should look like. There is a price to pay when we seek to mold our relationships around what we see in social media. We have to be aware that we are accountable to how the world sees how we treat our mates or spouses. I try to be that role model for my sons. - **TARZAN, 56**

I think that there is a warped sense of black relationships. I don't blame people for dating whomever they want to date but if we're able to be in a black on black relationship, it's like a very rare flower and it's the best thing in the world. It's just like in advertising, you can't do shit without color, you can't sell anything. So, we need to understand how rich our melanin is! There are black women walking around here with these blond wigs talking about black power. So there are different levels of understanding. Also, there are a lot of road blocks between us and so many distractions keeping us from really connecting. We are not accepting each other for who we really are. When some black men get to a certain level financially and they start to feel a certain way about things, he's feeling like he can now stretch his boundaries and date outside his race. There is a reprogramming and a debriefing that needs to happen. This is why I'm a firm believer that relationships are better when people are older versus when they are younger because we are more aware of why we are together. As opposed to now I have acquired this status and I can date outside my race because all these different women are attracted to me now. It's just ignorance to me. We need to find our 'home' in each other. - **MM, 56**

I still think black relationships are good. Society makes us think that black relationships are not good, and because of this we make assumptions about our love. I don't know where they get their statistics from or who they're polling, but I see black love around me every day either on social media or with the people that I work with. The love is there, people want to pretend it's not. There are plenty of people who have been in long term committed relationships, there is black love on every level. - **ORLANDO, 56**

I think there is definitely a difference in black relationships compared to other relationships. It seems like there is a model that people have about how they're supposed to be. There are some men who can't stand dating black women because of the expectation that there is a "black way " to be in a relationship. No one even knows what this is. People will say that there is a certain way to be in a black relationship, but it is elusive. I think black women are in some kind of mental rebound or there's something in their DNA where they're looking for a certain kind of way to be treated that's based on fiction. I don't know what it is. For example, I put up a Facebook post with a picture of an engagement ring with this teeny-weeny diamond in it, and I asked a lot of women, both black and white, "If a man offered you this ring in proposal, would you marry him?" The black woman said "No". They wanted a ring with a bigger diamond. Whereas the white women didn't say anything about the ring size at all. They were more concerned if the man really loved them and if they could see a future with the man then the ring was not important. So I posted other items about cars, houses, etc... and every single time for the black women it was all about possessions and with the white women it was a totally different issue. A black woman sees her man as what he owns, versus who he is. They see his car, his job and his clothes, they don't see the man. That's why a lot of black men will go to any other ethnicity but black. Other ethnicities can see through what he owns versus who he is. - **DN, 58**

Black relationships today are in trouble. If you look around, we don't see the "happy" black families. We see the angry black families, but the happy black families. If we look at the programming on television, we don't see the happy black family unit. What we're seeing is the mixed family unit. And seeing this continues my theory of the total disrespect of the black man. We

have to understand what is happening now. You can talk to 20 couples and of those 20 couples you may only find one that is happy together. The other couples aren't happy because they bought into the fantasy of marrying your college sweetheart, getting the house with the white picket fence, the dog that looks like a rat on a string and 2.5 children... This is a fantasy. Instead they should be saying, "What are we going to build together?" As opposed to wanting a bigger house or another car or acquiring more material things. So now the pressure is on because somebody has to pay for that crap.
- **KEITH, 60**


I think there is a lot of misogyny in terms of black men steering towards black women based on what we are seeing in the music and entertainment industry. It seems as though the Jewish people, since they control these industries, are dictating the outcome of how black people are portrayed. And this trickles down into how black people see themselves. I feel sorry that women feel like they have to wear their skirts so high that it shows their privates or that they have to have these breast augmentations or that they have to have butt implants, so forth and so on. Sexuality is so open these days. I kind of longing for the earlier days when things were so hidden and private and intimate. Now it's all kind of in your face. This behavior promotes the one-night stands and the lack of commitment. Also, the court system is liberal in locking up black men for lack of child or spousal support payments that it becomes impossible for black men to maintain a decent lifestyle. Particularly here in the southern states like Georgia.

It certainly saddens me to see the degree of divorce that's in our communities. I think that we are seeing some aspects of mis-education, particularly coming out of slavery. This is one of the factors that is influencing the rate of divorce that we see in our community and that is the science of marriage. In slavery we were just breeding machines for the masters or tools at his disposal. In my opinion we should be more engaged in marriage, 'till death do us part'. We are not seeing this in our communities, therefore we have a very high degree of divorce and family instability. - **PILOT, 61**

Times are very different then when I was coming up in my 20's. I'm not really judgmental because when I was in my twenties, I was a wild child. If I was twenty years old today, in 2020, I would probably be running around with my pants sagging and trying to get my dick sucked by every little chicken head on the corner. If I look at this from the point of view of a 40 year old, I see couples who are trying to stay together and stay married. This is a good sign and it feels really good. But when I look in magazines I see a bunch of us who are single. I think people have an unrealistic fantasy of what love and life should be, and because of this, we have a small percentage of happy couples and a very large percentage of individuals who just want to hang out. I think people need to mature in order to find stable relationships. The word mature has nothing to do with age. It has more to do with understanding of self, understanding of family and having an understanding of how to connect with another person. - **ANTHONY, 62**

# Chapter 13

## MEN'S LAST WORDS

I put away my sheet of questions and kept the tape recorder running as I asked the men if they had anything else they wanted to say that pertained to men and intimacy, relationships, women, or the book. Some of them were exhausted by answering the interview questions while others were still revved up and ready to share more. Those men continued talking freely as they were still under the guise of anonymity and they felt there was more to be said. There was no holding back as they talked about other areas of interest that needed to be brought to the forefront. These Black men were glad that their voices were being heard and their statements recorded in such a unique platform for their self-expression.

Being a male exotic dancer is challenging at times but very beneficial. It's challenging because I get judged a lot by females. It hurts to be judged in this way. If I like a girl and I tell her I'm an exotic dancer, they assume that I have girls all over the place. It's rewarding because I've been able to find confidence in myself that I didn't know I had. It brings me financial gain and I get to meet some great people, important people. Because I'm an exotic dancer, women who come to my show just want to sleep with me because they are turned on by what they see, so they judge me based on what they see. They may have husbands at home so they view me as just a fantasy. I've met so many women from all over the world. It's like they come out to Vegas just trying to get away and have some fun. These women will come to my show and pay me whatever they like. They'll expect me to automatically be open to going back to their hotel just because they paid me a certain amount of money. - **JOSHUA, 25**

I was cheated on by my wife. When I found out, it hurt. It really hurt like on a whole other level! In our marriage, I held myself to a higher level and felt as though it was my responsibility to take the lead, so when I found out my wife was sleeping with someone else it was like, damn! I didn't understand what more she needed. I was in the Navy and I was on deployment when it happened. All the money that I was earning was being sent home to her and then I found out that she was spending it on other things, this was really hard to take. - **LAWRENCE, 26**

I was being honest with women that I was dating and told them that I was just out here playing, so don't catch any feelings, I'm just playing. I was openly dating, I was openly polyamorous. I realized then that even though I was telling women the truth, they still would somehow misconstrued what I was saying. - **DONNIE, 27**

Sometimes a woman can become callus because women hold so much shit! What ever happened to you, don't bring it into the next relationship. That's how my ex-girlfriend was and after a while I couldn't deal with her anymore. - **DONNIE, 27**

A lot of women are so caught up in money, cars, social media and material things, so much so that it is hard to get past their exterior to find out who they really are inside. But then again, a lot of women really don't know who they are inside. If you remove the makeup, the lashes, (by the way, who invented that shit? Those lashes look like dead bugs on their eyes), the breast and butt implants, these women will probably be left with very low self-esteem. - **DC, 29**

Women are so busy trying to calculate what I have, my car, my home, my career, etc... they don't even take the time to really see the man that I am, they don't see me. There was a time when profiling and flexing was important to me. I had to have the flyest girl, with a banging body and pretty face. This is no longer important to me. Don't get me wrong, I ain't trying to be with no scrub, but she has got to see me beyond the things that I own. - **PHILLIP, 43**

I took an anger management class a while ago and I had to really take a look at myself. We did mirror work where I looked in the mirror and asked myself questions. I had to be honest with myself and answer these questions. There is nothing more powerful than looking in your own eyes, looking into your soul and being honest with myself. I learned so much about myself doing this work .- **LOGAN, 28**

The type of woman that would lock me down and keep me would be someone who understands me. She listens to me and she's submissive. And by submissive I mean she's soft, but not weak. She's interested in understanding me. If I ask her to do something, she has my back and will do it. There won't be any fussing and fighting about it. A woman that can cook would be a plus. And it's important that the woman respects herself because if she respects herself, she's willing to respect others. Also, if she's self-motivated, ambitious and supportive of me and my career. She pushes me to be the best I can be. I feel like a man is supposed to protect and provide for his woman. If I have a woman that supports me and pushes me to be my best, this is what I want. I just want her to tell me, "You can do it, you can be whatever you choose to be!" Her telling me, "You're a good father or you're a good coach", these affirmations are what I want and need to hear. If she does the things I ask of her then I feel like I can protect and provide for her. - **LOGAN, 28**

I dated this girl who was fine as fuck! She was beautiful, had a banging body, the sex was great, but that was it. That was all she was bringing to the table. She had no conversation whatsoever outside of what's happening on social media. I was so bored with her that I found myself seeking mental stimulation elsewhere. When we broke up I realized that I would never again be a woman who was so caught up in unnecessary things. I don't care how fine a woman is, ask any man, after a while that shit fades. I'm trying to grow as a man and if I don't have a woman who's growing with me then she ain't worth my time. I want a woman on my arm that I can take to a dinner party and be proud of. - **DC, 29**

"Love is found in freedom". This has been my experience. When I find that there is something that hinders me from being able to be free whether it's sexually or emotionally, or being able to freely communicate, or even just feeling free to be myself, "Freedom" is the word that keeps coming up. It comes up for me in different parts of my life and in different relationships. This is the one thing that has hindered me from being in love and staying in love and doing something fruitful, it's just freedom. So I would say that "Love is found in freedom". - **DAMIAN, 30**

I'm making a conscious effort not to be in a relationship right now because I've been in one relationship after another since I was a teenager and I haven't taken the time to be single. Here I am now, 30 years old, and I am just now embracing my life and intentionally trying to experience things being single. I'm getting to know myself as a single person. - **DAMIAN, 30**

My girlfriend and I haven't gone out in a while. I haven't seen her in a revealing dress and in high-heels, which she loves to wear, in a while. This is something I would like to see more of. I'd like to be able to meet her somewhere and act like we don't know each other. It's just something I'd like to do to spice things up in our relationship. - **JAMAR, 32**

Women come in all different shapes, sizes, and complexions, some women wear makeup, some don't. Some dress high-fashion and some dress artsy. For me as a man, each woman is like a gift-wrapped present. Each one is a different gift to unwrap. They even smell different once they're opened, LOL! - **JAMAR, 32**

A woman has the potential to raise her man. She can encourage him to do all the things he didn't think he could do. If she sticks by him and supports him during hard times, then together they can build a strong foundation. I honestly believe that a woman can control a relationship and a man can be in charge if she allows him to be. If a woman wants to stay in the relationship, and if I'm her dude, and she allows me to be in control, then this is the way it will be. Men these days are in control, they are not in charge. A man can only be in charge if a woman allows him to be. - **HUGH, 32**

It's so weird because a woman will be quick to tell her friends that she's not being pleased in the bedroom, but she won't tell her man. Women will not tell their men what they need in the bedroom, this just doesn't make sense to me. - **HUGH, 32**

When men get bored in relationships they can't blame the women. We have to take the responsibility and try new things as well. To build a relationship we can't just have sex, we have to build a friendship with women. We have to do things that are going to create a bond together. Men have to change their thoughts on relationships and try new things. - **HUGH, 32**

Most black men walk around thinking we're OK when we're really messed up! - **ANDRE, 33**

I started to know that I was attracted to both men and women around the age of 12. I felt alone because a lot of people said I had to choose. It's either one or the other, you can't like both, and I genuinely liked both. It was just weird for me. I suppressed my feelings towards men for a long time and I just dated women. I got a little bit too curious around college and I couldn't take it anymore so I started experimenting in my freshman year of college. I was on the DL (Down Low). - **KING, 34**

I've had mental health challenges my entire life. I've struggled with varying degrees of depression and anxiety. From the death of my grandmother, through bouts of homelessness, being broke, to other things that have been plagued by my youth. It got to the point where everything was coming down on me at once and I just broke down. I was always feeling like I had to fight every fight by myself. I felt like no one understood me, there was no empathy. In 2015 I tried to commit suicide. My life was falling apart. I felt like nobody cared about me. I almost lost my life in my own hands worrying about what people were doing, or not doing to me. This is no longer in the matrix of things that I care about. I just can't be worried about other people because they're too fickle. I'll be dead and in the dirt and they're still out here living how they're living. - **BRYCE, 35**

We live and operate in a world with high feminine energy. There are a lot of women running things, directing things, and telling us how it's supposed to go. While there is validity to all of this, what's missing that balance of male energy that has a different approach. There are a lot of women who try to operate in their masculine energy. There are women raising children who are really tough, and really abrasive and aggressive with them, trying to get them to do things, by yelling at them. This is not masculine, it's a woman's version of masculine. She thinks that being hard, rough and tumble is the way to get it done. - **BRYCE, 35**

I read a book, *The Way of the Superior Man*, and one thing that the author wrote about that I really identified with was how sometimes a man can just enjoy a woman's energy, even if he's married or not. He doesn't have to look at a woman and go holler at her or get her phone number. Sometimes as a man we just want that female energy around us. I notice now that I'm older and have a child, I'm not out hunting or looking for women, but sometimes I just want the company of a woman. So I find myself just hanging out with some of my female friends and just chilling with them, enjoying myself and enjoying their energy. I'm a guy's guy, I just love women. Not because of sex

alone, it's their energy. I'm a masculine guy, I just need that feminine energy.
- **ISAIAH, 35**

There are red-flags that come up in relationships and rather than talking about it, women are gone without saying a word! They won't even tell a man what he did wrong so that he can explain his actions and what happened. Maybe he didn't know that what he did bothered her or upset her. And if a man asks her what's wrong, she will say, "oh nothing, I'm good". And then next thing you know, a few days later, he hasn't heard from that woman and doesn't know what's going on. Two or three weeks go by and she doesn't even say 'hello'. Nobody wants to sit down and talk about what happened and expose their feelings about things. We have to talk to each other because maybe that man really didn't know what he said really upset or bothered her. If we don't know what bothers women then we won't know how to fix the situation. - **RL, 36**

Women have got to realize that money is only one aspect of a relationship. What about companionship and compatibility? What about good sex and communication? What about building a future together? I once had a woman tell me, "I don't need no man! I got a vibrator and a healthy bank account". She said all the good men are married. WTF! Does she even consider how she makes a man feel when she says things like that to him? Women today have to understand that they can either lift a man up or break him down with their words. We need to, both men and women, start using our words wisely and in an uplifting way.- **ZION, 37**

There are so many lonely women out here because they don't choose to see the value of a man pass his wallet or his bank account. My cousin was making six-figures working at AT&T. She wouldn't even look at a man if he wasn't pulling in the same amount, and you know what, she could never find a good man. All the men she was dating in that financial arena had two or three women they were messing with. When she lost her job and the money, she had a real reality check. Her pride and her ego were shot down. She ended up meeting a man with a dollar and a dream and together they are building a very successful company. - **ZION, 37**

Prayer is a big thing for me. The woman that I'm with has got to be able to pray with me and pray over me, just like I'll pray over her. If we're getting ready to eat we're going to pray over our food together, I don't care who's around us. I need her to know, if God isn't in it then we ain't in it. The woman that I'm with now has never had anybody pray over her. - **RL, 36**

There are men out here sleeping with two or three women, living with the fear of getting caught and being found out. In my mind, I'm like, man just tell women what you're doing and let them decide if they want to deal with you or not. Stop playing these games! - **RON, 39**

If a man is not ready to be with a woman, then no matter what she does he's not going to be with her. If he ain't ready, he ain't ready. - **RON, 39**

The hardest thing I don't understand is why women like to be mistreated by men. If a guy is really nice to a woman they say, "Oh he's too nice". But if a man literally beats a woman they keep going back. If I'm really nice and I'm really digging her and I'm giving then she thinks I'm too nice. I can never understand this. Other guys that I talk to say the same thing, "Yo, you gotta treat them badly!" I can't treat any woman badly but I think I have to change some things about myself. I have to hold myself back because they'll take me for granted. It's just weird that I have to play this game of being a bad boy… what the fuck! - **RON, 39**

Some men will just go along with women. Whatever that woman is attracted to, men will try to conform to what it is she wants. They will tell her what she wants to hear and show her what she wants to see versus just being real with themselves. - **VICTOR, 40**

When I was thirteen, I got my first mentor, he was my sixth grade teacher. He helped me to understand what was happening to my body. He introduced sex education to me from a healthy perspective. We spoke about everything from A to Z. We talked about school, women, books, sex, money, politics, African-American studies… everything! - **WES, 42**

There is a metamorphosis that happens to a man throughout his life. And there are a lot of elements that women are not privy to and will never be privy to because we put up a front. Not because we have to and not because we want to, but because it's societal. It can go back as far as slave masters control over black men, it could be cultural. There could be a lot of different dynamics in place. - **WES, 42**

I like older women because they taste better. It's like eating a piece of fruit. I prefer fruit that is juicy and ripe. It's like that juicy, sweet watermelon on a hot summer day. - **CHRISTOPHER, 42**

A woman that I was seeing was honest with me about cheating on her husband, and although we continued dating and sleeping together, I could never trust her. I never saw a future with her. - **PHILLIP, 43**

Women shouldn't have sex with men until they are REALLY ready to have sex with them. They shouldn't choose to have sex with a man just because they don't want him to go and get it from another woman. This becomes a lie and they don't give him 100% of themselves. I don't want 10% of a woman, I want 100% of her when we lay down together and have sex. I would rather be a "pleasure delayer". I will delay pleasure until it is boiled to a point. Being in Atlanta, you can have a one night stand every day. But there is nothing better the when you meet someone and you don't have sex with them right off. We're talking every day, we're getting to know each other. I am the master of a kiss on the cheek when we had a great date. A woman may start to think that there is something wrong with her because I'm not jumping all over her trying to get sex. However, when we do finally have sex, it's always amazing! - **PHILLIP, 43**

When I'm out with a woman, I don't like her to dress in a provocative way. Because if a guy says something to her or God forbid touches her, then I have to get involved. But not only that, she should have some respect for herself. -**PHILLIP, 43**

I do believe in monogamy but in this day and age, lack of communication and a disconnection happens once couples have been together for so long. - **KADEEM, 44**

Individuals should really take the time to get to know themselves and just spend some time alone quietly with yourself and your thoughts. If we as men can do this every day, I feel it's one of the best medicines for our lives and we get to evaluate ourselves without judgment. I think this will bring us together as a people and hopefully create the right energy between us, because right now we need that. I feel there are so many people lacking the energy of love and they're feeling lonely and feeling alone. We need to take the time to feel grateful. - **DOMINIC, 45**

When a man is no longer in a relationship with a woman and she means nothing to him, then this is a problem. There is no more evidence that you need to know that he was in the relationship for selfish reasons. He was not in the relationship to acknowledge love in the first place, He was in the relationship to get what he can for himself. Unfortunately, this is the case with 99.9% of people in the world. - **DI-AMEN, 47**

I have had real intimacy before and currently I'm building this with the woman I'm dating. But even after three years, we haven't been able to fully open this up because of her level of sensitivity and emotionality. It's quite clear that her challenges are stemming from her past experiences, not just in her relationships but even beyond that. Her challenges stem from her childhood on through her relationships, up to this present moment. It's not that we haven't had our share of challenges since childhood, but the difference is, I've dealt with mine. I've gone into a spiritual initiation system that has allowed me to master myself. And since I've undergone this process and she has not, there is a definite difference between the two of us and it is hard for us to sync our frequencies and to resonate and vibrate on the same level when it comes to that because she's not quite at the level of understanding of self as I am. Just knowing this allows me to be patient with her as well. - **DI-AMEN, 47**

A man can't start off thinking what he did sexually to the last woman he was with is going to please the next woman. He has to have a neutral set of actions to where it is enough to inspire the woman or to make her feel confident that he has enough to please her. A man may not hit the mark the first time but he's done enough to where she can now show him what she likes. Now he can master her. - **DI-AMEN, 47**

When a woman likes you, she will make herself available. When a woman is interested in you, she will call you, she will talk to you. So all these women out here who are playing "hard to get" they wouldn't do this if they were really interested.- **GYNUINE, 47**

I've experienced a lot of women who have this belief that they should judge a man based on his wallet. They don't understand that does not make him a man. I encounter a lot of women who want me to pay their bills. What these women don't understand is that their bills ain't got nothing to do with me. She had those same bills before I met her. I don't believe that I'm supposed to pay my bills and her bills, I don't agree with that. I had one woman say to me, "You're a man, you're supposed to be a provider". This whole concept is misconstrued. Why does it have to be an action with the woman and a financial responsibility for me?... I just don't agree with this. - **GYNUINE, 47**

I make good money in my profession as an IT Manager and I decided to do what everybody else does and date for status. So I met this woman a couple of years ago who was a surgeon, and on paper, she was everything that a man would want. We lived an hour apart from each other, I was in Buckhead and she was in Conyers. Our lifestyles were very different, however, after six months we ended up moving in together. I quickly discovered that her expectations of me were differences that we could not see eye-to-eye on. I went against my better judgement by dating a woman based on her status and how much money she made, and I was miserable. It was great when we spent time together on the weekends, but once we moved in together, I realized that she was everything that I was not. I was getting older, at the time I was 45, and as much as I enjoyed myself, I don't want to be 80 years old and the only way someone knows I passed away was because somebody can smell my body decaying from my loft. - **DEL, 47**

There are a lot of women in Atlanta who are dating the same men and they have become ok with having a piece of a man. The dude can have a wife and a girlfriend and so long as she is getting a piece of a man then she's willing to settle for that. Women are willing to "bust it wide open" and give everything of themselves to a man who isn't even giving a percentage of himself to her. When did women stop demanding more of themselves and more from the man that they want? - **DEL, 47**

Most women I've met don't truly know what it's like to be adored. There is a difference being lusted after and being adored. Most women don't know what it's like to be adored for the way they talk, or for their ideas, or even just for what they bring to the world. It's as simple as noticing that she has fake flowers in her home and I come over and bring her real flowers, this has just added some value to her. This is letting her know that I appreciate her. - **DEL, 47**

From my perspective, a lot of females feel like it's okay to keep two men. When I was younger, between the ages of 21 and 30, I didn't realize that this is how women are. I'm thinking that everything is going to go my way, the way I want it. Of course it doesn't necessarily go that way. I had to learn with experience, that there isn't a textbook solution to dating women. I can't learn how women act from reading books, it comes from my experiences with them. - **WILLIAM, 50**

I always bathe my women. I really love doing this, it's part of my routine. I would get in the shower with them and clean her everywhere. When I first did this for my wife she thought it was the craziest thing. She would say, "What, you don't think I know what I'm doing?" This is not a prelude to sex for me, it's a way of showing my appreciation and adoration in a way. I want her to feel loved and special. The responses I got when I did this when I was dating were, "I'm 38 years old, no man has ever bathed me before or this is odd". I don't understand how some women have never been bathed before. - **MAVERICK, 51**

A real man is a man that can be committed to one relationship. Because to be in a relationship with multiple women doesn't take a level of commitment when you're jumping from one person to another. But to be in a relationship when you are going through the trials and tribulations and sticking to it, to me, that's a level of manhood. - **ISAAC, 51**

I think life is like a box of chocolates, you never know what you're going to get. And I think with Black men and women and love, it's a chance. You can't love unless you take a damn chance. So open your box and be open! Communicate. Look at the choices. Don't be afraid to not get it right. This just means you learned a lesson and moved on. Keep living and choose something else. - **DEION, 51**

I'm a very physical man. I need sex every day! Every damn day! She may be feeling tired but if my dick is poking her in the back, then she needs to give me some. Is she the type of woman that's going to cock her leg and say, "Okay, go on and get it baby!" or is she going to roll over and say, "Leave me alone." We need to communicate our sexual needs so we are on the same page. - **DEION, 51**

Women who aren't balanced within themselves become vampires to their mates where they need a man to make them happy and motivate them. That constant need and sucking of energy from a man to give her nourishment and the energy that she needs can be completely draining. It's like sucking the energy out of a man like a vampire. If I want to go play golf on a Saturday morning, I don't need her sitting around complaining that she doesn't have anything to do. Get a hobby! - **DEION, 51**

I'm not an arguer. So if I'm dating someone, we're not going to be debating and having tiffs every day. I don't care enough about a topic to argue with someone that I'm sleeping with. I'd rather acquiesce and say, "You know what, you're probably right". I don't like agitation. I don't like to be agitated or to agitate other people. I'm a Taurus, so once I'm agitated it's a wrap. I'm going to sit here and hold my breath so I don't go off on her. - **MAVERICK, 51**

When a woman plays "Pussy-Politics" with me, and rationing out the sex, she doesn't understand that all she's doing is giving me time to go find someone else. Not to toot my own horn, but literally, I walk around Harlem and women will just give me their phone number. I'm not that dude, you can't do this to me. - **MAVERICK, 51**

My first wife was very disrespectful and flippant towards me. Because of this, I developed a knee-jerk response when she said something to me when I think she was being flippant, or If I think she was questioning my statement or questioning me in a way that's uncomfortable, then I go on the attack. This was the way she and I communicated. One morning I woke up, looked at my wife sleeping next to me and I said to myself, "I do not love this woman anymore, I have to get the hell up out of here". We had been married for about seven years and I no longer had the patience for her. I didn't want to put my hands on her so I had to go. - **MAVERICK, 51**

I had a woman approach me once and she said to me, "You're beautiful, let me know if you're available". At the moment I wasn't available, but I made myself available. This woman was amazing! Physically, she was out of this world and intellectually she was on point. She was an Atheist and that was hard for me. It wasn't because of the way she felt about religion per se, it was more about the disdain she carried for the creator. It was okay for her not to believe in God, but to make little bullshit comments about people didn't sit well with me . - **MAVERICK, 51**

Women have become okay with suppressing what they need emotionally and intimately from a man and if they are doing this, are they also suppressing other areas of their lives? Women have been trained to do this. How are they really okay with this? Where does this come from? - **MICHAEL, 53**

Respect is very important to me. I cannot tolerate a woman who feels the need to yell at me and treat me like a kid. There is a switch that goes off in my head when a woman is disrespectful towards me. I cannot tolerate it. - **JORDON, 54**

Even though I've been married twice, I'm not one of those types of people to say, "I'm never going to get married again!" I realize that I made two bad choices. I don't know if I'll never get married again but I will say I won't get divorced again because the next choice I make will be the right one. - **JORDON, 54**

Men want to be intimate if there is a safe space to do so. I had this girl once who asked me "What's on your mind?" and when I told her she got mad. See women want intimacy but they have to be willing to listen and not take things personally or make it about them when a man shares his feelings. If he is judged or if she uses what he said against him, then that man will shut down and not share his feelings anymore. He will end up going to having sex with another woman who won't use what he said against him. - **GREG, 54**

I just want to emphasize the importance of compatibility because I don't think a lot of people in general focus on really being compatible with someone. They think more about the need to love someone. All that is great, but if you're not compatible you will have problems and the earlier you recognize that the better. You have to be honest about it. I know a lot of lonely people, men and women, that want to be in a relationship so they settle. They don't realize that they're settling, but they are. If you have something that's important to you, and you tolerate that in a person just to be in a relationship with them then we're not compatible and sooner or later there's going to be a problem. - **JORDON, 54**

When I met my wife initially, it wasn't a sexual thing. We did not have sex until six months after we met. We spent our time building our relationship first. We had multiple diners and conversations getting to know each other, and eventually the sex part came. - **TARZAN, 56**

I learned that I should be evolving with my wife, but I must be honest and say that I was hard-headed. My wife gave me clues on how to open her "safe". She wants me to open her mind to get her goods, whether it's a sexual relationship or building an intimate bond with her. I understood that if I was able to do this then our relationship could flourish. - **TARZAN, 56**

I like to tease my wife sometimes. I am crazy and I am wild and I am playful. I would take my penis out of my pants and walk in the house like that. I would walk in and start poking her with it! She would say, "Boy put that thing up!" I would take a shower and walk through the house drying off, butt naked! And if she is sitting on the couch, I may come up from behind her and rub it on her neck. If men keep sex fun and do little silly and crazy things with their mates, (of course you have to test it out first an see if she likes it), then adding this element of playfulness with my wife helps to keep our relationship interesting and entertaining. - **TARZAN, 56**

Here's what's stupid about men. Some men think they need to impress a woman with his car, his job, and all the other things that don't really matter. He thinks these are all the things he needs to get this fly chick. In reality, it's really just a temporary fix because without all these things some men feel like they should not have this woman and they should not be with her. They feel like their worth is in their possessions. - **MM, 56**

Women have got to understand that they are either that girl, or she's "the" girl. A man could be seeing a woman, dating that woman, sleeping with that woman but that's not necessarily his woman. She could be in his house doing laundry, cooking meals for him and doing all this other stuff. This doesn't really mean that he wants to be with her at the end of the day. After she's finished doing everything she's doing, he's ready for her to go. He may want to see her on Thursdays, but he doesn't want to see her on Fridays or Saturdays. She was good for that day but he needs to go and do some other things. Now, if it's his "girl", the one that he really wants to be with, she may still be at his house while he's out rolling and he doesn't want her to leave. You see, there is a very clear distinction between the two women. Women get it confused, they think because they're in this man's house doing his laundry and cooking his meal that this is it. When really it's about communication. If they are not communicating about their situation then the woman is going to end up hurt. - **MM, 56**

A woman has to empower her man and make him feel like he's head of the household, even if she's making more money than him. If a man does not feel like the man in his household then he doesn't want to come home. If a man really loves his woman, he's already going into the relationship thinking about her. Women have to double up on their confirmation and adoration towards their men. And what I mean by double up is having a balance between being into her guy versus not being into her guy. As a man, I want to always go home, but if she can't create that "home" then I'm a little suspect stepping through that door. If I sense that a woman cannot make a home for me, then I don't see her as wifey material. I met a woman that I was not instantly attracted to but over time she won me over. I wanted that fly chick who's good in bed, and who represented me very well. But over time, she won me over and I know that if I was ready to be married then she would be "home" for me. As I get older I have to shift my thoughts about what it is I'm really looking for in a woman. - **MM, 56**

When I was younger, I wasn't into holding hands with women at all. As I've gotten older, if the woman that I'm dating makes that move to hold my hand when we are out, and if there is a natural flow between us, then it's cool. However, if it feels contrived or forced, this doesn't work for me. I don't want a woman to act as though it is my job to hold her hand, it has to be a natural flow between the two of us. - **M.M., 56**

In a man's mind, he always wants to think that the woman that he is with is a virgin, and this is because of his inadequacies, it is a lack of self-esteem. A man always wants to be the biggest dick, the longest lover, the only lover, and all this other kind of stuff. It gets in his head that his dick, that he's about to put in his lover's mouth, had another dick in it before.- **DN, 58**

I'm looking for a best friend that I can actually have sex with. I would be totally happy in all aspects. I wouldn't have to find another friend to fill out the parts that are missing with the current friend. Sometimes I need a friend that I can talk to, I don't want a wife who won't listen to anything that I say or she's tired of what I'm talking about and she just gives me 15 minutes of talking time. I just went through this shit! - **DN, 58**

So many people will have sex the first night they are together and they think there in love. How can they be in love when they really don't know each other? There are a lot of people going through the motions, thinking they're building intimacy. The average guy will stick his pecker into anything! Some guys can put a bag over a woman's head and enjoy the moment and some women will be happy with any pecker that comes along.- **KEITH, 60**

I hear a lot of women out here saying, "Well guys are with multiple women so we want to do that too". So if a man is a hoe then women want to be hoes too and they should be so upset when a man calls them one. A hoe is a person who has sex with multiple people. - **KEITH, 60**

When people talk about "love", what is love? Who made up what love is? It is a concept that makes no sense because the unions that actually work the best together are those that are like business arrangements. When couples see eye-to-eye and they both have the same goals and aspirations and they respect each other, then this type of union will work better than the fantasy one. When you look at couples today, 99% of them are following the fantasy. This is a concept that came out of Europe because if we look back at Africa, a man could have multiple wives only if he could take care of those multiple wives. This system seems to be more effective then what we see going on in America and in the world. The European way of one man and one woman, this system is not working, something is not right. - **KEITH, 60**

The reason I did not marry the mother of my two children is because I did not know my own desire. I was still searching for my own desire of what I wanted in a female and I had not defined it at that point in my life. I didn't want to limit myself because if I did find the woman that I desired, as I felt I would, I did not want to hurt my partner. I felt that I could somehow fulfill my desires better once I found out what my desires were. I had this facade in my mind that there would be some perfect woman out there that would live up to some unexplained, undefined, expectation that I had. - **PILOT, 61**

There were periods when I was alone and when being alone and loneliness came together, this was not a great place to be. Everyday became the same as the next day because I was just alone. During these periods, it would have been great to have someone to share my time with. I would go out alone and see women and think, maybe she could be a potential lover. I was in search mode all the time. - **ANTHONY, 62**

I literally took a two year period in my mid-forties to do self-reflection and self-examination. What I realized is that most of the women in my life had been sexual partners and that I was picking certain women specifically to be sexual partners and to not have intimacy because of the career that I had chosen. In other words, I was picking a certain kind of woman that I would never give 100% of myself to because I didn't want to set up a certain kind of intimacy with them since I only wanted to have sex. So at a certain point, the sex wasn't doing it for me. I kept getting a certain type of woman with whom I had already established that there would be no real intimacy. And because of this, I won't be able to find a wife that I wanted to go deeper and deeper with. I had to look at myself and ask, "Why am I picking these types of women?"

So what I did was I stopped having sex with all the women in my life and if I met somebody new then I wouldn't have sex for two years. It was really really weird, but what happened was I was no longer attracting women in my life who just wanted sex or just wanted what I could provide in terms of money or whatever. Once I made this choice I actually started to develop female friends. I had never in my life until my forties, ever had female friends. I had female sex partners who were friendly to me and I was friendly to them. But I never just had a female friend. So during this two year period, I started to identify that in me. I then started to understand and reshape what it was that I needed in my life for a woman to occupy that space. If a woman was going to be in my space, what is it that she will provide in that space for me? - **ANTHONY, 62**

In a lot of ways my ex-wife was what I would dream about. In my eyes she was very attractive to me, so much so that she would stop traffic walking down the street. The demise of our marriage was because of her insecurities and low self-esteem, both which were a mystery to me. - **PAUL, 66**

Society frowns upon a woman who is sexually free saying that a woman is a whore if she has several boyfriends, and a man is a stud if he has several girlfriends. I don't think it should be this way. When society makes women think and feel this way she's a little less likely to really express and enjoy the possibilities of sex that are afforded her. There are women who want to approach a man and hit on them, but society frowns upon this and that's not fair to a woman. - **PAUL, 66**

# Chapter 14

# ABOUT THE BOOK

Thank you for taking the time out to really dissect the Black male psyche and share it with the world in a way that they're going to be able to receive it. Nobody really takes the time to think about how Black men feel nor do they want to understand our mental process. The fact that you are doing this is amazing! And I hope this touches people around the world who are having problems with themselves, or with things that they always doubted, or with things they feel like they can't get through. Any person reading this book that has questions about themselves, just know that it all gets better. You just gotta take the time to figure it out and to be true to yourself.
- **KING, 34**

One of the key things I got out of being interviewed for this book and hearing myself talk and having this rhetoric back and forth, is that communication is key. I think that I need a woman who is in tune with herself. And if I don't have this then it's a no-go for the relationship. I've never said this out loud to anybody before. - **ISAIAH, 35**

I hope that through reading this book it will help more women to open themselves up to understand what black men go through. And that they will be that shoulder to lean on, be that confidant, and be that partner for men that they would want to have for themselves. I hope for men that they recognize there are also women who are willing and able to be that support for them as well. As men, we need to allow ourselves to open up and let women in. - **BRYCE, 35**

I just hope that people who read this book will understand that all men are different. You need to take our words into consideration when you go out there talking to Black men. A lot of people think that we come with a lot of baggage and negative attitudes. Although we go through a whole lot dealing with racism, cops, jobs and all that stuff, when we come home, if we have a good woman all of that stuff goes away. - **MALIK, 38**

I feel like everything you put out into the universe comes back to you. There are not enough people giving their honest opinions on things. I love the book, I love what you're doing because even if one person reads it and they decide to change, this can have a residual impact on the next person. Maybe black relationships will have a chance to be great in the next 10 to 15 years. Right now I'm not hopeful, but at the same rate, it's the audacity of hope. - **DEL, 47**

I like the concept of this book because I think more women need to understand what's going on from a Black man's perspective. Once they understand that, it will give them a certain frame of mind of how to look at Black men. I hope what I shared will inspire a lot of people to think for themselves and about themselves. I hope they are able to reflect upon themselves because this is really where the love has to start, from within. The Bible talks about the Kingdom of Heaven within and a lot of people miss this. To me, if the Kingdom of God is within, then God is in all of us. We are not choosing to activate that God power within us. We need to take the time out to connect with that part of us. It is an unlimited part of who we are. The more we can connect with ourselves, there is no limit to what we can tap into and achieve. We have to believe this is so. - **ISAAC, 51**

www.ingramcontent.com/pod-product-compliance
Lightning Source LLC
Chambersburg PA
CBHW060315030426
42336CB00011B/1061